Macroeconomic Problems and Policies of Income Distribution

Macroeconomic Problems and Policies of Income Distribution

Functional, Personal, International

Paul Davidson
and
Jan Kregel

Edward Elgar

Published by
Edward Elgar Publishing Limited
Gower House
Croft Road
Aldershot
Hants GU11 3HR
England

Gower Publishing Company
Old Post Road
Brookfield
Vermont 05036
USA

British Library Cataloguing in Publication Data

Davidson, Paul, *1931–*
    Macroeconomic problems and policies of income
    distribution: functional, personal, international.
    1. Income. Distribution
    I. Title II. Kregel, Jan
    339.2

Library of Congress Cataloging-in-Publication Data
Macroeconomic problems and policies of income distribution:
    functional, personal, international/[edited by] Paul Davidson and
    Jan Kregal.
    p. cm.
    Selection of papers presented at an international workshop titled
    "Problems in Income Distribution: Functional, Personal,
    International" held in Gatlinburg, Tenn. in June of 1988.
    Includes bibliographical references.
    1. Income distribution–Congresses. 2. Equilibrium (Economics)–
    Congresses. 3. Macroeconomics–Congresses. I. Davidson, Paul.
    II. Kregel, Jan.
    HB523.M36   1989
    339.2–dc20   89–23543 CIP

ISBN 1 85278 206 4

Printed and bound in Great Britain at
The Camelot Press Ltd, Southampton

Contents

Contributors

A. Asimakopulos is the Dow Professor of Political Economy at McGill University, Montreal, Canada.

Kenneth E. Boulding is Distinguished Professor Emeritus, Institute of Behavioral Science, University of Colorado at Boulder, USA.

Y. S. Brenner is professor of economics, University of Utrecht, the Netherlands.

Wendy Carlin is a lecturer at the Department of Economics, University College London.

Fernando J. Cardim de Carvalho is associate professor of economics at the University Federal Fluminense, Rio de Janeiro, Brazil.

John Cornwall is professor of economics, Dalhousie University, Halifax, Canada.

Sheldon Danziger is professor of social work and public policy at the University of Michigan, USA.

William Darity, Jr. is professor of economics at University of North Carolina, Chapel Hill, North Carolina, USA.

Peter Gottshalk is professor of economics at Boston College, Massachusetts, USA; and with Professor Sheldon Danziger is research affiliate of the Institute for Research on Poverty at the University of Wisconsin-Madison, USA.

J. A. Kregel is professor of international economics at the Johns Hopkins University, Bologna Centre, Italy.

Y. E. Mazeya is a lecturer at the Rensselaer Polytechnic Institute, Troy, New York, USA.

Basil J. Moore is professor of economics at Wesleyan University, Middletown, Connecticut, USA.

Sándor Nagy is director of the Post Graduate Center for Social Sciences of the Hungarian Academy of Sciences, Budapest, Hungary.

Brian Nolan is a researcher at the Economics and Social Research Institute, Dublin, Ireland.

Paul Singer is a professor of economics at the University of Sao Paulo and senior researcher, CEBRAP, Sao Paulo, Brazil.

Timothy M. Smeeding is professor of economics at Vanderbilt University, Nashville, Tennessee and is project director of the Luxembourg Income Study.

David Soskice is the Mynors Fellow in Economics, University College, Oxford, England.

A. H. G. M. Spithoven is a researcher associated to the International Centre for Social Economics at the University of Utrecht, Utrecht, The Netherlands.

Eduardo Matarazzo Suplicy is professor of economics at the Getulio Vargas Foundation, Sao Paulo, Brazil.

Andrea Szegö is a researcher at the Institute of Sociology of the Hungarian Academy of Sciences, Budapest, Hungary.

Donald F. Vitaliano is an associate professor at the Rensselaer Polytechnic Institute, Troy, New York, USA.

Editors' Introduction

There are fashions in economics that, much like cycles in the real economy, are determined by a combination of exogenous shocks and endogenous processes yet to be understood. One area of economics that has been most subject to changes in fashion and fluctuations of interest is the theory of distribution. If one accepts the classical economists as the origin of modern economics, then the study of distribution was a motive force in the birth of the subject. Adam Smith's attempt to identify the determinants of the Wealth of a Nation – by which he seems to have meant the per capita income of the population in terms of the ratio of productive to unproductive labour and the average productivity of productive labour – was directly linked to the question of distribution. Ricardo took up the point and argued that if income were concentrated in those classes, e.g. landlords, that spent their income on servants, savants and other unproductive workers, both growth and average incomes would be lower. On the other hand, if income were directed in favour of capitalists more inclined to invest in the employment of productive labour, this would increase the rate of expansion and the national wealth by increasing per capita incomes more rapidly. The Rev. Malthus joined the controversy in defence of unproductive labour (clerics were unproductive labourers) as a source of demand when Ricardo's capitalists flagged in their task of keeping up investment. Workers were left to one side in this distributive battle between landlords and capitalists because it was presumed that they would receive no more than subsistence wages.

Where Smith, Ricardo and Malthus diverged was in terms of the theory of prices, and in particular in terms of the determination of the rate of profits. Smith argued that as wealth increased with the increase of capital, the rate of profit, the price of capital, would be driven down. Ricardo, on the other hand, argued that the only cause of a fall in profits could be a rise in wages. This antagonism between wages and profits became the foundation of the Marxist theory of exploitation as well as the basis of the theories of the neo-Ricardian socialists. The discussion thus moved to the division of income between capitalists and workers; and hence the theory of income distribution became the basis for revolutionary social and political ideals.

In the classical theory distribution was important because it had an

1

effect on the level of output and on accumulation. It was linked primarily to the analysis of production, since, to adopt Marx's argument, it was difficult to explain phenomena such as profits by reference to producers charging high prices since in an interdependent production system every seller was also a buyer. If a trader were charging higher prices to create a profit he was also being charged higher prices by someone else trying to do likewise; in aggregate none could succeed.

The response to these considerations came in the analysis of a rather different type of interdependent system: general equilibrium. It is common to refer to Walras's theory, based on given preference sets, production functions and basic resource endowments, as the source of this theory, but it was introduced into economics, albeit in a slightly different version, by Gustav Cassel. Cassel was the source of the shift in neoclassical theory from the study of the theory of value and distribution as a subject separate from the study of money and fluctuations, to economics as the theory of price. Cassel rejected the utility theory of value of Say, Bentham and Mill which was the basis of the neoclassical demand theory, arguing that it is impossible to define an abstract theoretical unit to measure utility (not that it could not be measured in principle) and that no economy had ever existed which did not employ money, so that the only meaningful unit of measure acceptable for theoretical economics was money price. Thus, in Cassel's view,

> economic theory becomes essentially a theory of price. This theory must necessarily embrace the whole process by which prices are determined, and in this process not only prices of the consumers' goods, but also of intermediary goods and of elementary factors of production are included. As people's incomes are determined by the prices of their contributions to production, the whole process which is known in economics as 'distribution' is embraced in the theory of prices.

Since these prices are the result of the 'total process of price-fixing' there is no way of arguing that they could be anything other than they are. This serves as 'a serious warning against all sorts of social experiments which are essentially nothing else than an attempt at fixing particular prices in opposition to what that total process of price fixing requires' (Cassel, 1925, pp.63-4).[1] Since any attempt to change the distribution of income implied tampering with the competitive solution to the general equilibrium system, it clearly could only be achieved at greater general costs than the possible benefits it might generate for individuals. The theoretical study of distribution was thus subsumed in the theory of price and the social and political justifications were defused by a Candide-like argument that the existing distribution was the only, and thus the best, possible state of a perfectly competitive interdependent world.

Not surprisingly, the study of income distribution went out of fashion. What did remain were the remnants of the theory of marginal productivity as put forward by Clark, but which was never properly part of the general equilibrium system. Both approaches, however, remained firmly anchored within the assumptions of perfectly competitive conditions. When the imperfect competition revolution broke out, this was one of the regions that came under scrutiny and the modern recovery of interest in income distribution might be said to stem from Joan Robinson's 1934 article 'Euler's Theorem and the Problem of Distribution'[2]. Piero Sraffa, who had been instrumental in launching Joan Robinson and others on their way to the imperfect competition revolution, was himself working on a slightly different project, a theory of price which provided an alternative to the general equilibrium theory of price and which also incidentally demonstrated the weakness in the marginal productivity theory.

But it was not until economists recognized the importance of income distribution for things like the consumption function in Keynes's theory that the subject really came back into fashion. Keynes, however, had little to say about the question *per se,* and economists schooled in the works of the classical economists soon discovered that Kalecki, working from Marx, had worked out a theory of unemployment equilibrium which was much like Keynes's, but with one important exception: it was based on the explicit analysis of income distribution. This led away from the microeconomic study of distribution launched by Cassel, and back to the study of an aggregate theory of distribution.

The renewal of interest came on a number of fronts and nearly simultaneously. Pride of place goes to Kenneth Boulding who, in 1950, published *A Reconstruction of Economics;*[3] followed in 1956 by Kaldor's 'Alternative Theories of Income Distribution',[4] Joan Robinson's *Accumulation of Capital,*[5] and Sidney Weintraub's 'Macroeconomic Approach to the Theory of Wages', followed in 1958 by *An Approach to the Theory of Income Distribution.*[6] An expression of this widespread revival of interest may be seen in one of the editors' doctoral dissertation published in 1960 as *Theories of Aggregate Income Distribution.*[7]

The upshot of this renewed interest in aggregate theories of distribution, joined with the fruits of Sraffa's research into a coherent classical theory of price which was published in 1960 as *Production of Commodities By Means of Commodities,* produced the 'Two Cambridges' controversies which dominated macroeconomics for most of the 1960s and early 1970s and attempted to recover the classical linkages between growth, capital accumulation and distribution. The other editor completed his doctoral degree on the basis of a dissertation on this extension of distribution in 1971 as *Rate of Profit, Distribution and Growth: Two Views.*[8]

But, nearly as rapidly as the modern interest in distribution had appeared, it disappeared, as the dominance of general equilibrium theory once again reduced it to the study of individual prices and incomes and rational expectations turned all prices into market clearing equilibrium prices. Cassel's magic was again exercised, but with even great efficiency and technical wizardry. Yet the problems associated with the distribution of income still remain, and economists continue to work in the area, even if today it does not attract the attention of the 'high theorists'.

When the creation of the J. Fred Holly Chair in Political Economy at the University of Tennessee raised the possibility of a special conference, it seemed appropriate to choose income distribution as the theme, to show, on the one hand, that work was still being done, and on the other to try to rekindle interest in the subject. Thus, under the auspices of the College of Business Administration of the University of Tennessee and the *Journal of Post Keynesian Economics* the editors organized an International Workshop, 'Problems in Income Distribution: Functional, Personal, International', in Gatlinburg, Tennessee in June 1988 which was attended by some one hundred economists from throughout the world. This volume reproduces a selection of the nearly forty papers that were discussed at the Workshop with the aim of covering the broadest possible range of topics in the area of income distribution.

The book opens most appropriately with a paper by Kenneth Boulding, who has remained actively at work on distribution ever since he first rekindled interest in the problem with his 1950 book. It also represents the spirit of the book to present all sides of the problem by integrating personal distribution and macroeconomic theory. The papers which follow run from theory to policy, from domestic to international perspectives, and are all written in the tradition of those economists who reintroduced distribution into fashion. The book may be considered as a dedication to Ken Boulding, and to the memories of Nicholas Kaldor , Joan Robinson and Sidney Weintraub, in the hope that economists may once again come to consider the theory of distribution as part of the origins of theory and applied research in economics.

P.D., J.A.K.

NOTES

1. G. Cassel, *Fundamental Thoughts in Economics,* London: E. Benn, 1925.
2. J. Robinson, 'Euler's Theorem and Problem of Distribution', *Economic Journal,* September 1934.
3. K. Boulding, *A Reconstruction of Economics,* New York: Wiley, 1950.

4. N. Kaldor, 'Alternate Theories of Distribution', *Review of Economic Studies,* XXIII, 1956.
5. J. Robinson, *The Accumulation of Capital.* London: Macmillan, 1956.
6. S. Weintraub, 'A Macroeconomic Approach to the Theory of Wages', *American Economic Review,* December, 1956; *An Approach to the Theory of Income Distribution,* Philadelphia: Chilton, 1958.
7. P. Davidson, *Theories of Aggregate Income Distribution,* New Brunswick: Rutgers University Press, 1960.
8. J.A. Kregel, *Rate of Profit, Distribution and Growth: Two Views,* London: Macmillan, 1971.

1. The Implications of Macrodistribution for Personal Distribution*

Kenneth E. Boulding

The concept of distribution always refers to the division of something into parts, each part being identified in some sense as different from the others. Unfortunately, there seems to be no word in the English language for 'that which is divided or distributed', as the word 'dividend' has been appropriated to other uses. The only word I can think of is a 'totality', which is then perceived as divided into its components. Division into components, like the organs and other parts of the body, departments and hierarchies of an organization, is different from the mere division into pieces, like the cutting up of a pie, where the pieces are all the same and do not interact with each other. Here we immediately run into problems of measurement. Pieces can usually be measured. Any measurement of components is likely to be a very inadequate description of the truth. Thus, we can divide the total weight of a body among its pieces. A butcher can do that. But the pieces are not necessarily components. The head is a piece, but it is made up of many components – brain cells, nerves, muscles, eyes, tongue, and so on. We can, of course, theoretically identify all the components and then weigh them; that tells us something. We can find out the proportion of the total weight of the body contributed by each portion of it. This may give us some clues as to its general functioning and health. An enlarged heart or excess fat or a cancerous tumour sends out important signals. The operation of the body is not the sum of its components in the way that the weight is the sum of the weight of its components, even though the weight of the body and the proportion of the weight of the various components may be an important clue to identifying the health of its functioning.

We have a similar problem with the economy. The economy is certainly a component of the total social system of the planet, which in turn is a component of the overall total system of the planet – physical, biological and social. Measurement of the total system is difficult, for a lot of different measures may be significant and they cannot really be combined. Thus we can measure the total mass of the atmosphere and find out what

6

are the proportions of oxygen, nitrogen, water, ozone, and so on; these proportions may turn out to be quite significant in the light of the destruction of the earth's ozone layer. We can measure the volume or mass of water and its chemical compositions in the oceans, rivers, lakes and porous ground. We might be able to measure the volume or mass of soil, could we define it. We could hypothetically measure the total weight, mass or volume of the biomass and divide each total number among its innumerable species – trees, grasses, animals, fish, and so on. The distributions here might be significant. Then we have to look at the energy flows from the sun and out from the earth if we are worried about the 'greenhouse effect', but there seems to be no way of adding all these things up. We always have to come face to face with a structure, not with a number. Numbers can guide us towards the truth, but they can never represent the truth. The real world is topological rather than numerical.

The sociosphere – that is, the sphere of all human beings, their artefacts and their activities – is likewise a structure where some aspects can be measured, but where the aggregate cannot be measured. We can measure the human population, now at a level of over five billion. We can divide this into parts by gender, age, nationality, occupation, health, race, and so on. The boundaries between many of these parts are rather vague. Race, for instance, is a very minor component of the total genetic structure of the human race. We are all one species. We are all genetically different except identical twins, and how we categorize these differences is a very difficult and yet unsolved problem.

We could count human beings with some confidence, but how can we measure the content of their minds? And how is this content distributed? We could distribute this content first by languages, taking note of the people who can speak more than one language. Distribution by political views would be very difficult. We don't really have an adequate taxonomy here. Political and religious systems, like ideological systems, have an enormous impact on the economy and they are very hard to reduce to clear images.

So we come to the economy itself. Economists think, perhaps rightly, that the economy is easier to identify and to reduce to measurement than other elements of the system because of the 'measuring rod of money'. The economy can almost be defined as all those things which can be measured, at least roughly, in terms of monetary units of value. The principal activity of the economy is the production, consumption and exchange of human artefacts. In exchange, it is conventionally assumed – at least by cost accountants – that the values of quantities of commodities exchanged for each other are equal. Actually, if we had a record of the ratio of exchange in all exchanges, say, on a given day, we could select any one commodity as a measure of value and express the value of a given quantity of any other commodity in terms of the measure. If ten oranges exchange for twenty apples, and forty apples for one hat, then the hat is worth either forty apples or twenty oranges. An orange is worth two apples or 1/20th of a hat; an apple is worth half an orange or 1/40th of a hat. Commodities that are exchanged frequently soon become measures of value and then become liquid assets and stores of value. When a measure of value, like gold, receives an arbitrary unit in terms of coinage we undoubtedly have money, in which all values can be reckoned.

Now we can begin to think in terms of a number that expresses a totality of the economy, and which can then be divided among its component parts. We start off with the total stock of objects at a moment of time, to which a monetary value can be assigned. This is real capital or goods, the largest part of which in developed societies indeed is probably household capital – houses, furniture , clothing, cars, and so on. It includes industrial capital – factories, machines, equipment, and so on; goverment capital – roads, parks, electric power stations, wires, and so on. Then we have finance and financial instruments, which are rights to purchase goods or money – dollar bills, coins, bank deposits of many different kinds, loans, bonds, stocks and shares, futures contracts. The value of these fundamentally rests on the value of real capital. They are very important in determining the distribution of the total value of real capital, that is, total net worth, among the persons in the society. If I have a house with a mortgage, its contribution to my own net worth is the value of the house minus the value of the mortgage. The holder of the mortgage adds the value of the mortgage to his or her net worth.

A very difficult problem, still by no means resolved, is how to include the value of human capital – minds and bodies – in the total. Human capital is only valued in the market in a slave society. In a free society every person is his or her own slave. What is in the market is the productive operation of the person day by day, either expressed as a wage or as the value of an independent craftsman's work. One way of valuing the human capital of a person is to sum up the discounted value of the expected wage for the rest of life. This, of course, involves profound uncertainties both as to the future wage itself and to the rate of discount. Nevertheless, the human capital set probably has a total value three or four times that of physical capital. In developed societies labour income from human capital tends to be 75–80 per cent of the total, and income from physical capital is about 20–25 per cent of the total, and the average rate of return on each is probably roughly the same.

Income is to capital what births and deaths are to a population. Production adds to the capital stock as births add to a population;

consumption subtracts from the capital stock as deaths subtract from a population. Here we use consumption in the literal sense of the disappearance of items in the capital stock, whether by depreciation, eating, wearing out or being transformed into other things, like wheat into flour. The tendency of economists to define consumption as household expenditures is most unfortunate, as it neglects the tremendous importance of household capital. Production and consumption, like births and deaths, are flows, measured per unit of time. If the capital stock, like a population, is to be constant, production and consumption, like births and deaths, must be equal. If production exceeds consumption, or births exceed deaths, the capital stock or the population will grow. The capital stock is a bit like a river – the total amount of water in it is the capital stock. The amount of water that comes into it every day from rain or tributaries is income or flow, the value of production. The amount of water that is lost per day by evaporation, absorption into the ground or running out to sea is consumption.

A fundamental identity here is that the total population in an equilibrium population is equal to the average length of life multiplied by the number of births or deaths per unit of time. Similarly, the total amount of capital is equal to the production or consumption per unit of time multiplied by the average length of life per unit of capital from the time it is produced to the time it is consumed. This is the famous, rather misnamed 'period of production' of the Austrian economists. Similarly, the amount of water in a river or a lake is equal to the amount that comes in or goes out per unit of time, multiplied by the average length of time, in these units, that a molecule of water stays in the river or lake.

We have a problem with capital, and implicitly also with human capital and population. Capital consists of a very large number of different species and things, from nuts and bolts to the feeling of just having gone to an opera, and it is very hard to add up the physical quantity. If there is a monetary value put on each item, however, we can add up the money values. And if we could identify a price, then the quantity is the money value divided by the price, price being a money value divided by the quantity. If we have $1,000 worth of wheat at $2 per bushel, then we know we have 500 bushels. Some prices, however, are measured in bushels, some in tons or pounds, some in square metres like carpets, and some in simple units like suits or automobiles. This then raises a tricky problem: Is there twice as much automobile in one that costs $20,000 as there is in one that costs $10,000? If prices are constant, then an increase of the money value of an item of capital is a good measure of the increase in its quantity. On the other hand, if we have inflation or deflation, money value has to be corrected for this by some price level. Price levels can only be calculated accurately if the nature of the commodities does not change. There is no way in which we can put the price of a colour television set in 1920 into our price level, for it did not then exist. If we compare the first great clumsy computers with little modern computers, the price per pound may not have fallen very much, but the price per unit of computing ability, whatever that is, has fallen enormously. This means that we can add up the money value in current 'dollars' of total capital fairly easily. A conversion to 'real' dollars of constant purchasing power can only be done very approximately because of the impossibility of constructing an accurate price level.

When we talk about distribution in the economy we have to ask: what is the 'totality' which is distributed? There are two possible answers to this, which are, however, fairly closely related. One is that the totality is the sum of the net worths of all individuals. This adds up to the net worth of the economy, which is the value of its total stock of real capital (economically significant objects). The second is that the totality is income in some sense, which is the totality particularly favoured by economists, partly because of their obsession with consumption as a measure of economic well-being, going back again to the view that household purchases are consumption. I would argue, however, that if we include human capital in net worth, then the net worth is a much better measure of riches and poverty than is income, just as the amount of water in the lake is a much better measure of the size of the lake than is the flow through it. We get satisfaction mainly from the use of household capital, not from its consumption. I get very little satisfaction out of the fact that my clothes, my car, my house or my furniture are wearing out, that is, being consumed, though I do have to confess to getting some satisfaction out of eating. For the most part, however, consumption is undesirable. We would be better off if all our capital goods took longer to wear out. Measuring economic welfare by income neglects this factor, although, of course, if the average length of life of capital is constant, income is a fairly constant proportion of capital and hence is a pretty fair surrogate for the distribution of economic welfare.

The problem of economic distribution is greatly complicated by the existence of profit, interest and discounting, something that we do not have to worry about very much in demographic models. Profit, or negative profit (loss), emerges when assets are revalued, often at the moment of sale, sometimes through accounting revaluations. There is a certain distinction here between realized profit at the moment of sale and unrealized profit, which implies a potential sale that is not made. The production of any product, let us say a loaf of bread, involves costs, which consist of assets that are destroyed in order to increase the stock of bread by one loaf. These costs consist of the money paid out in wages and the purchase of materials, the wheat that is turned into flour, and the flour that is turned into bread, the fuel burned in the oven, the depreciation of machinery and tools. Some of this happens in indirect exchange, as when the wages are paid to get somebody to transform something, some by direct exchange as when money is paid for raw materials. Conventional cost-accounting assumes that all exchange, whether of money paid out for goods or the transformation of one form of capital into another form, for instance, flour into bread, is exchange of equal values. At the end of it we have a product, the loaf of bread, which has a cost. In all this, of course, net worth has not changed, for the value of the cost, that is, the loss of assets, is assumed exactly to equal the value of the product, that is, the loaf of bread. Then, however, if the loaf of bread is sold for more than it costs, the net worth of the baker increases and a profit has been made. In terms of social accounting, we should include in the cost the depreciation of the value of the baker, which will eventually have to be offset by raising and training another baker, but we can hardly blame conventional cost accountants for not including this difficult item.

Then the question arises: where does the profit come from? Why was the baker able to sell the loaf of bread for more than it cost? The situation is complicated by the fact that if the baker is in debt, there will be an interest cost on the debt over the time it has taken to bake the loaf of bread, which appears as a deduction from what might be called 'gross profit', which is then divided into interest and net profit. If the baker owns his own shop and equipment, the net profit goes to him; if the bread is baked by a corporation, the net profit goes initially into increasing the undistributed profit item in the balance-sheet, and this may be distributed later to shareholders. The principal justification for debt is that going into debt enables the debtor to increase real assets on the asset side of his balance-sheet, and that by the manipulation of these assets through buying, selling and producing, the debtor whether a person, an organization, or a corporation, hopes to increase gross profit by more than the interest to be paid on the debt.

We still have the question: where does gross profit come from? There are several views on this. There is the Marxist view that profit is simply the difference between the total product and that part of the product which is taken by wage-earners, who really produce the whole thing. This is the theory of 'surplus value', which simply says that the total income of society is equal to wages plus gross profit, or non-labour income, which is true but not very helpful in explaining the proportion. Certainly Marx's prediction of the immiseration of the working class has been completely falsified by experience, especially in the successful capitalist countries, where the proportion of national income going to labour has increased more or less steadily, until its recent stabilization.

Another view going back to Nassau Sr, Alfred Marshall, Irving Fisher and the Austrian economists, is that gross profit is in some sense a reward for abstaining from consumption, i.e. 'waiting'. This is refined into the marginal productivity school, arguing that both wages and capital are paid their marginal product as specified by some kind of production function, like the Cobb–Douglas function. This was preceded by what might be called the 'crude' wages fund theory, that wages are paid out of, and therefore depend on, that proportion of capital which is allotted to them. Marginal products still do not explain very well what determines the division of national income into wages and gross profit, and it certainly breaks down in the Great Depression, when profits became negative and the proportion of national income going to labour rose sharply. It would be hard to explain this by saying that labour had become very scarce and capital very plentiful. Finally, there is what I have called the 'K theory', which I espouse myself, going back to Keynes's 'widow's cruse' in the *Treatise on Money,* to Kalecki and Kaldor, and to Kenneth Boulding, which suggests that gross profits arise partly because the receivers of profit in terms of money spend that money on household goods.[1] That is one reason why the baker can get more for the loaf of bread than his cost in terms of wages and such like. Another reason is that the receivers of profit are prepared to expand real capital in investment, and so diminish the output of wage goods.

There has been endless confusion in economics over the concepts of saving and investment, receipts and expenditures, hoarding and investing, much of which goes back to the failure to recognize that the total system has properties which are very different from the properties of the parts. One key to understanding the total system is the recognition that exchange is the circulation of assets among owners. Whenever a purchase is made for money, the buyer transfers to the seller some of his or her money-stock and the seller transfers to the buyer whatever is bought. In the case of a household purchase, what is bought often stays within the household until it is consumed or depreciates, although not necessarily so, as the second-hand market indicates. In the case of a financial instrument, sometimes people buy a bond or a stock for a lifetime income and hold it for many years; sometimes they sell it almost immediately. In financial markets there is circulation of financial instruments just as there is of money.

Money is peculiar in that it is rarely consumed or destroyed, except in fires, bank losses and failures, and central bank sales of securities. It has to be thought of as a shifting cargo, shifting around among the balance sheets and holdings of the people. At Christmas it certainly shifts from households into businesses, and in January usually back from businesses to households again. In terms of expenditures and receipts, if the quantity of money is constant, the total of expenditures must equal the total of receipts (for every expenditure there is a receipt) and the total sum of balances of payments must be zero. A positive balance of payments on the part of an individual is an excess of receipts and an accumulation of money; a negative balance of payments is an excess of expenditure and a decumulation of money. In Gertrude Stein's famous remark, 'Money never changes, it is only the pockets that change'.

Financial assets, stocks and bonds, and goods, finished or unfinished, are also cargoes that shift between owners. Sometimes, however, these shifts have adverse effects. If money shifts into households, this may mean that finished goods inventories accumulate in the hands of businesses that cannot find buyers. This results in a lowering of their prices. Gross profits diminish and we may have a deflation. If, however, this increases real wages, which results in a shift of the money stock out of households into businesses again, and a diminution in unsold inventory, the situation may rectify itself. Generally speaking, deflation is unfavourable to gross profits, and especially unfavourable to net profits, as interest payments change very slowly. Similarly, inflation is favourable to profits and especially to net profits, as interest rates again do not adjust quickly.

If, now, we ask ourselves: what determines the distribution of net worth among the human population, the answer has to be found in the famous law that 'everything is what it is because it got that way'. Mr X has the net worth that he has, including his human capital, because of a long history, partly of inheritance, both economic and cultural, partly because of the life history of adding (or not adding) to his net worth more than he subtracted from it through, for instance, parsimony, and partly through holding his assets in a form which rises or falls in relative value, including human capital, which is added to by education and training, and diminished by bad habits, sickness and ageing. Net worth is also increased by grants to the person and diminished by grants from the person, like taxes. Grants, of course, may imply all sorts of reciprocity; there is a large grey area between grants and exhange. The random element in this process is quite important; what might be called the 'lottery of life' – good luck and bad luck. It is often very hard to tell good luck from good management.

There is a problem which plagues the human race, which is the instability of equality. If we start off with a society in which everybody has the same net worth, the random factors of good and bad luck would increase the net worth of some and diminish the net worth of others. Those who got richer would find it easier to get still richer. On the whole, the bigger the net worth, the bigger the net income; the bigger the net income, the easier it is to get consumption below production and so have assets increase. The smaller the net worth, the smaller the income, the harder it is to get production above consumption, so assets may tend to decline. There are offsets to this process. An increase in poverty may stimulate some people to greater effort. Riches can lead into the 'Rake's Progress', pictured so dramatically by Hogarth. In complex capitalist societies, there is a noticeable cycle out of poverty into the middle and back again, and a similar cycle from riches into the middle and back again, both for individuals and for families and groups. The overall culture, especially the religious culture, is important here. The religious group that stresses temperance and modesty in living, hard work, honesty and productivity, is apt to grow richer. The groups trapped in extravagant life-styles and in drug and alcohol subcultures are apt to grow poorer.

It is a very interesting question as to whether these offsetting processs lead to some kind of equilibrium. There is some evidence for this. The overall distribution of income and of wealth tends to be surprisingly stable over time. In the United States it has changed very little since 1947, when data first became available.

One of the great forces behind socialism and communism is the feeling that the distribution of wealth and income is too unequal, and this view is often held by people above the average wealth or income who feel a certain sense of shame about the deprivations of others. There is a widely-held concept of distributional justice, even if this is rather vague, which has led to widespread provisions of a 'safety-net', a level of poverty below which people are not allowed to fall. This goes back at least to the Elizabethan poor laws. The spectacle of poverty – beggars and the homeless and the slums – is an embarrassment to the sensitive rich, although they do not always do much about it.

Communism, however, has turned out to be very disappointing from the point of view of the creation of equality. It may have produced a slightly more equal distribution of income in some countries, but this has been achieved at the cost of enormous inequalities in power. A centrally planned economy involves a high concentration of power in the hands of the planners and the bureaucracy. In capitalist societies, at least the successful ones, economic and political power are quite widely distributed, even though there are some corporations, wielding a considerable concentration of power, that are larger than the smaller communist countries. Nevertheless, an active market is a very effective limit of power and has at least some of the aspects of an economic equivalent to political democracy.

However, in spite of the New Deal and the 'war against poverty' in the United States, poverty was mitigated more by making everybody richer and increasing the average income and net worth, than by redistribution. So-called 'moderate poverty' was halved between 1950 and the mid-1970s, though it has been increasing somewhat ever since. So-called 'severe poverty' was cut by almost 75 per cent. This again, though, has been increasing slightly. This may have been partly a result of redistributions, but the major impact is that of a general increase in income and wealth. If everybody becomes twice as rich, then we halve the amount of poverty.

Another somewhat neglected factor in distribution is the impact of the overall commodity-mix produced by an economy, and the quantities of goods characteristic of different income levels that are available. On the whole, the technology of the last century or so has been a great equalizer in those societies that have followed it successfully. Automobiles are a good example. In China, which has a strongly egalitarian ideology, there is approximately one automobile for every 50,000 – 100,000 Chinese. It is not surprising that these are distributed very unequally. It is virtually impossible to have 1/50,000 – 100,000 of an automobile. In the United States, there is roughly one automobile for every two to three people; they are very widely distributed and the possession of an automobile goes very far down the poverty line. This, incidentally, has intensified extreme poverty, as it has led to a virtual collapse of the public transportation system outside the major metropolitan areas, so the extremely poor are without automobiles *and* without public transportation. This makes them much worse off in regard to transportation than they might have been 50 years ago, when public transport was both readily available and fairly cheap. In the United States it is rare to find even a billionaire with more than 5 – 10 automobiles so cars simply have to be widely distributed, notably through the second-hand market. When it comes to housing and clothing, inequalities can be larger. Unequal distribution of land and property, going back to the Norman conquests, together with the rise in population and in rents, permitted the English aristocracy to inhabit 'stately homes' far outrivalling the humble cottages of the poor and the crowded misery of the city slums. Technical improvement in the production of what might be called 'poor people's goods' and moderately poor people's goods can lead to a much sharper diminution of poverty than anything that is likely in the way of government intervention and subsidy. The importance of human capital must be stressed here. In President Johnson's 'War against Poverty' by far the most successful enterprise was the Head Start programme, which offset at least some of the disadvantages of poor children gaining access to the educational system.

One source of redistribution which has received a good deal of attention from economists, although quantitatively it may not be very large, is monopoly power. We see this, for instance, in the medieval guilds and in craft unions with restrictive entry. We have seen it very dramatically in this generation with OPEC and the spectacular rise in the price of oil that it brought about. There are many other examples of cartels that have achieved some success. As OPEC itself demonstrates, however, monopoly power is fragile. It encourages production outside the monopoly. It also encourages the development of substitutes for the monopolized commodity and economies in the use of it. Monopoly also is apt to produce a decline in technological advance. Why bother with new technology when you have got such a high price for your oil? So new technology develops outside the monopoly. On the other hand, a certain amount of monopoly power, by eliminating uncertainties, may promote investment and technical change. Agriculture in the US after the imposition of price supports in the early 1930s is a good example. Uncertainty is a major obstacle to the commitment of resources to new investment and the diminution of price uncertainty certainly had a remarkable impact on US agricultural productivity. The success of the Soviet space enterprise in the face of a dilapidated and inefficient general economy may be the result of a very positive commitment of the government with little uncertainty. A vigorous democracy like the United States can easily hamper technical change. If anyone is against any change it becomes very easy to stop it.

A problem in macro-distribution that has received far too little attention from economists is the division of gross profit between net profit and interest. The distortion of macro-distribution here, of which the Great Depression is the best example, may indeed produce profound changes in personal distribution, largely through the development of unemployment. It is ironic, for instance, that in 1932 and 1933, when unemployment was 25 per cent, the proportion of national income going to labour had risen sharply from about 59 per cent in 1929 to 72 per cent in 1932 and 1933, simply because the price level nearly halved. Even though the total net national product declined sharply, the decline was more in investment goods than in wage goods. Many of the employed were probably better off in 1932 and 1933 than they had been in 1929, but the unemployed were very much worse off, so that the distribution of income within the working class had become much more unequal.

We can also look at macro-distribution to give us a clue as to why unemployment was 25 per cent in the Depression years. We see that in 1932 and 1933 profits were quite sharply negative as a result of the virtual collapse of gross private domestic investment, so there were no additions to the aggregate net worth of businesses from that source. There was also a sharp decline in household purchases. Interest, however, as a proportion of the national income almost doubled between 1929 and 1933, simply because the price level nearly halved. A much neglected feature in the study of the labour market has been the impact of this gap between interest and net profit. When an employer hires somebody he sacrifices the interest which he could have gained on the money spent on the wage in the hope of profit on the product of the work. In 1932 and 1933 it was almost literally true that anybody who hired another was either a philanthropist or a fool. In a period of deflation, money stocks bear a positive real rate of interest. The way to get rich is to sell all you have and hold on to the money, or lend it at interest until the deflation ends. If everybody had done this, of course, there would have been a still more catastrophic fall in prices. Profit is the reward of the employer, the enterprising and productive capitalist. Interest is the reward of the lazy capitalist who does nothing but risk default on the debt, an event that is actually suprisingly rare.

We see something of the same thing happening today in a way that is a little ominous, though it has not caused anything like the difficulties that it did in the early 1930s. Net interest has risen from about 1 per cent of the national income in 1950 to something like 8 per cent in 1988. This is quite a severe burden on the economy. Part of this is a shift in the financial structure towards bonds and away from stocks. But part of it is due to high real rates of interest, especially in the late 1970s and early 1980s, which has had a lot to do with producing a severe depression around 1981. It is curious that today's radicals seem to attack profit much more than they do interest, whereas in the medieval cultures, both in Europe and in Islam, interest was looked on as a dangerous villain to be regulated or even prohibited. The Western world perhaps has something to learn from Islamic banking, in which interest has to be disguised as a quasi-partnership so that the interest receiver has at least some kind of responsibility for the success of the borrowing enterprise.

It is clear that the macro-distribution problem, what might be called the division into functional shares, whether of income or of assets, is a very critical part of the economic process and has a very complex but important relationship with the distribution of both income and assets by persons. In the search for a healthy society the study of this relationship, which is still very imperfectly understood, should have a high priority.

NOTE

*   This paper was first presented at the international workshop on Problems in Income Distribution: Functional, Personal, International, organized by Professors Paul Davidson and Jan Kregel, Park Vista Hotel, Gatlinburg, Tennessee, 26 June – 3 July, 1988.
1. See Kenneth E. Boulding, 'Puzzles Over Distribution', *Challenge*, 28, 5 (Nov./Dec. 1985), pp. 4–10.

2. The Effects of Monetary Policy on Income Distribution*

Basil J. Moore

1. INTRODUCTION

The topic of this Chapter conforms closely to that of my doctoral thesis written exactly thirty years ago, 'The Implications of Counter-Cyclical Monetary Policy for the Earnings of Canadian Chartered Banks'. Redistributional effects of monetary policy was not a very popular topic then, and it is not now. There is virtually no literature on the redistributional effects of monetary policy.[1] Some of the reasons for the near-complete lack of published material on this topic will become evident. Suffice to say that we are exploring virgin territory.

Section 2 outlines the proximate control variable of monetary policy, the level of nominal market interest rates. Section 3 considers prevalent views on the significance of interest rates for the functional and personal distribution of income. Section 4 looks at some policy preconceptions of the desirability of low interest rates. Section 5, after outlining some conceptual measurement difficulties, presents some empirical estimates for the US economy over the post-war period of the effects of variations in interest rates on the functional and personal distribution of income. Finally, Part 6 provides a brief summary and conclusions.

2. MONETARY POLICY AND INTEREST RATES

Neoclassical monetary theory falls within the tradition of what Schumpeter terms 'real analysis'. Interest rates are viewed as determined by real forces, conventionally summarized under the headings of productivity and thrift, or investment and saving. These 'real' forces presumably lie behind the demand and supply of loanable funds. The rate of interest represents the price of a loan of present money in return for a promise to pay future money. Since interest is the price of credit, the factors determining interest rates rather naturally are analysed in terms of the supply and demand for credit or 'loanable funds'.

18

Keynes (1936) maintained that such an explanation was incorrect, since saving and investment are not independent variables but *ex post* identities. Both varied directly with the level of income, which in his theory adjusted to equate planned saving with planned investment in equilibrium. Keynes argued that there are fundamental differences between a modern capitalist economy using credit or bank money and a Say's Law economy using commodity money. Interest rates, rather, fall under 'monetary analysis', since their role is to equilibrate the demand and supply of 'liquidity'. The *General Theory* provoked a long and heated controversy over loanable funds versus liquidity preference theories of interest, which to this day has not been logically resolved. Textbooks still typically proffer two separate and logically quite distinct theories of interest in their micro- and macro-sections.[2]

There is now increasing consensus, at least among post-Keynesian economists, that the money supply should be viewed as endogenous, and interest rates exogenous. Banks are price-setters and quantity-takers in their retail loan and deposit markets. They mark up or down their administered loan and deposit rates depending on their degree of market power, based on the level of wholesale rates. Borrowers determine the change in loans, loans make deposits, and hence the money supply is credit-driven. Central banks ordinarily are not able to determine the quantity of credit money, but only the price at which they supply additional cash reserves to the system.

This Chapter will take for granted that the short-term supply function of credit money should be viewed as horizontal in interest money space, at a level of short-term nominal interest rates administered by the central bank.[3] Whenever the central bank raises or lowers its marginal lending rate to the financial system in pursuing its ultimate policy goals, the horizontal money supply function shifts vertically up or down. Unless the central bank commits itself in advance to pegging the level of interest rates over time at some pre-specified level, a long-term money supply function independent of demand forces does not exit. The nominal short-run supply of credit money is always perfectly elastic, at a rate based on the central banks' administered minimum lending rate. Real forces thus affect the level of nominal interest rates only indirectly, by determining the range over which rates will be moved by the monetary authorities in pursuit of their ultimate policy goals of full employment, stable prices, rapid growth and external balance.

The level of nominal short-term interest rates should thus be viewed as exogenously administered by the central bank. Short-term rates can still be regarded as determined by the supply and demand for loanable funds. But since the monetary authority is the residual monopoly supplier of credit money, it always possesses the ability to determine the marginal supply price.

Central banks exogenously determine the level of nominal short-term rates by setting the marginal supply price of liquidity to the banking system. The range over which rates are administered differs widely over time and space. It will depend on the goals of the public authorities, the variance of animal spirits, the sensitivity of private economic behaviour to changes in interest rates, the size and openness of the economy, the degree of capital mobility, the extent to which foreign exchange reserves and rates are allowed to fluctuate in response to market forces, the willingness of the authorities to impose controls and regulations on the economy, and the levels of interest rates ruling in foreign financial centres.

In open economies central banks must be willing to buy and sell foreign exchange and gold in addition to domestic securities. Anything that the central banks buy or sell affects their total assets and liabilities, and so the supply of domestic liquidity. Willingness to let the exchange rate vary increases the independence of domestic monetary policy by enabling domestic interest rates to diverge from foreign rates. Under fixed exchange rates, in small open economies with perfect capital mobility, central banks will be unable to move domestic rates very far from the levels ruling in foreign markets without creating massive capital inflow or outflow. Under floating exchange rates, covered arbitrage will permit a domestic–foreign interest rate differential to persist without causing capital movements, providing it is equal to, and so offset by, the spot-forward exchange rate differential.

Nominal spot and forward foreign exchange rates, like nominal short-term interest rates, must thus be viewed as an additional central bank exogenous policy control variable. These two policy instruments are interdependent. A policy of fixed exchange rates is exactly analogous to a policy of pegging the domestic interest rate at a constant level over time. In flexible exchange rate regimes, interest rate differentials among countries may lead to exchange rate overshooting in order to satisfy arbitrage conditions. With free capital markets ·a level of domestic interest rates below foreign rates will lead to increased borrowing by and lending to foreigners. The resulting capital outflows will cause foreign exchange reserves and the spot exchange rate to fall, and the forward rate to rise, until the forward premium is just sufficient to offset the interest rate differential and equalize *ex ante* returns. Similarly domestic interest rates above foreign rates will generate a forward discount. Forward discounts or premiums on exchange rates are well explained empirically in terms of international interest rate differentials, so that interest rate parity appears to be approximately maintained. As a result domestic interest rate coordination among central banks will be necessary to maintain exchange rates at their targeted levels. This will be difficult to achieve whenever conflict arises between internal and external balance.

The Federal Reserve System, the central bank of the world's largest economy, has the greatest discretionary range over which it is able unilaterally to raise domestic short-term rates, due to the extent it is able to induce parallel interest rate increases by other banks in defence of their own exchange rates. Policy coordination is more likely to be required for the Fed to induce parallel discretionary reductions in interest rates.

There is an important asymmetry in central bank ability to set both the level of domestic interest rates and foreign exchange rates. As the residual monopoly supplier of domestic liquidity, the monetary authorities are always able to *buy* unlimited quantities of assets for their portfolios. They are able to finance these purchases simply by issuing their own liabilities, which constitute the high-powered base component of domestic money. Consequently central banks are generally able to raise asset prices and so *reduce* nominal interest rates and foreign exchange rates to any desired level. But in order to reduce the price of these assets and raise rates, they must offer to *sell* more out of their own portfolios. Since they hold only a finite amount of domestic securities and foreign exchange reserves, after they have sold all their existing holdings and exhausted their swap commitments they will be unable to depress further the price of these assets. This may place an upper limit on their exogenous ability to *raise* interest rates and exchange rates.

This was the case in the US in the late 1930s, when total commercial bank excess reserves exceeded the total value of Federal Reserve security holdings. The Fed was then forced to raise bank cash reserve requirements, since it had completely lost its ability to increase domestic interest rates by open market sales. The constraint is typically much more binding and frequent for foreign exchange rates. After foreign exchange reserves are exhausted, central banks will be unable to continue to sell foreign exchange to increase or even maintain the exchange rate, unless they are able to borrow or 'swap' additional reserves from other central banks. They are then forced either to permit the exchange rate to depreciate, or to impose quantitative controls on capital and/or trade flows.

There is little doubt that central banks move domestic nominal short-term rates, and that a reduction in domestic nominal rates causes capital to flow out and exchange rates to weaken. But it is only nominal interest rates, and nominal interest rate differentials, that are under the control of central banks. Asset-holder investment and portfolio decisions are based on their *ex ante* estimate of real returns, i.e. the nominal rate minus the expected inflation rate. Unlike nominal interest rates, inflation rates are not under the control of the monetary authorities. The authorities are never able to reduce *ex ante* real rates below the anticipated deflation rate, since nominal rates can never be negative.

The conclusion that nominal short-term interest rates are exogenously administered over a significant range by national central banks is on reflection not really so startling, even within the corpus of mainstream theory. Only theorists with thoroughly trained incapacitation would deny that central banks have the ability to affect nominal short-term interest rates. After all, central banks have invariably maintained interest rates at low levels during wartime, in spite of very high government deficits as a proportion of GDP. The mainstream literature on monetary policy has long been riven by an ongoing debate as to whether central banks should focus on interest rates or the money supply as their target instrument (Poole, 1970). Similarly, in the development literature, a frequent policy criticism has long been that nominal interest rates are administered at too low a level to promote financial deepening (Shaw, 1973). In many LDCs *ex post* real interest rates were maintained at negative levels for decades.

Mainstream real theories of interest rate determination must apply to the level of real rather than nominal rates. The two are traditionally reconciled by the Fisher hypothesis, which holds that nominal rates can be decomposed into a relatively stable real rate, determined by real forces of productivity and thrift, plus a variable inflation premium, based on the expected inflation and the tax rate. Empirical evidence appears at last to have thoroughly discredited the Fisher explanation. First, the variance of real rates considerably exceeds the variance of nominal rates. Second, over the last hundred years there has indisputably been no systematic relationship between nominal rates and inflation rates (Summers, 1983). Nominal rates have varied over a much narrower range than inflation rates. As a result, real rates were typically negative in periods of high inflation, and high and positive in periods of deflation. The simplest explanation is that the level of nominal rates is exogenously administered by national central banks, while *ex ante* real rates, the variable incorporated into wealth-owner decision-making, are simply the nominal rate minus the anticipated inflation rate.

3.   INTEREST RATES AND INCOME DISTRIBUTION

In investigating how the social surplus was distributed, the classical economists regarded the rate of interest simply as some portion of the rate of profits, which were regarded as a residual share. They attempted to describe the factors which determine this proportion, and which prevent the rate of profits from falling to the level of the rate of interest. For Ricardo wages in the long run were determined ultimately by the level necessary for subsistence. Both rents and profits were the residual. He regarded interest simply as a proportion of the profit obtained from the employment of the capital, which the money loan enabled the borrower to obtain. Marx regarded profits as capitalists' appropriation of the social surplus produced by labour. He distinguished money capitalists, who own the interest-bearing capital, and industrial capitalists, who borrow money capital and employ it in the sphere of production to exploit labour and generate surplus value. Like Ricardo he argued that the rate of interest was simply some proportion of the average profit rate. Since it exists outside the sphere of production it has no natural rate, but was determined by custom, legal tradition and institutional factors (Panico, 1983).

In neoclassical theory the personal distribution of income was viewed as determined by the price at which individuals can sell the services of each of the factors of production that they own. The demand for all factor services was seen as ultimately derived from a factor's contribution to the value of output at the margin, i.e. its marginal revenue product. The return to all factors, both labour and capital, was viewed as compensation for the value of their marginal physical product. This, together with factor inputs, determined the functional distribution of income. Unlike labour, which consists simply of wages and salaries, property income takes several forms: interest, rent and profits. Rent was viewed as the scarcity payment at the margin for heterogeneous land. Interest was viewed as derived from the net physical productivity of capital as a factor of production. Interest was thus ultimately determined by the same real forces as the rate of profit viewed as a functional return. The two rates were regarded as equivalent in long-run equilibrium. The question whether profits in the short run should be regarded as a functional or a residual return was the subject of perpetual and heated controversy. Monopoly power, innovation and risk-bearing have each been recognized in the neoclassical literature as a distinct source of short-run pofits, whether viewed as a residual return or as a reward to entrepreneurial ability.

The orthodox theory of distribution, which relies on factor-price equilibrium based on demand as determined by marginal revenue productivity, and supply as governed by marginal sacrifice or disutility of factor services, has been subject to many different types of criticism. First, there was the appropriateness and realism of the assumption of constant returns to scale, necessary to ensure that the product was exhausted in equilibrium, the so-called 'adding-up' problem. Secondly, Keynes denied that real wages were equal to the marginal disutility of effort, since labour could bargain only for its nominal and not its real wage. He went on to construct a theory of employment which implicity denied that the real wage for labour was determined by its marginal product. A third criticism stems from Sraffa's elaboration of the classical concept of prices of production. Sraffa showed that there was no need to rely on marginal productivity or disutility to determine equilibrium prices. He also showed that once capital services are recognized as deriving from heterogeneous commodities, as Joan Robinson had long argued, the quantity of any stock of capital goods cannot be measured independently of its price. Sraffa's work denied the logical foundations of a demand curve for factor services based on marginal productivity. It thus completely vitiated the orthodox explanation of market determination of factor prices as a reflection of supply and demand conditions.

The modern post-Keynesian theory of income determination is derived from Kalecki (1954). It is characteristically summed up by the adage: 'Workers spend what they get; capitalists get what they spend.' Ignoring government, national income may be divided into wages received by workers, and profits received by capitalists. National product may similarly be divided into consumption by workers, and consumption and investment by capitalists. If it is assumed that workers spend all their incomes on consumption, profits must then necessarily be exactly equal to capitalists' expenditure for investment and consumption. As Keynes put it, capitalists' profits are like the widow's cruse, which cannot be emptied no matter how much is taken out of it.

Kalecki's other main contribution was to distinguish two broad sectors of the economy: a highly competitive 'flex-price' sector, comprising primarily agriculture and raw materials, where prices are determined by supply and demand as in the orthodox account, and an imperfectly competitive 'fix-price' sector, comprising manufacturing and services, where prices ordinarily are administered at some stable mark-up over normal average variable costs, which he calculated were broadly constant with respect to output. The mark-up is chosen to yield a level of retail profits, after depreciation, interest and dividend pay-out, sufficient to provide for the required degree of internal finance for planned investment expenditures. (In the US, 80–90 per cent of total corporate investment expenditures are internally financed.) Real wages, the ratio of nominal wages to price levels, are therefore determined in commodity markets rather than labour markets, by average labour productivity and the size of the average price–wage mark-up.

For Kalecki the degree of monopoly and the planned investment expenditures of firms determine the size of the mark-up, and so the division of national income between wages and profits. Increased capitalist consumption out of profits would lead to a higher mark-up and lower real wages. Profits would necessarily exceed investment in the same proportion as they are used to purchase capitalists' consumption goods. In contrast, increased worker saving reduces the proportion of investment expenditures that must be internally financed, and so lowers the mark-up and raises real wages. Workers' incomes then consist of wages plus some proportion of interest and dividend payments.

For both Keynes and Kalecki the volume of employment depends on aggregate demand, and not on the level of money or real wage rates. Variations in money wages primarily affect unit costs and so the price level, while real wages are determined by labour productivity and the mark-up over normal variable costs. The mark-up must cover fixed costs, such as depreciation and overhead, and yield sufficient profits after dividends to finance the bulk of planned investment expenditures.

From the viewpoint of classical, neoclassical and Marxian theories of distribution, a change in interest rates primarily creates a *redistribution of property income among capitalists*, between rentiers and dividend or profit recipients. Since labour and property income is determined by the marginal productivity of labour and capital, or by the degree of exploitation, *the functional distribution of income is not directly affected by changes in interest rates*. Of course, each of the above theories would recognize that there may be indirect effects, if e.g. higher interest rates lead to a restriction of investment expenditures, a reduction in aggregate demand, and so a fall in output, employment, wages and profits.

From the viewpoint of the post-Keynesian theory of distribution, the *functional redistributional effect of changes in interest rates centres directly on the responsiveness of the mark-up to interest rates*. As stated, prices in the fix-price sector are viewed as set at some mark-up over normal average variable costs, sufficient to cover fixed costs, dividends and the internal finance of planned investment expenditures. Average fixed costs fall as production increases and overhead costs are spread over a greater volume of output. *Ceteris paribus*, variations in aggregate demand and output leave prices unchanged, but affect net profits. These firms are assumed to set prices based on some expected normal rate of capacity utilization.

In practice, oligopolistic markets commonly lead to the emergence of price leaders, who effectively set the market price for the industry so as to yield their targeted profit rate. Firms that are price-followers live under this price umbrella. They may have higher or lower average costs, and so lower or higher mark-ups and net profits.

Once prices are established, the level of output is determined by aggregate demand. Firms in the fix-price sector are characteristically price-setters and quantity-takers. Firms declare their price, and then, as quantity-takers, produce the output the market demands. In addition they attempt perpetually to maintain a sufficient degree of excess capacity so as to be in a position to expand production in response to unexpected increases in demand. Since they sell at some mark-up above average variable costs, this enables them both to maximize profits over time and to maintain their market share.

The responsiveness of mark-ups to variations in interest rates will presumably depend both on the magnitude and the expected permanence of interest rate changes. Cyclical increases in interest rates, which are expected to be temporary, are likely to be absorbed by firms, and not passed on by a rise in mark-ups. This is particularly likely when they occur in boom periods when aggregate demand is high, capacity utilization and profits are above normal, and unit fixed costs are falling. Similarly, cyclical reductions in interest rates are also likely to be absorbed and not passed on in a reduction in mark-ups. Particularly when they occur in cyclical downturns, interest savings will be retained to help offset the tendency of average fixed costs to rise as overhead costs are spread over a smaller volume of output. Cyclical fluctuations in interest rates may thus, as Marx held, serve primarily to redistribute property income between profits and interest. They will then have no effect on the functional distribution between labour and capital, and only second-order effects on the distribution of personal incomes.

Nevertheless secular increases or decreases in the level of interest rates, changes that are expected to be permanent, must be passed on by firms as an increase or reduction in mark-ups. Interest is a cost, like depreciation, rent and other overhead charges, and thus must be passed on in prices if firms are to attain their profit targets sufficient to finance their desired dividend and investment plans.

The foregoing discussion was confined to the effects of interest rate changes on the private fix price business sector. While this is the largest single borrowing sector, the flex-price sector (agriculture and mining), households and governments are also very large debt issuers in absolute volume.

In the case of the flex-price sector, if long-run prices approximate normal total unit costs, interest rate changes would be expected to be passed on in prices over the long run, assuming the profit rate is unchanged. In the short run, when prices are governed by demand shifts and supply is equated to marginal or variable costs, they will be largely absorbed by producers. This is particularly the case for farmers, who as price-takers are characteristically unable to meet their debt obligations when agricultural prices fall sharply due to forces beyond their control.

The income redistributional effects of changes in interest rates for household sector debt will depend on how household financial asset-liability ratios vary by income level. Although the wealthy receive a larger proportion of their income from interest payments, and as net creditors will benefit from interest rate increases, their larger collateral permits them to maintain higher debt ratios as well.

Similarly, the redistributional effects of changes in interest rates for government debt will depend on how the progressiveness of government debt ownership compares with the progressiveness of government tax obligations. To the extent that government debt was issued to finance government transfer expenditures on current rather than capital account, i.e. is largely deadweight debt, the effects of interest rate changes will also be generationally redistributional. The net incidence will depend on the distribution of debt ownership relative to the distribution of tax liabilities. To the extent that ownership of government debt is more progressive than tax obligations, the rich will be net gainers from increases in interest rates paid by the public sector, and net losers from decreases. Since a large proportion of government debt is held directly by pension funds, money market funds, insurance companies and other financial intermediaries, and only indirectly by private sector households, and the estimate of tax incidence and shifting involves arbitrary assumptions, the calculation of these net redistributional effects for the government sector is not a modest task. Finally, as will be shown, the inverse response of capital gains and losses to interest rate changes seriously complicates the estimation of net distributional incidence for all sectors.

4.   KEYNES'S VIEWS ON THE REDISTRIBUTIONAL EFFECTS OF LOW INTEREST RATES

In the concluding chapter of the *General Theory*, Keynes, in a much quoted and very influential passage, made an impassioned case for the approaching 'euthanasia of the rentier'. He argued that up to full employment the growth of capital is not dependent on the abstinence of the rich, but rather is impeded by it. 'Only in conditions of full employment is a low propensity to consume conducive to the growth of capital, . . . One of the chief social justifications of great inequality of wealth is therefore removed.' (Keynes, 1936, p. 373). He then continued, 'For my own part, I believe there is social and psychological justification for significant inequalities of incomes and wealth, but not for such large disparities as exist today' (Ibid., p. 374).

Keynes's own policy inferences from his theory was first that the rate of interest should be reduced 'to that point relative to the schedule of the marginal efficiency of capital at which there is full employment' (Ibid., p. 375). Influenced possibly by the fashionable 'stagnationist' ideas in the air in the 1930s, he asserted, 'it would not be difficult to increase the stock of capital up to a point where its marginal efficiency had fallen to a very low figure. . . . The return from durable goods . . . would . . . just cover their labour costs of production plus an allowance for risk and the costs of skill and supervision' (Ibid.). This, he went on, would mean

> the euthanasia of the rentier, and, consequently, the euthanasia of the cumulative oppressive power of the capitalist to exploit the scarcity value of capital. Interest today rewards no genuine sacrifice, any more than does the rent of land. The owner of capital can obtain interest because capital is scarce, just as the owner of land can obtain rent because land is scarce. But whilst there may be intrinsic reasons for the scarcity of land, there are no intrinsic reasons for the scarcity of capital. (Ibid. p. 376)

This view encouraged many to view interest payments negatively as the 'dead hand of the past upon the present'.

There is fairly obviously something suspect about Keynes's formulation that a low savings rate is important whenever a country is less than fully employed, after which a high savings rate encourages capital accumulation. After all, he had previously argued that it was investment which determines savings. Since savings by definition are equal to investment *ex post*, no quantum jump in the savings rate will ever be observed as a country reaches full employment. Low savings is due to low investment, and not the reverse. Nevertheless Keynes's advocacy of low interest rates in order to ensure high levels of investment as consistent with full employment found a very receptive audience. It was, in particular, uncritically endorsed by most Third World governments, even though the notion of capital satiation in their case was patently absurd. Since governments were typically the largest borrower the argument was indisputably self-serving.

Keynes's belief that an increased rate of accumulation could deprive capital of its scarcity-value 'within one or two generations' (p. 377) sounds astonishing to us today, fifty years and nearly two generations later, particularly when we have recently experienced short-term interest rates of 20 per cent. With hindsight we can see that Keynes clearly underestimated the effects of technological change in raising the return on new investment. There are intrinsic reasons for the scarcity of capital.

From the viewpoint of our present argument, Keynes appeared apparently to have regarded it as self-evident that a reduction in interest rates would reduce the degree of income inequality, and by implication a rise in the level of interest rates would increase it. Perhaps he had in mind the historically regressive redistributional effects of large deadweight government debt, as in the UK in the nineteenth century, when bond-ownership was much more concentrated than tax liabilities. Note that his argument was long-run, and explicity assumed that profit rates would fall *pari pasu* with interest rates, as investment was expanded in response to lower interest costs and the marginal efficiency of capital was driven down 'to a very low figure'. Keynes's argument can unexceptionally perhaps be rephrased most simply as follows: wealth-ownership is much more unequally distributed than labour income. Therefore, if property income, comprising both profits and interest, falls, the inequality of the total distribution of income must necessarily decline.

Significantly, Keynes's interest rate redistribution argument overlooked the inverse effects of interest rate variation on wealth and so on income in the form of capital gains. As interest rates fall, the value of capital assets, as determined by the discounted value of their future income stream, necessarily increases, so that capital gains will occur in the process. While Keynes's explicit argument was that in the case of reproducible assets the future income streams would fall proportionately with interest rates, this would not be the case for land. Land values would thus rise enormously.[4] The tendency of wealth values and income in the form of capital gains to move conversely with interest income as interest rates vary complicates, to put it mildly, the measurement of the total redistributional effects of interest rate variation.

Low nominal levels of interest rates administered by governments and central banks have been the rule in most developing countries. Given the low level of individual savings, credit was viewed as an important way to promote capital formation, and special agencies were set up to provide cheap credit for the agricultural sector. In most such countries the nominal volume of such credit has grown rapidly, and absorbs a large portion of external funds channelled by international agencies. Despite a huge expansion of credit volume, only a small proportion of farmers in most low-income countries have ever received formal loans.[5] It has only gradually been recognized that such countries are in no sense accurately characterized as having excess savings and a lack of investment opportunities, but rather by numerous productive opportunities which cannot be taken advantage of because of credit unavailability. Low rates have created excess demand for credit, and necessitated administrative rationing to clear the market. Poorer borrowers with less collateral have, as a result, been denied credit completely. Investment projects have not been rationed efficiently by expected return, and the largest and safest borrowers have benefited from a substantial and highly regressive income subsidy.

The other role of interest rates is to attract savings into financial assets. Most poor countries maintained nominal rates at low levels despite the presence of inflation, so that interest rates in real terms were negative. This discouraged savers from acquiring financial assets, and encouraged them to hoard unproductive real assets such as land and stocks as inflation hedges. While in the short run the volume of nominal lending *by* the banking system determines the volume of nominal lending *to* the banking system, i.e. loans make deposits, in the long run in real terms this relationship is reversed. The amount of real loans the banking system can extend in the long run is governed by the amount of real deposits that the banking system can attract.[6]

5. EMPIRICAL ESTIMATION

To the extent that interest rates vary procyclically as a policy instrument, it is difficult to isolate empirically the income redistributional effects of interest rate variations from time-series data. Inflation, capacity utilization and unemployment rates, which may also have important redistributional effects, are all characterized by similar cyclical variations. Regression analysis suggests that labour's share is highly sensitive to the unemployment rate and to the direction and rate of change of the unemployment rate. It has been estimated that over the period 1948–81 an increase of 1 per cent in the unemployment rate was associated with a ½ per cent decrease in labour's share. With zero unemployment labour's share would rise by 3 per cent per year, so that the distributionally neutral employment rate was 6 per cent (Buchele, 1984, p.79). But since unemployment and interest rate variables are highly collinear, it is virtually impossible to isolate significant individual variable effects by regression analysis with time series data.

A related difficulty concerns the nature of the data on income distribution. First, long-run changes in the functional distribution of income between labour and property shares are dominated by changes in sectoral composition. The government sector is treated as if entirely produced by labour, since a return to capital is not imputed for the public sector. Much of the service sector is similarly predominantly labour-intensive. Finally, in the individual proprietors' sector, which includes much of agriculture, the division of proprietors' income into labour and property shares is dependent on a necessarily arbitrary assignment of opportunity costs. Long-run changes in the personal distribution of income are similarly dominated by demographic, ethnic and sociological facors which affect family size. As a result even highly statistically significant movements in the functional or personal income distribution may have little or nothing to do with the associated variation in interest rates, due to an 'omitted variables' problem.

The total income redistributional effects of changes in interest rates and inflation rates for financial asset-holders are impossible to estimate without including capital gains and losses. Consider a $1000 bond whose yield rises from 5 to 7 per cent, at a time when the inflation rate increases by the same amount. While the interest rate and the inflation rate increase by 2 per cent, the interest income flow increases by 40 per cent, from $50 to $70. Under such conditions the rise in interest income, rather than an increased return on capital, can alternatively be viewed as a return of capital. Over the year the value of the bond in real terms will fall to $980, so that the extra $20 of income just permits the bondholder to stay even. When interest rates rise the market value of long term bonds goes down. Existing bond-holders cannot receive the higher yield unless the bond is sold at a precisely offsetting capital loss. Finally, the extra $20 of interest that replaced the real depreciation of the bond principal is considered income under the tax laws and subject to tax. Thus while from the standpoint of income flow interest recipients look like big winners, after all balance-sheet effects are considered they may be big losers. Stockholders are also affected by changes in interest rates, to the extent dividend yields vary together with interest rates. A rise in interest rates ordinarily causes price–earnings ratios to fall, imposing capital losses on stockholders as well as bond-holders. As shown in studies of the income redistribution effects of inflation, the results differ markedly depending on whether one uses Census (cash) income or accrued comprehensive income (ACI), which includes income-in-kind, capital gains and losses from balance sheet changes, and tax effects (Minarik, 1979).

A final problem concerns the interrelatedness of different government policy actions. Upon taking office in 1980, the Reagan administration near simultaneously administered cuts in social spending, whose effects fell heavily on the poor, across-the-board tax cuts, which had a sharp regressive effect on after-tax disposable income, and a high interest rate policy. One of the effects of the latter was to cause the dollar to appreciate substantially, and so induce a wave of import penetration which effectively put an end to double-digit money wage increases. As is by now well known, the share of money income received by the bottom quintile of all families has fallen over the 1980s, while the share received by the top quintile has increased. The Reagan administration's identification of 'growth of the federal government' as the major cause of the long-term decline in the US growth rate since the early 1970s is now increasingly widely recognized as a 'Trojan horse' for a policy of less egalitarian income redistribution. It is thus extremely difficult to isolate the redistributional effects of the rise in interest rates from historical time-series at a time when so many other variables were changing. This difficulty speaks against

Figure 2.1.   Relative income shares.

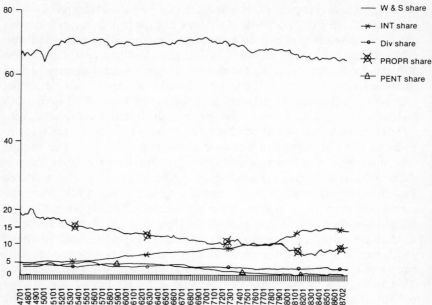

regression analysis and for policy simulation studies (Bluestone and Havens, 1986). Finally, households at any given income level are differentially affected by variations in interest rates. Since the elderly receive a larger than average share of their income from property, they are likely to be affected more like upper-income groups by interest rate variations, irrespective of their income level.

The behaviour of the functional distribution of income shares for the US economy over the postwar period is presented in Figure 2.1 and Table 2.1. The two most striking changes are the 10 per cent rise in the interest share, from 4 to 14 per cent, and the 10 per cent fall in the proprietors' share, from 19 to 9 per cent. Over the entire period, the share of wages, dividends and rents each fell slightly, from 1 to 2.5 per cent. These trends exhibited substantial variability over time. Over the period from 1948 to 1970, the proprietors' share fell by 8.5 per cent, accompanied by a broadly similar increase in both the wage share (4.7 per cent) and the interest share (3.9 per cent). Since proprietors' income is a combination of both labour and property income, a reasonable surmise is that before 1970 the rise in the labour and interest share represented primarily a transfer from

Table 2.1   Personal income share, 1949-87

Year	Wages, salaries, and other labour income	Interest income	Dividend income	Proprietors' income	Rental income
1949	66.0	4.0	3.3	18.7	3.3
1950	66.6	4.2	3.5	17.4	3.2
1955	69.3	4.6	3.1	14.9	3.9
1960	69.2	5.7	3.1	13.2	3.7
1965	69.2	7.0	3.4	11.8	3.4
1970	70.7	7.9	2.9	10.3	2.3
1975	67.1	9.3	2.2	9.5	1.0
1980	66.9	12.0	2.3	8.0	0.3
1985	65.1	14.3	2.3	7.7	0.3
1986	64.8	14.1	2.3	8.2	0.5
1987	64.6	13.6	2.3	8.8	0.6

Note:
The columns do not sum horizontally to 100 because transfer payments and contributions for social insurance have been omitted.
Source:
Survey of Current Business, Department of Commerce, Bureau of Economic Analysis.

proprietors' income. In contrast over the period 1970–87 the proprietors' share fell by only 1.5 per cent, while the interest share continued to rise by 5.7 per cent, and the wage share fell by 6.1 per cent.

Table 2.2 presents the behaviour of unit labour costs and the implicit price deflator for the non-farm business sector, which may be considered a reasonable proxy for the 'fix-price' sector. As seen, the implicit price deflator follows unit labour costs closely. Over the entire forty-year period, both the mark-up and its inverse, labour's share for the non-farm business, were extremely stable with no sign of trend. There was some variability within the period. The mark-up fell slightly to 1960, then sharply to 1970, before rising again. But the substantial 6 per cent fall in the share of wages and salaries and rise in the share of interest in total personal income since 1970 (Table 2.1) was reflected by only a 2 per cent rise in mark-ups and fall in labour's share in the non-farm business sector (Table 2.2). The 4 per cent rise in the interest share of personal income and fall in the share of wages and salaries over the period 1970–80 (Table 2.1) must have been due to the general rise in debt levels and total interest payments by all sectors of the economy, since over that period the average mark-up in the fix-price sector actually fell slightly (Table 2.2). However, since 1980 the 2.3 per cent fall in wages' share in personal income (Table 2.1), was more than fully reflected by the rise in average mark-ups

Table 2.2   Unit labour costs, prices and mark-up, non-farm business sector (1977 = 100)

Year	Unit labour costs (WN/Q)	Implicit price deflator (P)	Average mark-up k = P/(WN/Q)	Labour's share (WN-PQ)
1948	36.7	36.4	.992	1.008
1950	37.1	37.5	1.011	.989
1955	42.9	43.1	1.004	.996
1960	49.7	48.5	.976	1.024
1965	50.9	51.9	1.020	.980
1970	65.2	63.4	.972	1.028
1975	89.2	88.3	.990	1.010
1980	132.9	127.8	.962	1.039
1985	165.6	164.6	.994	1.006
1986	169.3	168.1	.993	1.007
1987	172.6	171.8	.995	1.005

Source:
Monthly Labour report, Department of Labour, Bureau of Labour Statistics.

by firms in the fix-price sector (Table 2.2) in response to the sharp rise in interest rates and the cost of debt finance.

The rise in interest as a proportion of personal income from 4 to 14 per cent was due to the rise in the ratio of debt to income as well as to the increase in interest rates. As is well known, interest rates increased nearly five-fold over the period. Short-term interest rates averaged about 2 per cent in the 1950s, 4 per cent in the 1960s, 6 per cent in the 1970s, and 9 per cent in the 1980s. Since 1970 debt ratios have also risen substantially for all sectors. As shown in Chart 2.1 the ratio of total debt to GNP was about 1.5 in 1965 and 1970, 1.6 in 1980, and 2.2 in 1987. As shown in Charts 2.2–2.8, a general sharp rise in debt ratios since 1981 has been evident for the US, coincident with the rise in interest rates.

In order to explain the effects of changes in interest income for the distribution of personal income, it is necessary first to examine the distribution of wealth ownership. Wealth data are very imperfect, and the *Survey of Consumer Finances*, 1983 probably provides the best recent estimate of household wealth distribution. Oversampling of high-income households has effectively reduced the differences between survey-based and flow-of-funds estimates of wealth aggregates (Avery, Elliehausen and Kennickell, 1987). Estimates of the proportion of wealth owned by upper-income families (the top 10 per cent of families with 1983 incomes above £50,000) are shown in Table 2.3.

**Chart 2.1   Debt levels relative to GNP[a]
total: all sectors**

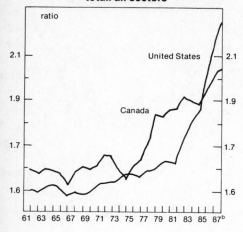

**Chart 2.2   Debt levels relative to GNP[a]
financial sector**

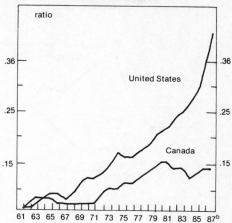

**Chart 2.3   Debt levels relative to GNP[a]
non-financial sector**

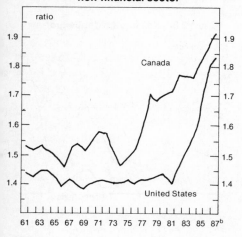

**Chart 2.4   Debt levesl relative to GNP[a]
private non-financial corporations**

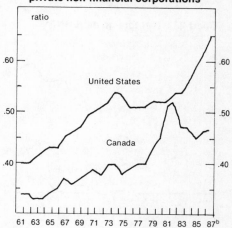

Source:
Canada: National Balance Sheet & National Income Accounts.
United States: Flow of Funds & National Income Accounts.
Notes:
[a] Ratio, debt to GNP.
[b] Scotlabank Economics estimate for 1987.

Chart 2.5   North American debt/equity ratios[a]

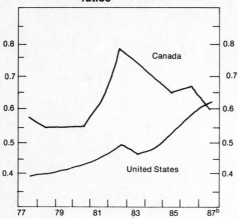

Source:
Canada: Industrial Corporation Financial Statistics.
United States: Quarterly Financial Report.
Notes:
[a]Total manufacturing and resource industries.
[b]To 1987 Q3.

Chart 2.6   Debt levels relative to GNP[a] government sector

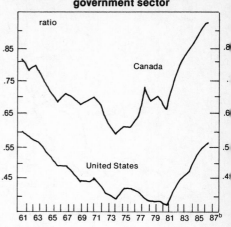

Source:
Canada: National Balance Sheet & National Income Accounts.
United States: Flow of Funds & National Income Accounts.
Notes:
[a]Ratio, debt to GNP.
[b]Scotiabank Economics estimate for 1987.

Chart 2.7   Net foreign debt/GNP[a]

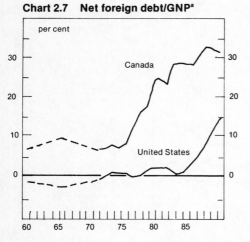

Note:
[a]Data available at 5 year intervals 1960–1970.

Chart 2.8   Net foreign debt/exports[a]

Note:
[a]Data plotted at 6 year intervals 1960–1970.

The top 10 per cent of all families received 30 per cent of total income, and held 63.5 per cent of total household assets, 68 per cent of net worth, 90 per cent of stocks, 95 per cent of bonds and trusts, 91 per cent of business equity, about 50 per cent of fixed income liquid assets, and 32.7 per cent of total debt held by the household sector. As shown in Tables 2.3 and 2.4, the degree of income and wealth inequality have both increased since 1963, as has the share of total debt issued by upper-income families. The extent of income and wealth concentration is shown by the fact that, in 1983, the top 1 per cent of all families owned more than 30 per cent of total wealth, and received more than 10 per cent of total income. The top $\frac{1}{2}$ per cent of all families, while receiving 6.5 per cent of total income, held nearly 25 per cent of total wealth, and issued nearly 10 per cent of total debt.

About 40 per cent of the wealth of the top 10 per cent was held in the form of corporate stock and business equity, compared with only 70 per cent for the lowest 90 per cent. Such assets are only indirectly affected by variations in interest rates, and do not directly generate interest income.

Even though the top 10 per cent hold only a relatively small proportion of their total wealth in the form of fixed income financial assets (18 per cent), they accounted for 70 per cent of all fixed income assets held by the household sector. The share of fixed income financial assets in total household assets was 17 per cent in 1983 (Table 2.3). As may be seen from Table 2.1, the increase in the share of interest income in total personal income from 1963 to 1983 was about 7 per cent. The rise in the share of interest income accruing to the top 10 per cent (4.8 per cent) thus accounted for most (85 per cent) of the total increase of 5.6 per cent in the share of income received by the top 10 per cent, from 23.8 to 29.4 per cent, from 1963 to 1983.

6.   CONCLUSIONS

Over the entire post-war period the share of interest in personal income rose by 10 per cent, while labour's share remained remarkably stable. This stability conceals a 5 per cent rise in labour's share to 1970, which appears to reflect the concurrent fall in proprietors' income, and then a 6 per cent fall to 1987. The latter was accompanied by a similar rise in interest income, while proprietors' income fell only slightly. About one third of the 6 per cent shift in the functional distribution of income from wages and salaries to interest income since 1970 can be explained by the rise in average mark-ups and fall in labour's share in the fix-price sector.

Table 2.3   Wealth of U.S. Households, full sample 1983 SCF

	All households		0-90th %		Percentile of net worth 90-99th %		2nd 1/2%		UPPER 1/2%	
	AMOUNT ($ B)	% OF GRO AS	AMOUNT ($ B)	% OF ALL HH	AMOUNT ($ B)	% OF ALL HH	AMOUNT ($ B)	% OF ALL HH	AMOUNT ($ B)	% OF ALL HH
Gross assets	12103.6	100.0%	4418.3	36.5%	3861.7	31.9%	849.3	7.0%	2974.2	24.6%
Principal residence	3778.9	31.2%	2456.4	65.0%	1013.4	26.8%	119.5	3.2%	189.6	5.0%
Other real estate (gross)	1871.3	15.5%	410.4	21.9%	677.2	36.2%	123.5	6.6%	660.1	35.3%
Public stock	1075.3	8.9%	109.6	10.2%	351.6	32.7%	144.0	13.4%	470.2	43.7%
Bonds and trusts	851.8	7.0%	47.6	5.6%	212.3	24.9%	52.1	6.1%	539.9	63.4%
Cheque accounts	122.3	1.0%	66.7	54.5%	34.8	28.5%	9.1	7.5%	11.7	9.6%
Savings, CDS, money Mkt	1062.0	8.8%	522.0	49.2%	387.8	36.5%	61.0	5.7%	91.2	8.6%
Life insurance cash value	270.6	2.2%	175.0	64.7%	66.6	24.6%	10.0	3.7%	19.0	7.0%
Business Assets (net)	2364.4	19.5%	209.4	8.9%	908.2	38.4%	306.6	13.0%	940.2	39.8%
Automobiles	375.6	3.1%	298.5	79.5%	65.9	17.6%	5.1	1.3%	6.2	1.6%
Miscellaneous	331.6	2.7%	122.8	37.0%	143.9	43.4%	18.5	5.6%	46.3	14.0%
Debt	1541.4	12.7%	1037.2	67.3%	310.6	20.1%	44.9	2.9%	148.7	9.6%
Automobile debt	91.5	0.8%	82.0	89.6%	8.7	9.5%	0.3	0.4%	0.5	0.5%
Consumer debt	228.5	1.9%	136.6	59.8%	50.9	22.3%	13.1	5.7%	29.7	12.2%
Principal residence debt	883.0	7.3%	696.6	78.9%	152.0	17.2%	14.5	1.6%	19.9	2.3%
Other real estate debt	338.4	2.8%	122.0	36.1%	99.1	29.3%	16.9	5.0%	100.4	29.7%
Net worth	10562.2	87.3%	3381.1	32.0%	3551.1	33.6%	804.4	7.6%	2825.6	26.8%
Income (gross)	2330.0	19.3%	1644.1	70.6%	451.9	19.4%	83.4	3.6%	150.7	6.5%
Number of observations	4103		3343		490		90		180	
Number of households	83917968		75525808		7552554		420631		418987	
Minimum wealth ($'S)	−73400		−73400		218094		1479941		2660357	
Maximum wealth ($'S)	86852000		217882		1477888		2656841		86852000	

Source:
Avery, Elliehausen and Kennickell, 1987.

However the entire fall in labour's share since 1980 can be explained by the rise in the average mark-up in the fix-price sector, as firms raised their mark-ups in response to the secular increase in interest levels, thus substantiating the post-Keynesian theory of income distribution. Most of the rise in the interest share over the period 1970–80 must thus have been due to the general rise in interest rates and debt–income ratios across all sectors of the economy.

With regard to the personal distribution of income, the high degree of concentration and the increase in the ownership share of upper-income groups in both income and wealth from 1963 to 1983 have been noted. Since upper-income groups are substantial net creditors, they gain on income account from increases in interest rates. Even though 70 per cent of upper-income wealth is held in the form of corporate stock and business equity, the rise in interest income can explain 4.8 per cent of the observed increase of 5.6 per cent in the income share received by the top 10 per cent of families. However, given the importance of realised capital gains in the adjusted gross income of upper income taxpayers (35 per cent of AGI in

Table 2.4   Wealth of U.S. Households, full sample 1963 SFCC

| | All households | | 0-90th % | | Percentile of net worth | | | | | |
| | | | | | 90-99th % | | 2nd 1/2% | | UPPER 1/2% | |
	AMOUNT ($ B)	% OF GRO AS	AMOUNT ($ B)	% OF ALL HH	AMOUNT ($ B)	% OF ALL HH	AMOUNT ($ B)	% OF ALL HH	AMOUNT ($ B)	% OF ALL HH
Gross assets	4942.5	100.0%	2081.6	42.1%	1460.6	29.6%	318.9	6.5%	1081.3	21.9%
Principal residence	1494.2	30.2%	1134.7	75.9%	287.7	19.3%	29.8	2.0%	42.0	2.8%
Other real estate (gross)	416.5	8.4%	115.0	27.6%	192.3	46.2%	27.7	6.7%	81.4	19.5%
Public stock	721.0	14.6%	62.1	8.6%	210.4	29.2%	112.2	15.6%	336.3	46.6%
Bonds and trusts	295.6	6.0%	21.4	7.2%	38.7	13.1%	10.5	3.5%	225.1	76.1%
Cheque accounts	76.9	1.6%	36.3	47.2%	22.6	29.4%	3.8	5.0%	14.2	18.5%
Savings, CDS, money Mkt	428.3	8.7%	228.8	53.4%	159.8	37.3%	11.0	2.6%	28.7	6.7%
Life insurance cash value	193.3	3.9%	106.9	55.3%	58.7	30.4%	10.3	5.3%	17.4	9.0%
Business Assets (net)	978.3	19.8%	187.9	19.2%	398.9	40.8%	86.0	8.8%	305.5	31.2%
Automobiles	178.6	3.6%	142.3	79.7%	30.7	17.2%	3.0	1.7%	2.6	1.4%
Miscellaneous	159.9	3.2%	46.3	28.9%	60.7	38.0%	24.6	15.4%	28.2	17.7%
Debt	721.2	14.6%	556.3	77.1%	108.4	15.0%	15.4	2.1%	41.2	5.7%
Automobile debt	57.5	1.2%	51.5	89.6%	5.7	10.0%	0.0	0.1%	0.2	0.4%
Consumer debt	112.1	2.3%	67.6	60.3%	16.8	15.0%	6.9	6.1%	20.8	18.5%
Principal residence debt	466.9	9.4%	409.6	87.7%	49.7	10.7%	4.8	1.0%	2.7	0.6%
Other real estate debt	84.7	1.7%	27.5	32.4%	36.1	42.6%	3.7	4.3%	17.5	20.7%
Net worth	4221.2	85.4%	1525.4	36.1%	1352.2	32.0%	303.5	7.2%	1040.1	24.6%
Income (gross)	1217.4	24.6%	927.6	76.2%	205.0	16.8%	21.7	1.8%	63.1	5.2%
Number of observations	2557		1730		444		95		288	
Number of households	57926992		52143696		5202442		288998		291845	
Minimum wealth ($'S)	−62889		−62889		138212		816731		1390218	
Maximum wealth ($'S)	76169104		138063		814614		1387081		76169104	

Source:
Avery, Elliehausen and Kennickell, 1987.

1982 IRS Individual Income Tax Returns, compared to 1.8 per cent for all taxpayers) the indirect effects of interest rate changes and inflation on wealth values and capital gains income may be of equal importance.

This leads to an additional and separate argument for the policy goals of low interest rates and price stability. In a world of more rapid inflation, central banks must administer nominal interest rates at a higher level than in a world of less rapid inflation, as consistent with the desired growth of real aggregate demand. The market value of total financial assets must fall, since asset values are inversely related to the nominal interest rate at which future income streams are discounted. Moreover, the warranted wealth–income ratio of an economy depends positively on its saving/investment ratio, and negatively on the rate of growth of its nominal income (Moore, 1988). As a result both financial wealth values, and the ratio of wealth to income, fall as interest and inflation rates rise, and conversely rise as interest and inflation rates are reduced. In so far as wealth is an argument in everyone's utility function, people as a whole are better off in a world of price stability where interest rates are lower and wealth-income ratios are higher, than in a world of inflation. The effects of inflation should thus be viewed as not primarily to redistribute wealth, but to destroy it.

Nevertheless, since the distribution of wealth is much more unequal than the distribution of income, in a world of low inflation and low interest rates where wealth–income ratios are higher, the distribution of wealth would be even more unequal, in so far as the rich would gain proportionally more than the poor. The effect of interest rates and inflation on total utility may thus depend ultimately on the strength of the green-eyed monster.

NOTES

*   This paper has benefited substantially from the comments of Christopher Niggle made at the Post-Keynesian Workshop on Income Distribution.
1.   In researching this Chapter, I first conducted a data-base search of the literature. The *Economic Literature Index*, which contains about 200,000 records for the period 1969–87 for all journals covered by the *JEL*, keyed more than 4000 files for 'Interest Rates or Monetary Policy', and about 2000 for 'Income Distribution or Redistribution'. But the intersection of these two sets yielded only five files; three on the distributional effects of interest rate regulations, one on rural financial markets in LDCs, and Tracy Mott's 'A Post-Keynesian Formulation of Liquidity Preference' in the *JPKE*. I then tried *ABI-Inform*, a larger database containing nearly half a million records from 660 economic, business and trade periodicals from 1971 to June 1988. This keyed about 19,000 articles on 'Interest Rates or Monetary Policy', and 18,000 on 'Income Distribution or Redistribution'. But the intersection of these two sets was again minuscule. The search yielded only 38 records, representing about 0.01 per cent of the total.
2.   For a discussion of real and monetary theories of interest see Moore (1988), ch. 10 'Interest Rates: a real or monetary phenomenon'.
3.   For an extended development of this position see Moore (1988), Part I.
4.   Some indication of the effect of low interest rates on land values may be had from the current situation in Japan, where the value of the grounds of the Emperor's palace in Tokyo currently exceeds on paper the value of all the land in the state of California! (*Economist*, 11 June 1988, p. 33).
5.   It has been estimated that only about 5 per cent of the farmers in Africa, and perhaps 15 per cent in Asia and Latin America have had access to formal credit. Typically 5 per cent of the borrowers have received about 80 per cent of the amounts disbursed (Gonzales-Vega, 1983, p. 366).
6.   See Moore (1988), ch. 13.

REFERENCES

Avery, R. G. Elliehausen and A. Kennickell 'Measuring Wealth with Survey Data: An Evaluation of the 1983 Survey of Consumer Finances', mimeo, 15 May 1987, Federal Reserve System.

Bluestone, B. and J. Havens, 'How to Cut the Deficit and Rebuild America', *Challenge* May/June, 1986, pp. 22–9.

Buchele, R., 'Reaganomics and the Fairness Issue', *Challenge* September/October, 1984, pp. 25–31.

Gonzales-Vega, C., 'Arguments for Interest Rate Reform', in J. D. Von Pischke, D. Adams and G. Donald (eds), *Rural Financial Markets in Developing Countries*, Baltimore, Johns Hopkins University Press, 1983, pp. 365-72.

Kalecki, M., *Theory of Economic Dynamics*, New York, Rinehart, 1954.

Keynes, J. M., *The General Theory of Employment, Interest and Money*, London, Macmillan, 1936.

Minarik, J., 'Who Wins, Who Loses from Inflation?', *Challenge* January/February, 1979, pp. 26-31.

Moore, B. J., *Horizontalists and Verticalists: The Macroeconomics of Credit Money*, New York, Cambridge University Press, 1988.

Panico, C., 'Marx's Analysis of the Relationship Between the Rate of Interest and the Rate of Profits', in J. Eatwell and M. Milgate (eds), *Keynes' Economics and the Theory of Value and Distribution*, London, Duckworth, 1983, pp. 167-86.

Summers, L., 'The Nonadjustment of Nominal Interest Rates: A Study of the Fisher Effect', in J. Tobin (ed.), *Macroeconomics, Prices and Quantities*, Washington, D.C., Brookings Institution, 1983, pp. 201-34.

3. Keynes, Income Distribution and Incomes Policy

J. A. Kregel

1

The role of income distribution in Keynes's theory has always been something of an enigma. He appeared to be more concerned with the problem in the *Treatise on Money* than in the *General Theory* where it gets only passing attention.[1] The adoption of the wage-unit as the unit of measure in the *General Theory* has led some commentators to argue that Keynes assumed output and employment to be independent of monetary factors such as the relative levels of money wages and prices despite his clear dissent from such a position. John Hicks has gone further and stated that Keynes's theory employs a 'labour standard' (in difference from, e.g., a 'gold standard') and therefore requires not only a constant, but a rigid nominal wage level (cf. Hicks, 1985).

It would thus appear that Keynes treated distribution as primarily a monetary, rather than a real, phenomenon, related more to price than to output determination. The object of the present chapter is to try to discover whether the absence of discussion of distribution in the *General Theory* is consistent with this view, and to trace the implications for the analysis of incomes policies to control inflation.

2

Hicks suggests that Keynes was led to the assumption of rigid wages as the result of his experience during the 1920s return to the Gold Standard. (The implicit reference is to the difficulty in reducing miners' wages and the subsequent General Strike in 1926.) But Keynes was careful to argue that his objection to traditional analysis did not concern the influence of changes in wages on output and employment, but rather the method of analysis of how this might occur.

There is, however, more than an implicit historical reference to the idea of a 'standard' in Keynes's theory. Sir John's reference to a 'labour standard' may have been an unconscious recollection of Keynes's criticism in the *Treatise* of Fisher's 'cash-transactions standard' and the Cambridge 'cash-balances standard', and his suggestion to analyse instead a 'purchasing power standard' or a 'labour standard', because these latter standards

> are fundamental in a sense in which price-levels based on other types of expenditure are not. Human effort and human consumption are the ultimate matters from which alone economic transactions are capable of deriving any significance; and all other forms of expenditure only acquire importance from their having some relationship, sooner or later, to the effort of producers or to the expenditure of consumers. I propose, therefore to break away from the traditional method of setting out from the total quantity of money irrespective of the purposes on which it is employed, and to start instead . . . with its twofold division (1) into the parts which have been *earned* by the production of consumption-goods and of investment-goods respectively, and (2) into the parts which are *expended* on consumption-goods and on saving respectively.

Keynes goes on to state the condition for price stability as the equivalence of the two proportions, for only then the 'price-level of consumption-goods will be in equilibrium with their cost of production' (1930, pp. 120–1). Keynes extends this proposition in terms of a 'fundamental equation' for the price of consumption goods:

$$P = (1/e) W + (I' - S)/R$$

where W is the rate of earnings per unit of human effort, e is the efficiency or productivity of labour, $(1/e)W$ the rate of earnings per unit of output, R, or unit labour costs. When $I' = S$ the second term on the right-hand side vanishes and $P = (1/e) W$.

The purchasing power standard may thus be expressed as $1/P$ and the labour standard as $1/W$. It is also possible to say that in equilibrium, defined as stable P, the 'labour' and 'purchasing power' standards are equivalent when corrected for the differences in the efficiency of labour effort, or that $1/e = P/W$, or $WN = PR$ or $W/P = R/N$. This means that money wages have the same amount of *purchasing* power over goods for labourers (W/P) as the money wage buys *producing* power of goods for the entrepreneur (R/N).

Keynes argues that since the quantity of money cannot influence any variable of the fundamental equation directly, it cannot affect the labour or purchasing power standards; it is thus redundant as an explanation of prices for it has no effect on the 'effort of producers or the expenditure of consumers'. It thus follows that the quantity of money will not have any direct effect on output or employment, for if it does not disturb the equilibrium between costs and prices, it creates no incentive to change normal levels of production. All impact comes indirectly through the impact of money on interest rates, and of interest rates on the second term of the fundamental equation, $(I' - S)/R$.

This result stems from the fact that Keynes's theory of prices is based on the proportions in which earnings are divided into consumption and saving and in which expenditures on labour are divided into production of investment and capital goods. Only those factors which change these proportions will have an effect on prices, profits, and thus on output and employment decisions.

3

In the *General Theory* the two independent decisions concerning expenditure by households and the composition of output by firms is replaced by the decision of the entrepreneur concerning the operating level for existing capacity and the increase in capacity through net investment. With only a single decision-maker, the entrepreneur, it was more natural to adopt the standard of greatest relevance to the entrepreneur's profit, the 'labour power of money or the earnings standard' which measures 'the purchasing power of money over units of human effort', recognizing that

> the chief obstacle in the way of computing this standard is to be found in the difficulty of finding a common unit in which to compare different kinds of human effort. For even if we agree – as we must – that it is proper to ignore degrees of skill in this connection and to mean the rate of earnings per unit of effort averaged over all grades of skill actually prevailing in the community, we ought still, theoretically at least, to take account of variations in the intensity, distastefulness and regularity of work. (1930, p. 56)

The adoption of this standard will require the assumption of a fixed distribution of skill levels and a fixed, associated set of wage differentials, if it is to be used as an 'index of the labour power of money . . . the average hourly money earnings of the whole body of workers of every grade' (ibid.). It would seem that the adoption of the wage-unit was not so much intended to provide a method of aggregation or of translating from nominal to real values, as to provide an adequate standard for the decisions of entrepreneurs. Since the 'wage-unit' or the 'labour standard' is a 'real value' as far as the entrepreneur is concerned, it does not necessarily follow that the wage-unit must be rigid if it is to be used as a standard, although it is necessary that wage differentials should be constant and independent of the level of output. The fundamental assumption of the 'labour standard' is rigid wage differentials, not rigid money wages.

There is some evidence, however, to suggest that this is an assumption which Keynes did take from experience (cf. 1936, pp. 13–14); his insistence that labour would attempt to use money wages to protect their *relative* real wages earned the charge that he assumed that labour suffered from money illusion when he was in fact assuming that labour recognized that real wages were determined by factors which were outside the wage bargain.

4

Keynes was also usually careful to distinguish between two propositions: the impact of a change in the level of wages on the level of output and employment at a point in time, and the impact of a change in the level of output and employment on the purchasing power standard, i.e. on the real wage. The latter was not of direct importance to the invariance of the labour standard, although there will also be an influence of changes in the level of wages on the level of output and employment because of the impact on the labour standard.

With respect to the second proposition, in the *General Theory* Keynes had assumed that real wages would move inversely with changes in the level of employment, primarily due to decreasing productivity. This caused two diverse sets of problems. First, it allowed critics such as Pigou to argue that Keynes's policy would work only because it reduced real wages and increased profits, which was the traditional explanation. Second, if higher wages and prices were required to reduce real wages, rentier opinion would clearly be hostile to full employment policy. Harrod, on the other hand, worried that the real wage reductions implicit in Keynes' proposals would make the trades unions hostile. But these were 'political' impediments, not economic factors. Indeed, when it was pointed out, first by Harrod, and then by Dunlop and Tarshis, that statistical evidence showed that increased output could be produced at lower costs and prices, these factors became irrelevant and the discussion centred on the impact of wage changes on the decisions of entrepreneurs, i.e. on the labour standard.

The question was resolved by reference to the behaviour of costs. In conditions of constant costs and flexible prices there is no difference between the impact of a rise in money wages and the impact of a change in effective demand on real wages. In conditions of decreasing costs it is possible for both the purchasing power and the producing power of wages to rise. It would seem that Keynes reached a conclusion similar to the exclusion of the rate of interest from the propensity to consume – since the impact could go either way it is best left out. By assuming the wage-unit constant neither money nor real wages could have any direct effect on employment in the short period.

5

There was, however, a loss in clarity in the passage from the 'two-standards' system of the *Treatise*, to the single standard system of the *General Theory*. As already noted, equilibrium in the *Treatise* could be expressed in terms of an equivalence between the labour and purchasing power standards: $1/P = e/W$ (or $WN = PR$ or $W/P = R/N$). In disequilibrium, I' departed from S, and the two standards diverged, with $1/P$, and thus W/P, falling relative to W/e. The *producing* power of labour remains unchanged while its *purchasing* power falls, the difference giving rise to 'windfall profits'. The relative movement of the two standards reflects the movement of prices and total profits (which include normal remuneration of entrepreneurs plus windfall profits).

By defining the average product of labour as $e = R/N = W/P = A$, and the windfall profits per unit of consumption good as $(I' - S)/R$ the fundamental price equation may be written $P = K(W/A)$, where $K = [(I' - S)/R]/(W/A)$ and $k = 1 + K$. Then k becomes the measure of divergence of the two standards, or as it is more commonly known, the degree of monopoly or the mark-up of prices over costs.[2] In 'normal' conditions $k = 1$.

Although changes in k reflect changes in the distribution of income, this is insufficient to build a theory of distribution, for there is no explanation of the base or 'normal' distribution which is implicit in the equilibrium position $k = 1$. Since K is a function of investment decisions relative to savings, the mark-up on consumption goods, k becomes a function of the rate of interest (which makes consumption goods prices similar to capital goods prices which in the *Treatise* are also determined by interest rates). Changes in distribution can then be traced to divergences of the interest rate from its natural level. But the natural interest rate is defined as that which preserves the 'normal' position of equilibrium, so it does not provide an explanation of distribution.

As Nell (1973) has pointed out, there is no theoretical basis which explains either absolute or relative real earnings. In such conditions it would seem appropriate to extend Chick's (1985) suggestion that Keynes's use of the wage-unit is meant to reflect historical circumstances governing wage levels, to include historically-given skill and wage differentials. The base or 'normal' distribution of income between wages and profits is then given historically, as is the natural rate of interest which produces $I' = S$ and $k = 1$. The question that then has to be confronted is why wages should ever depart from their normal position, for it is clear that unless changes in money wages can influence the rate of interest they cannot change the prevailing distribution of income.[3]

6

To see more clearly the different role played by the distribution of income in Keynes's theory, it is useful to reconsider the traditional analysis of the effect of changes in wages on the level of employment. The traditional argument is that the profit incentives will lead the firm to produce at the point where price is equal to marginal cost given existing plant. If any firm is producing below this level it can increase profits by expanding employment because marginal revenue from a marginal unit of output exceeds the marginal wage cost of producing it at any level of output below this point. If, when all plants are operating at this position, there are still unemployed resources (labour), then unemployed workers should offer to work for wages below the prevailing market wage, which through competition should reduce wages all round. This shifts the average cost curves for all firms down and creates a profit incentive to expand production since the profit-maximizing position of marginal cost–marginal revenue equality occurs at a higher level of output. The new short-period equilibrium is one in which price exceeds average cost and leads in the long-run to either the entry of new firms, the use of previously scrapped machinery, or investment in the now slightly larger, profit-maximizing, plant. The limit to this process of expansion of investment and the increase in capacity is given by long-period full employment when the fall in the average cost curve due to declining wages comes to a halt.

The process of expansion caused by the impact of a reduction in wages on profits creating the incentive to increase output is, however, unchanged whether the average revenue curve is horizontal or negatively sloped, i.e. in conditions of perfect or imperfect competition in output markets, a uniform reduction in the average cost curve will increase the profit-maximizing level of output and create excess profits that will lead to new investment that will eliminate excess profits whether they are judged relative to the competitive norm or the imperfectly competitive norm (in which case the so-called equilibrium with 'excess capacity' argument comes in). In equilibrium, prices equal average unit costs of production and 'excess' profits are zero.

This process looks very much like the equilibrium scheme of the *Treatise* where equilibrium is defined as the position where prices equal costs. But the *Treatise* adjustment dynamic is different because the level of demand is directly linked to costs through the households' decisions concerning the proportion of income to save and consume. This suggests that the important point is not the slope of the cost curve as determined by the assumption made concerning returns, or the slope of the demand curve facing the firm, but rather the direct dependence of demand on costs or

Figure 3.1

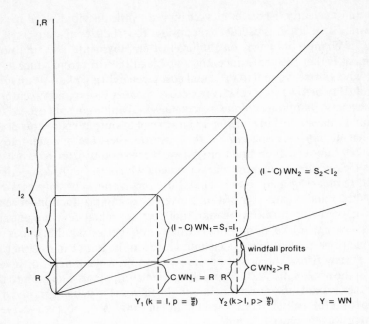

earnings. This interdependence is, in fact, the point that is stressed by almost all of the economists who were involved in attempts to link imperfect competition and less than full employment equilibrium in the 1930s and 1940s (e.g. Harrod, Kahn and Sraffa).

7

The precise points at which the *Treatise* argument differs from the traditional approach may be expressed graphically as in Figure 3.1. When household savings from earnings are zero, equilibrium requires that investment is zero. This equilibrium can be expressed by a 45° line in earnings-output space. This may serve as a benchmark position. When households' decisions on the proportion of their incomes to spend and save are independent of entrepreneurs' decisions to employ labour to produce consumption and investment goods, households' spending decisions (remember that this also includes entrepreneurs' spending from normal profits) may be represented by a ray from the origin lying below the 45° line. The vertical distance between the ray and the 45° line shows saving from normal earnings. The results of the producers' expenditure decisions on labour to employ in the production of consumption and investment goods at normal wages and prices are given by the horizontal lines showing consumption R (= WNr) and investment I (= WNi). When the households' decisions on the proportion of earnings to devote to consumption goods produces expenditures equal to entrepreneurs' costs of production for consumption goods then k = 1, P = W/e and I' = S.

If there were unemployed labour in this situation and wages fell, what would be the result? Both R and I would shift down, WN falls, but there is no reason for N to change, P still equals W/e but is lower by Δ W/e. There is no change in profits. Profits cannot increase by decreasing costs; the only way to increase profits is to increase investment expenditures, WNi. If I rises to I_2 (and c is the proportion of households' expenditure to income) so that c(WN) > WNr = R then k > 1 and there are windfall profits: p > W/e. If these profits lead to a revision of what were considered normal investment and employment, and thus to an additional increase in investment, then employment increases and the limit to the process is full employment. Note that as long as e remains constant W/P falls as employment increases. The expansionary cycle is thus accompanied by a change from the initial normal distribution of income between workers and entrepreneurs in favour of the latter.

The completion of this process may be described by an accelerator process such as Harrod worked out in his *Trade Cycle*, producing fluctuations with full employment as a ceiling and deep depressions as a floor. Keynes himself notes that the expansionary boom phase of this process will be very likely to produce a change in W as a result of the decrease in the share of wages in national income including windfalls. This he defines as an 'incomes inflation' which augments the 'capital inflation' already underway and makes it impossible to control inflation by operating on interest rates. Even restoring the old 'normal' distribution of income in such conditions may not be sufficient to restore stability.

8

In the *Treatise* Keynes followed Wicksell and called the rate of interest which brought I' and S into equality the 'natural rate of interest'. But later (1936, p. 242), he recognized that there is no reason for this rate to be either natural or unique. There will be a unique rate, or the 'neutral' rate asssociated with full employment, but there may be different 'natural' rates of interest for every level of investment relative to consumption and its associated level of employment. There will thus be a natural rate for

Figure 3.2

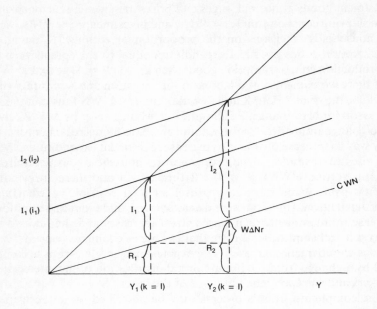

every position of $P = W/e$ and $I' = S$ which is associated with a different ratio of WN_i/WN_r and its related equilibrium value of $c(WN)/WN$. It would be possible to plot these combinations in 'natural interest rate'–income space. If it is assumed, as Keynes did, that the aggregate value of investment goods, I, and thus the total cost of production of new investment goods, I', is higher the lower the natural interest rate, while e is independent of the level of I, then these combinations of natural interest rates and income would generate a relation similar to the familiar 'I–S' curve. It would have as a property that P is stable at W/e, given W, for every value of Y because $I' = I = S$ at every value of Y. The value of k would thus equal to unity for every point on the curve.

While it is intriguing to note that stable prices are required by the equilibrium construction of the IS curve, without reference to any *ad hoc* assumption, such as is found in the textbook versions of IS–LM, that prices are fixed or that wages are assumed to be rigid, this fact has a more important corollary: the distribution of income is also constant for every level of Y. The analysis of income distribution must then take place via an analysis of disequilibrium price adjustment which has no representation in the diagram.

9

It is even more interesting to note that this I–S curve could also be generated in the more traditional manner by assuming that the level of investment is an inverse function of the interest rate, but that I is a constant proportion of Y. Then with the consumption ray fixed, an increase in I from I_1 to I_2 due to a lower rate of interest would increase WNi (and WNr in the same proportion); an increase in investment would then be represented as an equiproportionate rise in *both* I and R. This assumption moves the analysis from the *Treatise* to the *General Theory*, for in such conditions the consumption goods market is always in equilibrium for expenditures equal costs of production; windfall profits are replaced by higher consumer goods, production and the multiplier is introduced to assure that the higher level of investment is balanced by an equivalent increase in saving, S, resulting from the expansion of income by a multiple 1/s of the change in investment. It is the multiplier process which thus hides from view both the effect of interest rates on investment relative to consumption (and thus on k, the divergence of prices from costs) and of the distribution of income on prices, because the distribution of income is effectively frozen. In the *General Theory* an increase in investment is implicitly an equiproportionate increase in both investment and consumption goods production; since the WNi/WNr ratio is constant there can be no change in the distribution of income, nor can there be any affect of distribution on prices (or vice versa).

In these conditions the effect of changes in real wages can only be analysed by means of *ad hoc* assumptions concerning the shape of the cost curves in the consumption goods industries (which is what Kahn's short-period theory as set out in his 1931 article is all about), i.e. on changes in 'e'. This is, perhaps, an unnecessary step backwards towards Marshall, but it allowed Keynes in 1939 to respond to his friendly critics that their discovery of rising real wages made little difference to his theory, for if costs are constant we are back to the given 'e' and constant real wages, while if they are decreasing 'e' is rising which allows either real incomes or wages to rise without profits falling.

10

Whichever behaviour of costs is adopted, Keynes's argument concerning the possibility of less than full employment equilibrium still holds in the sense that any increase in employment will produce losses and any reduction will open up possibilities for profit by expansion. In the *Treatise* case consider the decision of a single consumption goods producer to expand output by one unit. This implies an additional labour requirement of 1/e and an expenditure on wages of W/e or of W in standard labour units. But if the entrepreneur makes this expansion he will discover that his revenues can at most increase by c(W) < W so that he will make losses unless investment is increased by (Ni/N)*W = (1-c)(W). This is the same argument which is applied for total output expansion in the *General Theory*.

Now this is also the argument that clinches the case against the use of wage reductions to increase employment for no matter how low the wage a worker offers, the entrepreneur's current position maximizes profits for any expansion of employment, given current wages, will produces losses of (1-c)W. For example, if a worker offers a wage equal to cW, which is the entrepreneur's expected revenue, as long as he does not spend all of it on his employer's output and saves some of it, his employer's increased revenues will be below the additional outlay on increasing employment. There is then no wage bargain that the worker can offer to the employer which will convince the entrepreneur that he can recover the costs of increasing employment at a profit.

This result is independent of the degree of competition in the traditional sense; k remains equal to unity at the point of equilibrium output, while it is less than one on the right and greater than one on the left. This is just the opposite of the traditional relation where to the right of the point where price = marginal cost equilibrium profits exceed costs, and vice versa. The problem is not the shape of the demand curve, but the relation between costs and demand created by the existence of a propensity to consume which differs from the share of investment in output.

In the *Treatise* Keynes insisted on the variability of investment relative to saving as the main cause of the cycle. In the *General Theory* the source of the problem is shifted to the behaviour of the propensity to consume. The underemployment equilibrium results because the propensity to consume responds only slowly to the requirements of equilibrium. Indeed, in the analysis above, it is the fact that the propensity to save is constant that requires the distribution of income to be constant.[4]

11

We thus reach the conclusion that there is no rational support for the use of a change in wages to change the level of employment, nor real incomes. Indeed, there are good reasons to avoid random changes in money wages, for at best they will simply increase prices, and at worst they may cause a reduction in the efficiency of capital; and thus a reduction in output. It is to this extent that Keynes suggests that they have uncertain impact on the system for increases or decreases may produce the same result of a fall in output and employment. This is the point at which we find the justification for incomes policies which aim to keep wage changes in line with changes in productivity in order to keep W/e stable.

But this is precisely where Keynes's decision to use the labour standard creates difficulties. If relative wages are given historically, along with wage rates, then wage stability requires that differentials remain constant. But productivity changes at different rates in different industries and in different categories of labour within the same industry. Any rule which requires that wages rise at an average rate of productivity growth will keep the labour standard constant, but it will not necessarily equal the change in the purchasing power standard for individual groups of workers. An incomes policy is meant to stabilize a labour standard, not a purchasing power standard.

12

The most important aspect of the money wage rate lies in the fact that it determines the value of money in which labour contracts are specified. The labour contract represents a speculative position concerning the changes in the labour and purchasing power standards over the life of the contract. To the extent that changes in wages are without impact on any real variables, the only effect will be on the relation between these two standards for different classes of labourers and different income categories. Since these changes will be non-systematic they cannot be captured or avoided systematically by any single group of workers or income class. There will thus be an incentive to eliminate them. If this can be done through wage stabilization then there will be a general interest for all parties to adhere to policies which stabilize average money wages in order to stabilize the relation between the labour and the purchasing power standard. Thus, in much the same way as each individual entrepreneur has an interest in his competitors paying high wages as long as he can pay low wages, every entrepreneur has an interest in stable wages as long as he can vary the wage when it is necessary in order to meet changes in his own labour and product markets. It will also be true that labourers will also have an interest in stable wages as long as they can use wages to defend their own relative wage differentials.

The labour contract thus also represents a speculative decision on two quite distinct sets of decision variables: the general level of prices and wages on the one hand, and the relative wages and relative profitability of labour and entrepreneurs on the other: or better, on wage and price levels and wage and price relativities. While there is a clear interest in both parties in stabilizing the value of the unit of account used to express the labour contract, this same confluence of interests is not always true for the latter. This is because changes in relative prices and wages may not have an impact on labour and employers in the same sector.

On the aggregate level a fall in aggregate prices will leave the relative profitability of a single producer unchanged for the prices of the outputs of all other producers also fall. Neither should absolute profitability change for if all prices are lower money wages can be lowered without changing real wages. On the other hand, if the price of one producer falls relative to that of another, his relative profitability will be reduced. Since there is no guarantee that the fall in prices will apply to the goods purchased by his labour force, any attempt to lower money wages to preserve profitability will lead to reductions in real wages which will be resisted. The only other response is to change 'e', the productivity of labour. Thus, he can either reduce real wages or decrease employment.

Likewise, labourers in a particular sector may find their wages falling behind those of other similarly skilled workers without the profitability of their employers having increased as a result. Any attempt by labour to restore differentials will then reduce their employers' relative profitability and be resisted.

Even when aggregate wages and prices are stable, changes in the relative wages and prices of individual groups of workers or employers will create conditions in which there may be a particular interest to use money wage changes to restore wage or profit differentials or relativities. This incentive will always be stronger than any general interest in overall price stability. The problem is then to identify the conditions which cause changes in relativities and formulating methods to make them compatible with overall wage stability. Just as the adoption of the labour standard in the *General Theory* led to the constancy of the distribution of income when combined with the multiplier, its use required the constancy of wage relativities. Neither assumption is of particular help to the analysis of incomes policies which are crucially related to both problems.

NOTES

1. Of course, Keynes discusses the impact of decreasing returns on prices and thus on real wages given money wages, and the role of income redistribution on the propensity to consume, but it is not explicitly considered as a determinant of the level of employment. Indeed, many post Keynesians consider Kalecki's theory of employment to be superior to Keynes's because it is derived directly from an analysis of the distribution of income.

2. On Weintraub's definitions k is Z/wN so that 1/k becomes a measure of labour share in national income (but note that for Keynes W covers full costs including entrepreneurs' remuneration, overheads, etc.).
3. Here is one of the places where Keynes argued that wage changes could have an effect, given the quantity of money, Cf. 1936, p. 263; clearly he did not consider it highly probable that unions should start to use wage policy as a proxy for monetary policy.
4. In his *Theory of Wages* (1963, p. 59) Sidney Weintraub criticises Kaldor on this point and offers an alternative explanation, arguing 'that the savings ratios are constant because the wage share is constant'.

REFERENCES

Chick, V., 'Time and the Wage-unit in the Method of *The General Theory*: History and Equilibrium', in T. Lawson and H. Pesaran (eds) *Keynes' Economics: Methodological Issues*, London: Croom Helm, 1985.

Harrod, R. F., *The Trade Cycle*, Oxford: Clarendon Press, 1936.

Hicks, John, 'Keynes and the World Economy', in F. Vicarelli (ed.), *Keynes's Relevance Today*, Philadelphia: University of Pennsylvania Press, 1985.

Keynes, J. M., *A Treatise on Money* Vol. I, Vol. 5 of *The Collected Writings*, London: Macmillan, 1930 (1973).

Keynes, J. M., *The General Theory of Employment, Interest and Money*, Vol. 7, of *The Collected Writings*, London: Macmillan, 1936 (1973).

Nell, E. J., 'The Fall of the House of Efficiency', in S. Weintraub (ed.), *Income Inequality*, the Annals of the American Academy of Political and Social Science, September 1973.

Weintraub, S. *Some Aspects of Wage Theory and Policy*, Philadelphia: Chilton, 1963.

4. Public Debt and the Size Distribution of Income

Donald F. Vitaliano and Y. E. Mazeya

1. INTRODUCTION

The mounting pilè of US Federal Government debt is a continuing source of concern to policy-makers and economists. Attention has largely been focused on the implications for capital formation and long-term economic growth. This Chapter deals with the relatively neglected potential effect of the payment of debt-service interest on the size distribution of income. Net interest payments amounted to more than $75 billion dollars in 1983, the year under investigation (Economic Report of the President, 1985). We analyse the pure transfer effect of servicing the debt (including payment of interest on foreign-owned debt), as well as the estimated effect of debt on real output via changes in capital formation. The two highest income quintiles are found to be losers in the transfer process, but all income classes gain on balance from debt due to a predicted rise in real output.

Because it is conceptually more satisfactory to analyse the distributional effects of marginal changes in debt, our analysis involves only the interest and taxes on the 1983 increment in debt, as distributed among Census-defined families.

2. CONCEPTUAL FRAMEWORK

Abba Lerner's (1948) phrase 'we owe it to ourselves' captures one view of the burden of the debt. From the perspective of a particular generation alive at a given point in time, the Lerner model views the debt–interest circuit as a pure transfer process – the aggregate consumption possibilities of that generation are unaffected by internally borrowed debt. The Lerner model is perhaps most compatible with Musgravian tax–interest imputation analysis carried out in this paper.

Another conceptualization of what constitutes the relevant burden of the debt focuses on the impact of debt vs. tax finance on private capital formation and growth. This view was stressed by Modigliani (1961). In the full-employment setting assumed here, and with his life-cycle consumption function, the bonds issued by government become a form of household wealth, which induces a cumulative rise in consumption and decline in saving (= investment) equal to the original amount of debt issue. Future generations are poorer because they inherit a smaller capital stock than if only tax finance had been employed. The smaller level of real output caused by the reduction in capital formation is deemed to represent the 'true' burden of the debt.

The relevance of the Modigliani view has been challenged by Barro's (1974) Debt Neutrality Hypothesis, whereby persons are assumed rationally to discount the future taxes implied by current debt issue. In consequence, people feel no richer due to the tax cut made possible by debt issue, consumption is unaffected, and the tax cut proceeds are saved and lent to the government. No impairment of capital formation occurs.

The approach taken here is eclectic. It combines the Lerner view of interest and taxes as a transfer with an estimate of the effect of debt on the private capital stock, and thence upon the level and distribution of income, in order to derive an appropriate counterfactual to the existing distribution. In addition, we incorporate an estimate of the effect of payment of interest on foreign-held debt upon the domestic size distribution of income.

3.   INCIDENCE METHODOLOGY

The methodology employed here is that of 'imputation' and is most closely associated with Musgrave's pioneering studies of tax and fiscal incidence (1948, 1974). Gillespie (1965) and Pechman (1985) have used essentially the same approach as Musgrave. The basic technique involves allocating or 'imputing' among the income classes the various taxes and items of expenditure, assuming all the while that the gross or pre-fiscal size distribution is unaffected by the resource withdrawal occasioned by taxation and the injection caused by expenditure. The main drawback of the Musgrave technique of imputation is that it employs a partial equilibrium model to work out what is essentially a general equilibrium problem when the entire system of public expenditure and taxation is analysed. Because we are concerned here with only a small piece of the overall fiscal picture, the partial equilibrium use of differential incidence seems quite reasonable, provided that one extends the notion to include any differential effects on the gross level and size distribution of real income of changes in the private capital stock attributable to the change in debt.

During the 1980s the federal government has run a substantial deficit in each year. In order to avoid the awkward question of the incidence of interest paid out of further borrowing, we allocate by income class only about two-thirds of the net interest paid by the Federal Government, because about one-third of the revenue pool out of which interest was paid in 1983 was raised by further borrowing.[1]

Typically, tax and budget (i.e. combined tax and expenditure) incidence studies employ a variety of shifting and incidence assumptions, one for each major tax or expenditure item. Total taxes and spending are then allocated among the various income classes using various distributional indices or proxies. Where no shifting and incidence consensus exists, the authors usually present alternative versions, leaving it to the reader to choose. Most of the difficult tax incidence questions that have required use of alternative assumptions in other studies are avoided here because 77 per cent of the potential tax-revenue pool out of which debt interest is paid consists of individual income taxes, whose unshifted incidence is widely conceded. By contrast, the corporation income tax, whose incidence is least certain, accounts for only 10 per cent of the allocable tax pool. The remainder of tax revenues originate in customs and excises, and estate and gift taxes, the incidence of which is fairly straightforward.

Our conceptual framework is long-run comparative statics. This is the standard approach in incidence studies, where the burden of taxes and benefits of expenditure are those deemed to result from the full adjustment of the economy to the postulated change in fiscal policy. We also assume that appropriate monetary policy adjustments occur to maintain full employment and stable prices. Because the standard model of tax incidence employs a competitive framework, consistency suggests a similar assumption for expenditure incidence, and we do so in the analysis of the incidence of debt interest. Since some readers may object to our assumption of a perfectly competitive economy, or view the incidence picture differently, we present an alternative allocation of debt interest that incorporates assumptions polar to our benchmark case.

4.   DEBT AND CAPITAL FORMATION

Servicing the public debt can affect private capital formation by creating positive and negative wealth effects resulting from the receipt of interest and payment of taxes. Changes occur in the full-employment growth path of the private capital stock because debt-induced wealth effects can alter the volume of private saving.

Given the fixed level of government spending implicit in the differential incidence framework, the substitution of borrowing for some portion of current taxation implies $dD = -dT$, where D is debt and T is tax revenue. (In this chapter, changes are denoted with d, thus dD denotes an increment in debt.) In tracing through the effects of debt, we make several simplifying assumptions. For example, we ignore second-round effects of increased saving, leading, via higher income, to further increases in saving by assuming additional income from higher saving is consumed. And we neglect any changes in wealth capitalization caused by interest-rate changes.

We employ Modigliani's life-cycle model to analyse the saving impact of debt issue. At the time of debt issue $(t = 0)$, households enjoy a tax cut, translated by households into some perceived change in net worth which, in turn, induces a rise in consumption and saving. Given full employment and fixed government expenditures, any rise in consumption must crowd out some private investment. The effects on capital formation in period 0 are transitory: in the long run any initial-period adverse effects are offset by a compensatory rise in saving and investment in subsequent periods (Cavaco-Silva, 1977, pp. 104–16). The reason is that the fall in household wealth of equal magnitude will, in turn, trigger a long-period compensatory fall in consumption (rise in saving/investment) designed to repair the damage. Regardless of what taxes are cut in period 0, or whether or not people suffer fiscal illusion regarding debt-related taxes and interest, any period 0 *actual* displacement of investment will eventually trigger a corrective reaction. However, in later periods $(t > 0)$ when taxes are levied and interest is paid on debt issued in 0, there may be positive or negative net wealth effects that, in turn, trigger changes in saving/investment and long-run capital formation. Our model and data indicate that these debt-service wealth effects, when combined with differences in the propensity to consume out of different types of household wealth, induce a long-run rise in capital stock of 21 cents per dollar of debt issued at time 0. That outcome stems from the predicted rise in saving caused by the tax-induced negative wealth effect overbalancing the predicted fall in saving induced by the positive wealth effect of receipt of debt interest.

Our model places minimal reliance upon rational expectations as a source of influence upon household behaviour. Adjustment to debt occurs only after taxes have actually been levied to finance debt and the interest has begun to flow to bond-holders. All we assume is that households capitalize the value of future taxes and interest, once they come into existence.

We lay out the full model, whose results are presented here in summary form only, in another paper (Vitaliano and Mazeya, 1988). With regard to government debt held only by the *domestic private sector*, the long-run impact on the private capital stock (K) of issuing dD of debt paying interest perpetually at the rate i is given by:

$$dK = idD \left[\frac{\alpha_2 (1 - b - c)}{\alpha_3 \theta} + \frac{c}{\phi} - \frac{\alpha_4(1 - b)}{\alpha_3 \phi} \right] \quad (1)$$

where α_2 = marginal propensity to consume out of human income-based wealth.

α_3 = marginal propensity to consume out of non-human income-based wealth.

α_4 = marginal propensity to consume out of government bond wealth.

$1 - b - c$ = fraction of debt service taxes imposed on human income.

b = fraction of gross interest on debt "recaptured" by taxing it.

c = fraction of debt service taxes falling on non-human income (other than bond interest).

θ = discount rate applicable to human source income.

ϕ = discount rate applicable to non-human source income.

The first two terms inside the brackets of equation (1) refer to the positive impact on capital formation of the taxes imposed to pay debt-interest. Taxes on human and non-human income are capitalized as reductions in wealth, which induce increased saving. The last term in (1) incorporates the capitalized value of debt interest which, by creating positive wealth effects, induces reduced saving and capital formation.

Table 4.1 presents estimates of the key parameters required to determine dK from equation (1). The propensities to consume out of various wealth forms was estimated from a time-series life-cycle aggregate consumption function using maximum likelihood Cochrane–Orcutt methods. The human and non-human wealth series are from Kendrick (1976); government bond wealth (including state–local debt) is expressed at market value in constant dollars from Seater (1981). The consumption function was fitted to 1929–69 data because that is the time-frame of the Kendrick series. t ratios are shown for data estimated by us. The discount rates i, ϕ and θ are drawn from the literature, as is the share of taxes falling on human and non-human income.

Utilizing equation (1) and the parameters in Table 4.1, we estimate dK = .21dD: a one dollar increment in public debt outstanding induces, in the long run, a rise in private capital stock of 21 cents above what it would otherwise be. It must be emphasized that the predicted effect refers to the longest period of adjustment, whereas most discussions of debt and capital formation are concerned with the 'crowding-out' effects in the year of debt issue. The key to the estimate of a positive effect lies in the relative

Table 4.1   Values of parameters used to determine effect of
debt on capital formation

1.	Human wealth propensity to consume	$\alpha_2 =$	.163
		$(t = 21.4)$	
2.	Non-human wealth propensity to consume	$\alpha_3 =$	.114
		$(t = 12.05)$	
3.	Bond wealth propensity to consume	$\alpha_4 =$	.039
		$(t = 3.01)$	
4.	Human wealth discount rate	$\theta =$	.19
	(net private rate)		
5.	Non-human wealth discount rate	$\phi =$	.10
	(after tax)		
6.	Government bond rate	$i =$	.05
7.	Human income share of taxes	$1-b-c =$	.54
8.	Interest recapture	$b =$	.15
9.	Non-human income share of taxes	$c =$	.31

Note:
t ratios in parentheses on lines 1–3.

Sources:
1–3. Vitaliano and Mazeya (1988).
4. Psacharopoulos (1973).
5. Jorgenson and Griliches (1967).
6. Seater (1981).
7–9. Musgrave and Musgrave (1973).

The tax shares refers only to taxes deemed relevant for financing debt interest.

size of the α propensities to consume and the allocation of the tax burden. The fact that labour income bears over half of the tax burden to pay interest means that its negative wealth effect triggers a significant fall in consumption ($\alpha_2 = .16$), while the taxes that fall on property income trigger a smaller fall ($\alpha_3 = .11$), and the receipt of debt interest causes only a slight rise in consumption since $\alpha_4 \approx .04$. An equation similar to (1) is derived by Vitaliano and Mazeya (op. cit.) to determine the effect of foreign-held debt. In that case we predict $dK \approx 0$, largely because the drain on domestic savings required to service foreign-held debt offsets the positive effect of debt-related taxes on long-term saving.

The next step in determining the appropriate counterfactual to the actual distribution of income is to use the predicted change in capital stock to forecast the change in the level and distribution of real income that it causes. For that purpose we fit a Cobb–Douglas-type aggregate production function to the human and non-human wealth stocks.[2] The coefficient on private capital stock is then used to predict $dY = \Omega dK$, where Y is real GNP and Ω the predicted effect of dK on dY. Having once determined the value of dY by which we adjust actual 1983 real output to arrive at the 'no debt' (really, less debt) scenario, we must next allocate dY among the income quintiles that characterize the size distribution of income.

The national debt grew by $213.7 billion in 1983 (Treasury Bulletin, 1986, p. 29). Since only two-thirds of debt interest was tax-financed (see note 1), we consider here only the effect of $141 billion of the debt increment. Of the latter sum, $8.3 billion was purchased by foreigners (ibid.), leaving $132.7 billion as the relevant increment of debt from which to estimate dK by means of equation (1). Therefore dK = .21 ($132.7) = $27.9 billion. The private capital stock would be $27.9 billion less in the long run, if tax finance had been used instead of borrowing in 1983.

The production function estimate of Ω, the output–capital ratio, is .25; thus real GNP in 1983 is $7 billion greater with debt than without. Because our distribution analysis employs the Census concept of family money income, we take the ratio of that concept to GNP in 1983 as the fraction of the change in GNP to allocate among the income classes: *$3.760 billion*. We turn to the allocation of this predicted change in family money income among the income classes.

All taxes and debt interest are allocated by money income quintiles to families because broader measures of income and finer details of distribution are not available on a consistent basis over the time-period covered by our econometric estimation, i.e. since 1947. We employ the data and definitions of the US Census's Current Population Survey.

5.   INTEREST RECEIVED BY OTHER PARTS OF THE FEDERAL GOVERNMENT

In 1983 more than 25 per cent of US government debt was held by the Federal Reserve system and various government accounts, such as the social security trust funds (Economic Report of the President, 1985, p. 327). Any 'surplus' interest received by these debt-holders is handed back to the Treasury and is not part ot the net interest paid to the private sector. However, part of the interest received by the Fed and trust funds is spent to operate the central bank, provide transfer benefit payments or help fund some other activity such as the federal government's various bank deposit insurance schemes.

It is assumed here that the debt-interest payments to US governmental holders have no net effect on the income distribution. In the absence of the debt (or marginal change thereof), these expenditures would be financed by the same taxes used to raise the interest at present.

6. ESTIMATING THE SIZE DISTRIBUTION OF INCOME

The Lorenz curve of income distribution is described by the following equation of Kakwani-Podder (1973):

$$N = \pi e^{-\tau(1-\pi)} \tag{2}$$

where N is the cumulative proportion of income, π is the cumulative proportion of income-receiving units (e.g. families), τ is an empirically determined parameter and e the base of the natural logarithm. If $\tau = 0$, income is equally distributed: $N = \pi$. The larger the absolute value of τ, the more unequal the size distribution of income. We estimate τ with (2) in log form, using least squares regression and the quintile values of N and π from the Current Population Survey for families for each year from 1947 to 1985. Thus we have a summary statistic τ of the quintile size distribution for 38 years. There is relatively little change in the degree of inequality over time, as measured by τ. Inequality appears to have declined modestly up to 1980, but by 1985 it had increased to about the same level as in the late 1940s.

The distribution parameter τ is next regressed on several variables thought to influence the size distribution of income: capital stock, human capital, taxes, transfers and a time trend (Haley, 1968; Blinder, 1974).[3] The coefficient on the capital stock variable is then multiplied by the estimated $27.9 billion increment in capital stock to adjust the value of τ for 1983. The counterfactual size distribution is then constructed by utilizing this predicted value of τ to allocate the $3.760 billion change in family money income estimated in 4 above. The result is presented in Table 4.4, line 1. Next, we turn to the pure transfer aspect of debt service: the incidence of interest paid on the debt increment and the taxes levied to finance that interest.

7. AMOUNT OF INTEREST TO BE ALLOCATED

Two steps must be taken in order to carry out the debt-interest allocation exercise. The amount of interest attributable to each ownership category of debt-holder must be determined, then the incidence of that interest must be decided, i.e. among shareholders, customers of firms, taxpayers and so forth. We start by estimating the amount of interest attributable to each category of debt-holder.

The US Treasury does not record the interest received by the various debt-ownership categories. The approach employed here for allocating debt interest among ownership categories is to use the Treasury's data on subscriptions for public marketable securities by investor category (Treasury Bulletin, 1984). This gives a breakdown, by maturity, of debt purchased by each investor category during 1983, thus corresponding to our incremental analysis of debt issue. Use of the appropriate interest rate for each maturity class permits determination of the total interest payable by the Treasury to each category. However, approximately 43 per cent of original-issue debt was purchased by dealers and brokers, who are presumed to be acting as middlemen since they own only a tiny fraction of outstanding debt. This interest was allocated by investor class according to the pattern of subscriptions of the remaining investor classes. In addition, interest credited to the catch-all investor category All Other, consisting of foreign, savings and loan and not-for-profit organizations, was apportioned according to their relative ownership of total debt outstanding in 1983. A total of $24.261 billion in interest was thus attributable to debt issued in 1983. However, since our concern is with the allocation of tax-financed debt interest attributable to families, that sum is reduced to $10.888 billion after making those adjustments.[4] The ownership categories and amount of interest, in descending order, credited to each are (in billions): Banks ($6.146), Individuals ($1.754), Non-financial corporations ($1.319), Foreign and international ($0.639), Not-for-profit organizations ($0.596), Insurance companies ($0.133), State and local government (general and pensions) ($0.184), and Private pension plans ($0.054).

8.   INTEREST INCIDENCE

Although a vast literature on tax incidence exists, the incidence of the spending side of the public household is a relatively neglected subject. In what follows, we attempt to employ the same type of reasoning employed in analysing the shifting and incidence of taxes when allocating the interest received by owners of public debt.

Debt interest is allocated using a variety of distributional indices: consumption by income class, ownership of savings bonds, liquid assets, homeownership,etc. Table 4.2 lists all the indices employed here, the distribution of each by family money income quintile, and the source of each index. The allocation of the interest credited to each domestic investor category is distributed among the income classes in Table 4.3. The analysis underlying each imputation is discussed next.

Banks

This category includes commercial banks, savings and loan associations, mutual savings banks and mutual funds. Banks are credited with more

Table 4.2   Indices of allocation (percentages)

Index	Family money income quintile					
	1	2	3	4	5	Total
1. Liquid assets	6.6	10.6	15.3	21.7	45.8	100
2. US savings bonds	7.1	16.0	19.7	19.8	37.4	100
3. Marketable US securities	3.4	9.0	12.1	16.5	59.0	100
4. Life insurance equity	1.9	5.2	10.4	21.2	61.3	100
5. Consumption expenditure	8.8	12.2	17.6	23.7	37.1	100
6. Expenditure on vehicles	6.9	12.3	19.1	25.7	36.0	100
7. Expenditure on owner-dwellings	6.1	8.7	14.1	24.2	46.9	100
8. Social security benefits	15.8	28.8	24.6	15.7	15.1	100
9. Household net worth	5.5	6.3	12.8	19.6	55.8	100
10. State–local tax burden	6.9	10.8	16.9	23.1	42.3	100
11. Expenditure on education	2.5	4.5	10.6	19.9	62.5	100
12. Expenditure on health	12.7	19.3	19.2	22.9	25.9	100
13. Expenditure on entertainment	7.0	9.3	15.8	26.6	41.3	100
14. Dividends	2.9	9.9	14.3	21.8	51.1	100

Note:
Totals may not sum due to rounding.

Sources:
1 and 9, Board of Governors of the Federal Reserve System, *Survey of Consumer Finances, 1983*, first and second reports.
2 and 3, US Dept of Commerce, *Household Wealth and Asset Ownership: 1984*, Series P–70.
4, US Dept of the Treasury: *Tax Reform for Fairness, Simplicity and Growth*, 1984.
5, 6, 7, 8, 11, 12, 13, 14, Bureau of Labor Statistics, *Consumer Expenditure Survey*, 1978, 1982–82.
10, estimated by the authors.

than half the total interest, and thus the treatment of this category of ownership is important. A modern fractional reserve-multiple expansion system allows banks to earn interest by lending out a portion of deposits left in their charge. Assuming some normal rate of profit is required to induce banks to provide services, and a long-run tendency to zero above-normal profit, receipt of debt interest allows fees to be lower or interest paid to depositors to be higher. Therefore, we assume that debt interest received by banks is shifted forward to depositors.[5] In turn, bank depositors consist primarily of individuals and businesses. Individually-owned demand and time deposits are attributed interest according to the ownership of liquid assets by income class. Interest credited to business-owned deposits, mostly demand deposits, reduces business costs and is assumed shifted forward to consumers of final products via a zero

Table 4.3   Allocation of Domesticly-received debt interest in 1983
(billions of dollars)

Investor category	Income quintile					
	1	2	3	4	5	Total
Banks	.494	.740	1.033	1.414	2.465	6.146
Individuals						
Savings bonds	.068	.154	.189	.190	.359	.960
Other securities	.027	.071	.096	.131	.469	.794
Corporations	.116	.169	.232	.313	.489	1.319
Not-for-profit						
Education/research	.005	.009	.021	.040	.124	.199
Health	.027	.042	.042	.050	.056	.217
Social service	.010	.017	.015	.010	.010	.061
Arts, religion	.022	.023	.023	.024	.025	.117
Insurance companies						
Property/casualty	.005	.008	.011	.014	.023	.061
Life insurance	.001	.004	.008	.015	.044	.072
State and local government	.009	.014	.022	.030	.055	.130
Pension plans						
Private	.010	.015	.021	.028	.044	.118
State-local	.004	.006	.009	.012	.023	.054
Total $	.798	1.273	1.722	2.270	4.186	10.249
Per cent allocation	7.8%	12.5%	16.9%	22.2%	40.5%	100%

Note:
Totals may not sum due to rounding.

economic profit competitive equilibrium, and is distributed according to consumption by income class.

Savings and loan associations and mutual savings banks are assumed to behave in the same manner as the time deposit component of commercial banks, i.e. interest is shifted to depositors and allocated according to the ownership of liquid assets. Interest received by mutual funds is attributed to fund investors, based on the ownership of liquid assets by income class, on the assumption that competitive pressures ensure that fund managers earn only normal profits.

Individuals

Private individuals received $1.754 billion of debt interest in 1983. Government bonds held by households are assumed to confer their interest benefit on their owners because of the absence of subsequent market transactions via which changes may occur to shift the interest received. Debt held by individuals consists of non-negotiable US Savings Bonds and marketable securities. (Economic Report of the President, 1986, p. 350). The interest earned on US Savings Bonds is allocated according to ownership; and interest on marketable debt is allocated according to the ownership of US securities (which includes Treasury and other US government securities). (Household Wealth and Asset Ownership survey, 1986).

Corporations

Non-financial corporations received $1.319 billion in interest income. It seems reasonable to suppose that receipt of debt interest by corporations is 'incidental' to the central working of such organizations. That is, it does not directly affect marginal revenue and marginal cost, and thus short-run output. In a long-run competitive framework, any above-normal profits arising from receipt of debt interest would be eroded by entry of new firms. In this scenario, the incidence of debt interest is shifted to consumers of the products of the corporate sector via lower product prices. The relative distribution of total consumption by income class is therefore the appropriate allocation index.

Foreign and International

Interest on debt held by foreigners does not become part of the domestic income flow, but must be paid for by taxes imposed on US residents. In consequence, the $0.639 billion credited to foreign-held debt is treated as a negative item in the domestic income distribution: $0.639 in taxes are deducted according to the presumed incidence thereof, but the corresponding amount of interest is not credited to any domestic recipients. This is shown in Table 4.4.

Given the sharp rise in foreign-held debt since 1983, it is interesting to note that the same general pattern would obtain for the larger sums of interest now being sent abroad, provided that the relative incidence of taxes among the income classes has not changed very much.

Not-for-profit Organizations

This category of debt ownership includes a diversity of organizations: educational and research organizations, social services organizations, health care organizations, and arts, cultural and religious organizations. Educational, research and health-related organizations received about 70

*Table 4.4   Summary of total effect of debt on income distribution (1983)
(billions of dollars)*

Type of effect	Income quintile					
	1	2	3	4	5	Total
1. Output effect	.196	.214	.451	.936	1.936	3.760
2. Domestic interest received	.798	1.273	1.722	2.270	4.186	10.249
3. Taxes to pay domestic interest	.221	.563	1.278	2.433	5.754	10.249
4. Taxes to pay foreign interest	.014	.035	.080	.151	.359	.639
5. Domestic transfer effect (line 2 – line 3)	.577	.710	.444	– .163	– 1.568	0
6. Domestic & foreign transfer effect (line 5 – line 4)	.563	.675	.364	– .314	– 1.927	– .639
7. Total effect (line 1 + line 6) (benchmark case)	.759	.889	.815	.622	.036	3.121
ALTERNATIVE CASE*						
8. Domestic interest received	.395	1.101	1.521	2.168	5.064	10.249
9. Domestic transfer effect (line 8 – line 3)	.174	.538	.243	– .265	– .690	0
10. Domestic & foreign transfer effect (line 9 – line 4)	.160	.503	.163	– .416	– 1.049	– .639
11. Total effect (line 1 + line 10)	.356	.717	.614	.520	.914	3.121

Note:
The alternative case allocates all interest attributed to consumers in the benchmark case (see Table 4.3) instead to receivers of dividends. Totals may not sum due to rounding.

per cent of all endowment-related income attributed to the not-for-profit sector (James and Rose-Ackerman, 1986, p. 8).

Private non-profit organizations lie between traditional for-profit firms and government agencies. Like ordinary firms, they often serve markets for goods and services (e.g. health care or education), and like government agencies there are no residual profit claimants.

Following James and Rose-Ackerman (*op. cit.*), consider a NPO (not-for-profit) firm producing a single product sold at a unit price P, which also receives donations and earns interest on endowment assets. Neither interest nor donations are directly related to output Q, and thus they constitute a form of 'fixed revenue' F. The firm's average revenue (AR) function is thus $AR = P + F/Q$. A profit-maximizing firm would not alter output in consequence of the receipt of interest, since the latter does not alter marginal revenue or marginal cost. However, the NPO will expand output up to the point of its budget constraint that total revenue = total cost. Increased output will reduce AR until it equals average cost; the latter is assumed to be conventionally U-shaped. If in the short run, average revenue equals short-run average cost but is above long-run average cost, free entry of additional NPOs will reduce AR into equality with average cost. We therefore conclude that the benefits of interest on debt owned by not-for-profits accrue to their customer/clients.

The \$0.596 billion in debt interest attributed to NPOs as a group is apportioned among the following constituent organizations, based on the relative ownership of all NPO endowment assets: health care (36.4%), education/research (33.3%), religion (15.2%), social service (10.3%), community development (3.6%), and art and culture (1.2%) (ibid.).

The health and education interest is distributed by income class according to health and education expenditures. Religion and community development are treated as pure public goods and allocated on a per capita basis. Receipt of social insurance benefits is the proxy used to allocate interest paid to social service organizations. Art and culture is distributed based on entertainment expenditures.

Insurance Companies

The interest allocated to insurance companies amounts to \$0.133 billion. The discussion of the insurance industry is divided between life companies and property and casualty companies. Based on their relative ownership of debt, life companies are attributed \$0.072 billion in debt interest and property and casualty companies \$0.061 billion (Federal Reserve Statistical Digest, 1984).

Interest earned by property and casualty insurers is assumed to be shifted forward to their policy-holders based on the assumption that perfect competition assures that prices (i.e. insurance premiums) cover only the expected value of losses, administrative overhead and a normal profit. Any above-normal profit resulting from interest earned on insurance company reserves is competed away by free entry.

Property and casualty interest is attributed to individuals and businesses, which represent the bulk of property and casualty insurance written, based on the relative amount of insurance in force. Among individuals, homeowner and auto insurance accounts for about 90 per cent of the value of policies (Property and Casualty Fact Book, 1984–85);

the interest related to each is distributed according to consumer expenditure on homes and vehicles. The remaining portion of individual insurance interest and all business-related interest are allocated according to total consumption by income class.

An analysis similar to that employed for the property and casualty sector is applied to the life insurance industry. The interest thus attributed is allocated according to the ownership of life insurance equity by income class.

State and Local Government

Interest attributed to state and local government units is typically earned in connection with the investment of temporarily idle funds arising from the mismatch between the timing of receipts and expenditures, and from the investment of employee pension funds. The latter are treated below, together with private pension funds.

Because debt interest represents only a minor source of state–local revenue, it typically does not alter spending plans and, instead, is used as an offset against own-source taxation. This seems reasonable because the amount of idle funds is often unpredictable and is not viewed by budget officers as a reliable enough revenue source upon which to base spending commitments. Thus, state and local taxpayers are deemed to benefit from debt interest, and it is allocated according to the incidence of state and local taxes.

State and Local Tax Incidence

Included here are property taxes, income taxes, sales taxes and miscellaneous taxes and charges.

Following the near-standard view of property tax incidence, we assume it is borne by owners of all capital and allocate the tax burden by income class according to the distribution of household net worth. This follows the Harberger factor-price equalization model, where capital is deemed to move in the long run among different jurisdictions so as to equalize net returns. Excise or price effects of the tax due to the inflow and outflow of capital among jurisdictions are assumed to cancel each other.

State and local income taxes are assumed unshifted and allocated according to estimated payments made by income class (BLS Consumer Expenditure Survey, 1982–83).

Sales taxes and miscellaneous taxes and fees are assumed to be shifted forward as higher product prices, and are allocated according to the distribution of total consumption spending by income class.

The overall incidence by income quintile of the state and local tax system is shown in Table 4.2. It is the weighted average of the allocation of each type of tax, the weights being the amount of revenue due to each tax. The resulting incidence pattern is used to distribute $0.130 billion in debt interest received by state–local government general fund accounts.

Pension and Retirement System funds

This category includes the $0.118 billion interest paid to private pension funds and the $0.054 paid to state and local government pension schemes.

Modern labour economics views pension plans as a form of deferred compensation, whose incidence falls primarily upon the wage-earner (Ehrenberg and Smith, 1985, pp. 333–47). That is, fringe benefits such as pension plans are 'paid for' by reduced cash compensation over the long run. Most pension plans are of a defined benefit type, where the employer promises a fixed benefit to the worker. The employer is the residual contributor to the fund, and any interest earned on fund assets reduces the amount of the employer's contribution. In a competitive framework, total compensation is market-determined, but its composition varies according to employer–employee preferences. Workers cannot receive above-market compensation and employers do not earn above-normal profit. It would thus appear that final product prices must be lower in the long run in consequence of the receipt of debt interest by private pension plans: higher wage benefits or above-normal profits due to pension plan interest is eroded in the long run by labour and capital mobility. Therefore, the $0.118 billion in private pension plan debt interest is allocated according to total consumption spending by income class.

State and local government pension plans differ from private ones primarily in that they are seriously underfunded and, of course, free entry and the profit motive are absent (ibid., p. 424). In this situation, the reasonable assumption seems to be that receipt of debt interest relieves state and local taxpayers of part of the cost of funding pension benefits. The $0.054 interest paid to state –local pension plans is allocated according to the state and local tax burden.

Table 4.3 presents the allocation of debt interest by income quintiles resulting from the preceding analysis of each ownership category. An alternative incidence scenario that dispenses with the perfectly competitive, zero economic profit assumption is incorporated in summary distribution in Table 4.4.

9.   FEDERAL TAX INCIDENCE

The analysis of the burden of federal taxation deemed to finance debt interest is fairly straightforward. Tax revenues available for the payment of debt interest in 1983 amounted to $377.1 billion, consisting of individual income taxes (77 per cent), corporate income taxes (10 per cent), customs and excises (11.6 per cent) and gift and estate taxes (1.6 per cent) (see note 1).

We assume individual income taxes do not shift and we allocate them by family money income, based on the BLS Survey of Consumer Expenditures (1982–83). Corporate tax incidence is assumed to be borne by owners of all capital, in line with the Harberger model (discussed in the preceding section) in relation to the incidence of the property tax. Household wealth is the index of allocation employed here. Excises and customs duties are assumed to be shifted to consumers and allocated by total consumption. Estate and gift taxes are assumed not to shift and are allocated entirely to the top income quintile. Table 4.4 presents the incidence of the federal tax system used to finance interest on the public debt.

10.   COMBINED EFFECTS

The output, domestic and foreign transfer effects on income distribution of that portion of the 1983 increment in federal government debt serviced by taxation is presented in Table 4.4. Line 1 of the table distributes the increase in real output due to the rise in capital stock estimated above (pp. 58–64). The $3.760 billion increase in family money income is distributed using the predicted value of the distribution parameter τ, which incorporates the effect of the changed capital stock on the size distribution. Over 50 per cent of the higher output is received by the top income class, reflecting the considerable degree of inequality in family money income.

Line 2 of Table 4.4 allocates the domesticly received debt interest, carried over from Table 4.3. The taxes used to pay for that interest are shown on line 3, and line 4 uses the same relative tax burden to distribute the interest sent abroad to service the increment in foreign-held debt in 1983.

Considering just the Lerner-type domestic tax-interest circuit, it is clear from line 5 that servicing the national debt has a net equalizing impact on the size distribution of income. The two top quintiles pay more in taxes than they receive in interest. Even though they receive together 63 per cent of the interest, the top two quintiles pay 80 per cent of the tax burden. This result is strongly influenced by the heavy reliance in 1983 upon the progressive personal income tax to finance debt interest. Any changes incorporated in the Tax Reform Act 1986 that lessen the degree of progressivity of the overall tax system would tend to lessen the redistributive effect of servicing the debt.

Combining the output, domestic transfer and foreign interest burden of the debt, we see in line 7 of Table 4.4 that all income classes are net gainers at the margin, from financing public spending by debt versus current taxation. The top income classes gain more in factor earnings from the predicted rise in capital stock than they lose from the redistributive effect of paying interest on the debt.

Before assessing our findings, we consider an alternative debt incidence scenario. In our view, the main assumption that readers might question is the systematic imputation to final consumers of the interest received by banks, non-financial corporations, insurance companies and private pension plans. Those who view the economy as less than perfectly competitive might assume that interest would not be shifted forward and, instead, assume that profit-receivers are the beneficiaries. We implement that assumption by allocating all the debt interest received by banks, corporations, insurance companies and private pension plans according to the receipt of dividends. This is shown in lines 8–11 of Table 4.4. Not surprisingly, the effect of the alternative incidence assumption is to increase the share of interest attributed to the top quintiles: the two highest classes now receive about 70 per cent of domestic interest. Nevertheless, the two top classes are still net losers in the domestic tax-transfer process (line 9), although their combined losses are more or less halved vis-à-vis the benchmark scenario of line 5. Similarly, all income classes are still net gainers when output, transfer and foreign effects are combined in line 11; but the lowest classes gain much less and the richest gain much more, as compared to the benchmark case (cf. lines 7 and 11). We therefore conclude that our basic result that the transfer effect of deficit finance has an equalizing effect is robust against the most plausible alternative assumption.

11.   SUMMARY AND CONCLUSION

Two broad conclusions emerge from our analysis. First, so far as the pure transfer, 'we owe it to ourselves' view of debt is concerned, the three lowest income quintiles are net gainers at the expense of the top two. The bottom three quintiles receive about 37 per cent of debt interest, but pay only about 20 per cent of the relevant tax burden. Thus, although the wealthiest families receive the lion's share of debt interest (63 per cent), that is more than offset by the 80 per cent of the tax burden that they bear.

Our second main conclusion is that servicing the debt exerts a favourable long-run effect on private capital formation. All income strata benefit from the increased real income caused by the predicted increase in real capital stock, but the two highest quintiles gain 77 per cent of it. Indeed, the better-off gain more from the output effect of debt than they lose from the transfer effect.

Combining the transfer, output and foreign effects of a marginal increase in debt indicates that all income classes are net gainers: all enjoy higher real incomes, and that income is more equally distributed than if government spending were tax financed.

NOTES

1. Treasury interest payments, net of interest returned by the Federal Reserve, were $75.2 billion in fiscal 1983. Tax revenues net of earmarked social security taxes were $377.1 billion. Outlays, net of social insurance payments financed by social insurance taxes (i.e. inclusive of the social security 'deficit'), were $584.8 billion. Debt interest is part of the latter sum. The fraction of taxes deemed to pay debt interest is 0.64 (= $377.1/$584.8).

   The amount of each type of tax is as follows:

Individual income taxes	$289.0 billion
Corporate taxes	37.0
Customs and excises	44.0
Gift and estate taxes	6.0
Other	1.1
	$377.1

   Income taxes represent 77 per cent of taxes that are a potential source of interest payments on the debt, corporate taxes 10 per cent, customs and excises 11.6 per cent, and estate and gift taxes 1.6 per cent. *Source*: Economic Report of the President (1985), Table B-71.

2. Assume a Cobb–Douglas production function $Y = A(t)K^aL^b$, where Y is real output and K and L the stocks of real capital and labour, respectively. A(t) is a technological shift parameter as a function of time t. $dY/dK \cdot K/Y = a$, and therefore $dY = (a \cdot Y/K)dK$. The term $(a \cdot Y/K)$ is defined as Ω in the text. Utilizing a Cochrane–Orcutt maximum likelihood procedure, real output from *Historical Statistics* (1975) was regressed on the stocks of capital and labour (Kendrick, 1976). The following equation was estimated for the years 1929–1969 (t-ratios in parentheses):

$$\ln Y = -0.183 + .561 nk + .391 nL + .063 \text{ time} \quad \text{(A1)}$$
$$(-6.88) \quad (6.84) \quad (4.35) \quad (6.0)$$

Adj.$R^2 = .99$.

The output/capital ratio Y/K averaged .44 over the period 1929–69. Thus $\Omega = .56 (.44) = .25$, as given in the text.

3. The distribution parameter τ was regressed on the same stocks of capital and labour used in text Table 4.1 and in note 2 above. In addition, total taxes, transfer payments and time were included regressors; the result, using Cochrane–Orcutt maximum likelihood, with t-ratios in parentheses:

$$\tau = -4.57 + .00050K + .00081L - .0016\text{Taxes} - .014\text{Transfers} - .22\text{Times} \quad \text{(A2)}$$
$$(-18.2) \quad (2.05) \quad (1.53) \quad (-1.26) \quad (-2.15) \quad (-1.57)$$

Adj $R^2 = .80$.

This equation was estimated using 1947–69 data, since the capital and labour series overlap the τ series only for that period.
4. The adjustment is based on the 0.64 fraction of interest paid out of taxation (see n. 1), and that 0.69 of total interest from all sources attributed to households was received by families (Current Population Reports, P-60, 1985).
5. A commentator on an earlier version of this paper suggested that we consider borrowers as customers of banks, in addition to depositors. That interesting idea could not be implemented because of the lack of a suitable allocation index.

REFERENCES

Barro, Robert J., 'Are Government Bonds Net Wealth?', *Journal of Political Economy*, 82, Nov.–Dec. 1974, pp. 1095–117.

Blanchard, O. J., 'Debt, Deficits and Finite Horizons', *Journal of Political Economy*, 93, April 1985, pp. 223–47.

Blinder, Alan, *Towards an Economic Theory of Income Distribution*, Cambridge, Mass.: MIT Press, 1974.

Brennan, G. and Buchanan, James M., 'The Logic of the Ricardian Equivalence Theorem', *Finanzarchiv.*, N.F. 38, 1980, pp. 4–16.

Board of Governors of the Federal Reserve System, 'Survey of Consumer Finances, 1983', *Federal Reserve Bulletin*, 70, September 1984, pp. 679–92.

Board of Governors of the Federal Reserve System, 'Survey of Consumer Finances, 1983: A Second Report', *Federal Reserve Bulletin*, 70, December 1984, pp. 857–68.

Board of Governors of the Federal Reserve System, *Annual Statistical Digest*, 1984.

Board of Governors of the Federal Reserve System, *Federal Reserve Bulletin*, 74, January 1986.

Cavaco-Silva, Anibal, *Economic Effects of Public Debt*. New York: St Martin's Press, 1977.

Economic Report of the President, Washington, D.C.: US Government Printing Office, 1985.

Economic Report of the President, Washington, D.C.: US Government Printing Office, 1986.

Ehrenberg, Ronald G. and Smith, Robert S., *Modern Labor Economics*, 2nd edn, Glenview, Ill.: Scott, Foresman, 1985.

Gillespie, W. Irwin, 'Effect of Public Expenditure on the Distribution of Income', in R. A. Musgrave (ed.), *Essays in Fiscal Federalism*, Washington, D.C.: Brookings Institution, 1965.

Gupta, M., 'Notes and Comments on Functional Form for Estimating the Lorenz Curve', *Econometrica*, 52, September 1984, pp. 1313–14.

Haley, Bernard, 'Changes in the Distribution of Income in the United States', in J. Marchal and B. Ducros (eds), *The Distribution of National Income*. New York: Macmillan, 1968.

Insurance Information Institute, *Insurance Facts: 1984–85, Property/Casualty Fact Book*. New York, 1985.

James, E. and Rose-Ackerman, S., *The Non-Profit Enterprise in Market Economics*, London: Harwood, 1986.

Jorgenson, Dale and Grilliches, Z., 'The Explanation of Productivity Change', *Review of Economic Studies*, 34, July 1967, pp. 249–83.

Kakwani, N. and Podder, N., 'On the Estimation of the Lorenz Curve From Grouped Observations', *International Economic Review*, 14, June 1973, pp. 278–91.

Kendrick, John *The Formation and Stocks of Total Capital*. New York: NBER, 1976.

Kochin, L., 'Are Future Taxes Anticipated by Consumers?', *Journal of Money, Credit and Banking*, 6, August 1974, pp. 385–94.

Kormendi, Roger, 'Government Debt, Government Spending and Private Sector Behavior', *American Economic Review*, 73, December 1983, pp. 994–1010.

Lerner, Abba, 'The Burden of the National Debt', in *Income, Employment and Public Policy: Essays in Honor of Alvin Hansen*. New York: Norton, 1948.

Levy, F., 'Changes in the Distribution of American Family Incomes, 1947 to 1984', *Science*, 236, May 1987, pp. 923–7.

Miller, Herman P., *Income Distribution in the United States*. Washington, D.C.: US Government Printing Office, 1966.

Modigliani, Franco, 'Long-run Implications of Alternative Fiscal Policies and the Burden of the Debt', *The Economic Journal*, 71, December 1961, pp. 730–55.

Modigliani, Franco, 'The Role of Intergenerational Transfers and Life Cycle Saving in the Accumulation of Wealth', *The Journal of Economic Perspectives*, 2, Spring 1988, pp. 15–40.

Musgrave, Richard A., et al., 'Distribution of Tax Payments by Income Groups', *National Tax Journal*, 4, March 1948, pp. 1–53.

Musgrave, Richard A. and Musgrave, Peggy B., *Public Finance in Theory and Practice*. New York: McGraw-Hill, 1973.

Musgrave, Richard A., Case, K. and Herman, L., 'The Distribution of Fiscal Burdens and Benefits', *Public Finance Quarterly*, July 1974, pp. 259–312.

Psacharopoulos, G., *Returns to Education*. New York: Elsevier, 1973.

Pechman, Joseph, *Who Paid the Taxes, 1966–85?* Washington, D.C.: Brookings Institution, 1985.

Pen, Jan, *Income Distribution: Facts, Theories and Policies*. New York: Praeger, 1971.

Prest, Alan, 'Statistical Calculation of Tax Burden', *Economica*, August 1955, pp. 234–45.

Radner, D. and Hinrichs, J., 'Size Distribution of Income in 1964, 1970 and 1971', *Survey of Current Business*, October 1974, pp. 9–31.

Reynolds, Morgan and Smolensky, Eugene, *Public Expenditures, Taxes and the Distribution of Income*. New York: Academic Press, 1977.

Seater, J. 'The Market Value of Outstanding Government Debt', *Journal of Monetary Economics*, 8, July 1981, pp. 85–101.

Seater, J., 'Are Future Taxes Discounted?', *Journal of Money, Credit and Banking*, 14, August 1982, pp. 376–89.

US Department of Commerce, Bureau of the Census, *Historical Statistics of the United States, Colonial Times to 1970, Part 1 and 2*. Washington, D.C.: US Government Printing Office, 1975.

US Department of Commerce, Bureau of the Census, *Current Population Reports, Money Income of Households, Families and Persons in the U.S., 1983*, Series P-60, No. 146, April 1985, Washington, D.C.: US Government Printing Office.

US Department of Commerce, Bureau of the Census, *Current Population Reports, Money Income of Households, Families and Persons in the U.S., 1985*,

Series P-60, No. 156, August 1987, Washington, D.C.: US Government Printing Office.

US Department of Commerce, Bureau of the Census, *Household Wealth and Asset Ownership, 1984*, Series P-70, No. 7, July 1986, Washington, D.C.: US Government Printing Office.

US Department of Commerce, Bureau of the Census, *Statistical Abstract of the U.S. 1986*, Washington, D.C.: US Government Printing Office, 1986.

US Department of Labor, Bureau of Labor Statistics, *Consumer Expenditure Survey; Total Expenditures and Income for the U.S. and Selected Areas*, Bulletin 1992, Washington, D.C.: US Government Printing Office, 1978.

US Department of Labor, Bureau of Labor Statistics, *Consumer Expenditure Survey: Diary Survey, 1982–83*, Bulletin 2245, Washington, D.C.: US Government Printing Office, 1986.

US Department of the Treasury, *Tax Reform for Fairness, Simplicity and Economic Growth*, November 1984, Washington, D.C.: US Government Printing Office.

US Department of the Treasury, *Treasury Bulletin*, Fourth Quarter, Washington, D.C.: US Government Printing Office, 1984.

Vitaliano, Donald F., 'The Payment of Interest on the Federal Debt and the Distribution of Income', *Journal of Economics and Business*, 25, Spring 1973, pp. 175–86.

Vitaliano, Donald F. and Mazeya, Y. E., 'The Effect of Servicing the Public Debt Upon Private Capital Formation', (paper), 1988.

Von Furstenberg, George, *Capital, Efficiency and Growth*. New York: Ballinger, 1980.

5. Increasing Inequality in the US: What We Know and What We Don't*

Sheldon Danziger and Peter Gottshalk

1. INTRODUCTION

Post-Keynesians have focused primarily on changes in the functional distribution of income. In this chapter, we analyse the major changes which have occurred within the personal distribution of income. Since much of this change has occurred within labour income, we hope that our work will encourage post-Keynesians to expand their analysis to explain changes within this major functional component.

The economic record of the past fifteen years in the United States, and in many industrialized countries, differs markedly from that of the immediate post-war period. Unemployment rates have been higher, real income growth has been slower, and inequalities within and between various demographic groups and regions have increased.

Ten years ago, academic conferences and papers examining the historical record in the United States discussed 'The Fading Effect of Government on Inequality' (Reynolds and Smolensky, 1978) and more ideologically inclined scholars asked, 'How Much More Equality Can We Afford?' (Browning, 1976). The conventional wisdom was that poverty had been declining rapidly and inequality had been relatively stable. Today, after a decade of stagnation, two back-to-back recessions, and a bugetary retrenchment, attention is directed to such issues as 'The Shrinking Middle Class' (Bradbury, 1986), 'A Surge in Inequality' (Thurow, 1987), 'Cycles of Deprivation and the Underclass Debate' (Wilson, 1985) and 'The Impact of Budget Cuts and Economic Conditions on Poverty' (Danziger and Gottschalk, 1985a). Despite a robust recovery, poverty remains high and inequality is still increasing.

It is ironic that the following statement, written in 1920 by Hugh Dalton, can serve as an introduction to this chapter:

The question whether the inequality of income is increasing or decreasing in modern communities is one of the most important questions in economics. Many writers have attempted to answer it, but their answers do not generally carry much conviction. To determine whether, under modern conditions, inequality tends to increase or decrease, involves the enumeration of a large number of distinct and conflicting tendencies and the weighing and balancing of them one against the other. (Quoted in Brady, 1951, p. 4)

More than sixty years after Dalton, we still attach normative significance to the trend in inequality, often cannot agree as to what the trend actually has been, and rarely understand its underlying causes. What is common to all of these studies is the failure of analysts to do much more than describe trends and then to advocate a policy response that fits the data and their personal views. That is, the degree of inequality and its trend are a topic of intense policy interest, but of little economic understanding.

We illustrate this point with respect to the question, prominent in the literature at least since Kuznets (1955), 'What is the effect of economic growth on inequality?' and, because of the special focus on poverty in the United States, 'What is the effect of economic growth on poverty?'

This chapter is organized as follows. The next section discusses trends in the level and distribution of family income. We then discuss the conceptual links between economic activity, inequality and poverty and point out some factors that now limit the inequality-reducing effects of economic growth. We then present some empirical results which illustrate why the effects of economic growth today differ from those in the post-World War II era. Finally, we turn to an evaluation of some hypotheses that attempt to explain increasing inequality.

2.   TRENDS IN FAMILY INCOME INEQUALITY AND POVERTY IN THE UNITED STATES

To appreciate recent trends in family income inequality and poverty, it is useful to contrast this experience with that of the 1950s and 1960s. As the data in column 1 of Table 5.1 and Figure 5.1 reveal, median family income adjusted for inflation grew by about 40 per cent between 1949 and 1959 and by about 40 per cent between 1959 and 1969. Poverty as officially measured (column 2) dropped by about 10 percentage points and the income share of the bottom 40 percent of families (column 3 and Figure 2) increased by 0.8 percentage points during each decade. In fact, between 1949 and 1969, real year-to-year changes in the median (not shown) were positive sixteen times, unchanged twice, and negative only once. The period since 1969, especially since 1974, is in marked contrast. Real median family income in 1985 was at about the same level as in 1969,

*Table 5.1   Family income, poverty, inequality, unemployment,
and government transfers, selected years, 1949–1985*

Year	Median family income (1985$) (1)	Official poverty rate[a] (2)	Income share of bottom 40% of familes (3)	Umployment rate (4)	Cash transfers per household (1985$) (5)
1949	$14,021	34.3%[b]	16.4%	5.9%	$ 832
1954	16,678	27.3[b]	16.6	5.5	1059
1959	19,993	22.4	17.2	5.5	1676
1964	22,783	19.0	17.1	5.2	2060
1969	27,680	12.1	18.0	3.5	2465
1974	28,145	11.2	17.5	5.6	3249
1979	29,029	11.7	16.8	5.8	3626
1985	27,735	14.0	15.5	7.2	3693

Notes:
[a]Percentage of all persons living in units with income below the official poverty thresholds.
[b]Estimate based on unpublished tabulations from March Current Population Surveys by Gordon Fisher, US Department of Health and Human Services.

Source:
US Bureau of the Census, Current Population Reports, Series P-60.

Figure 5.1   Median family income ($ 1967)

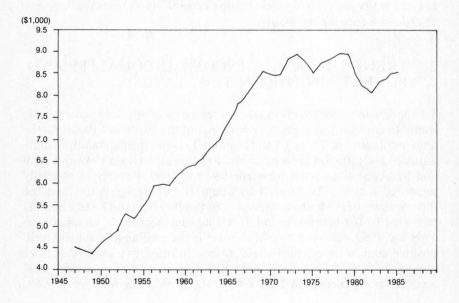

Figure 5.2   Share of bottom 40 percent of aggregate family income

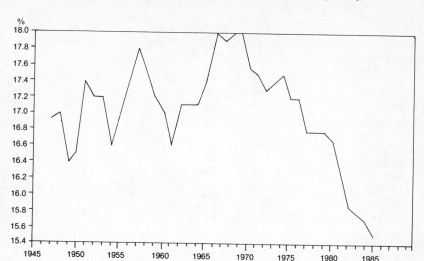

poverty as officially measured was higher, and the income share of the bottom 40 per cent was lower than at any time in the post-war era. Since 1969, there have been eight positive year-to-year changes in the median, two years of no change, and six years of negative changes. And unemployment (column 4) throughout the 1980s has been high by historical standards.

Macroeconomic conditions since the early 1970s have refuted two key assumptions that guided anti-poverty policy and views about economic growth and inequality. Conventional wisdom held that poverty could be alleviated against a background of healthy economic growth because the business cycle could be controlled. This was a reasonable assumption in the mid-1960s, as median family income growth had been positive for each year from 1958 to 1969. It was also believed that in an economy with low unemployment rates and with anti-discrimination policies and education and training programmes in place, everyone – rich, poor, and middle class – would gain. At a minimum, it was expected that economic growth would be proportional and that all incomes would rise at about the same rate. At best, income growth for the poor would exceed the average rate, and poverty and inequality would continue to fall as they had in the prior decades.

Table 5.2   Mean per capita income of quintiles of households (1985 dollars)

	1	2	3	4	5	Mean
Non-elderly families with children						
1967	$2,070	$4,348	$6,054	$8,172	$13,680	$6,864
1973	2,343	5,150	7,258	9,735	16,128	8,123
1985	1,734	4,529	7,096	10,139	17,784	8,256
% Δ 1967–85	− 16.23	+ 14.16	+ 17.21	+ 24.07	+ 30.00	+ 20.28
Elderly (65 +) households						
1967	1,954	3,623	5,200	7,987	18,889	7,531
1973	2,855	5,013	6,832	9,909	22,508	9,424
1985	3,455	5,799	8,243	12,198	25,852	11,110
% Δ 1967–85	+ 76.82	+ 60.06	+ 58.52	+ 52.72	+ 36.86	+ 47.52
Other non-elderly households						
1967	3,231	8,260	12,075	16,637	28,402	13,721
1973	4,024	9,658	14,194	19,641	33,778	16,259
1985	3,624	9,342	14,326	20,433	36,743	16,894
% Δ 1967–85	+ 12.16	+ 13.10	+ 18.64	+ 22.82	+ 29.37	+ 23.13
All households						
1967	2,173	4,760	7,192	10,844	21,535	9,301
1973	2,744	5,951	8,774	13,121	26,674	11,453
1985	2,499	6,099	9,508	14,491	28,713	12,262
% Δ 1967–85	+ 15.00	+ 28.13	+ 32.20	+ 33.63	+ 33.33	+ 31.84

Note:
Each household is counted once. Quintiles are computed separately for each demographic group for each year. These three categories are mutually exclusive. Price adjustment is via the Consumer Price Index.

Source:
Computations by authors from March Current Population Survey computer tapes.

Instead, despite the increase in government income transfer payments (column 5), poverty and inequality increased as growth faltered. But it would be incorrect to conclude from Table 5.1 that government transfers have been ineffective in reducing poverty and inequality. Most government transfers in the United States are targeted at the elderly, and, as the data in Table 5.2 indicate, the elderly experienced both an above-average income increase and a reduction in inequality during the period when aggregate income growth slowed. For the elderly, per capita income growth was fastest for the lowest quintile, and slowest for the top quintile. In contrast, the bottom quintile of households with children were actually worse off in 1985 than in 1967 – their per capita income fell by 16.23 per cent. Inequality among households with children increased, with the greatest income gains going to the highest quintile.

What are the underlying economic relationships among poverty and inequality, economic growth and government transfers? The simple story which emerges from this brief review of the data is that the early period of poverty and inequality reductions was due to strong economic growth, declining unemployment rates and large increases in government transfers. All three factors contributed to decreasing poverty and inequality. The recent increases in poverty and inequality seem to result from offsetting factors. The rise in unemployment rates and the slowdown in growth were partially offset by increases in government transfers. Non-elderly households that receive little in the way of government transfers and are most affected by market conditions fared much worse than elderly households that receive relatively large amounts of transfers and are mostly insulated from market conditions.

Such simple stories, while plausible, ignore the inherent difficulty in separating the impact of demographics, changes in macroeconomic conditions, and growth in income transfers on poverty and inequality reduction. We now turn to a more rigorous attempt to account for changes in the level and distribution of income.

3.   CONCEPTUAL LINKS BETWEEN ECONOMIC ACTIVITY, INEQUALITY AND POVERTY

The degree to which changes in economic activity affect the level and distribution of income depends crucially on the underlying economic process generating the change in economic activity. While declines in cyclical unemployment and economic growth both lead to increased economic activity, they have different impacts on inequality and poverty. Each reflects changes in conceptually different underlying processes which generate the income distribution.

Cyclical Unemployment

Changes in economic activity arising from reduced cyclical unemployment have two important features. First, the mean of the income distribution unambiguously increases when cyclical unemployment decreases. Not only is the sign unambiguous, but the annual rate of increase is very rapid compared to annual increases in the mean associated with economic growth. For example, real mean family income grew by 3.3 per cent between 1983 and 1984 and by 2.6 per cent between 1975 and 1976, two sets of years of strong cyclical recovery from recessions. By contrast, real median family income grew by only 4.9 per cent over the entire decade between 1969 and 1979. Since these are two years of close to full employment, this increase primarily reflects economic growth.

Reductions in cyclical unemployment also reduce the spread of the income distribution, leading to further reduction of inequality and poverty. The countercyclical change in the spread of the income distribution is consistent with economic theory. If employers share in the cost of training or screening, then they will find it to their advantage to institute a seniority-based lay-off policy. The first to be laid off will be those in whom the firm has the least investment. These workers, who are either newly hired or working in firms which offer little training, are likely to be in the lower tail of the earnings distribution.

Thus, while there may still be substantial disagreement about the role of economic growth in reducing poverty, we know of no one who would seriously question the primary importance of tight labour markets in reducing poverty rates for persons able and willing to work. It is unambiguous that both the location and spread of the income distribution change in a poverty-reducing direction as a result of decreases in cyclical unemployment.

This discussion has emphasized increases in cyclical conditions. But, by definition, cycles are independent of the secular trend, and thus have a downside during which poverty and inequality increase. To the extent that economic policies can dampen the business cycle, they can moderate cyclical swings in poverty and inequality. But only secular changes can lead to permanent changes in the level and distribution of income.

Economic Growth

As long as the fruits of economic growth are taken in the form of higher income, economic growth will be accompanied by increases in the mean of the income distribution. However, poverty will not necessarily decrease if growth is accompanied by a sufficiently large, offsetting increase in inequality. Unfortunately, the impact of growth on inequality is not nearly as clear, either theoretically or empirically, as its impact on the mean of the distribution.

Growth and the distribution of income are the joint results of a complicated set of underlying economic processes, reflected in changes in supplies of and demands for factors of production. Arguments that inequality is necessary for growth or that growth necessarily reduces inequality ignore the process generating growth and inequality simultaneously. Any correlation between these two variables is likely to be spurious – it is not growth *per se*, but how that growth is achieved, which determines inequality.

Technological change and increases in the supply of labour or capital offer two routes to economic growth. They are, however, not on equal footing. Since the amount of labour or capital cannot be increased indefinitely, only technological change can offer a permanent increase in the rate of growth of output. The two also differ in the ways in which they affect the distribution of income.

Technological change may increase or decrease inequality. The initial impact of technological change is to alter the demands for labour and capital. This in turn changes prices, which may call forth a supply response as workers flow to those jobs for which demand and hence wages are greater.

While technological change may increase the demand for all skill classes, this is by no means necessary. The result may be an increase in both economic growth and poverty. For example, a labour-saving technological change may lower the demand for low-skilled workers. The resulting decrease in wages of those at the bottom of the distribution will have two effects – some workers will drop out of the labour force, while others will be induced to gain skills in response to the drop in the relative wages of unskilled workers. Whether or not poverty increases depends on the relative magnitude of these two changes.

Since it is by no means simple for government to alter the rate and form of technological progress, public policy has tended to focus on the intermediate goal of increasing the quantity and quality of labour and capital. Inasmuch as taxes reduce the supply of labour and capital, government may be able to raise the rate of economic growth by undertaking policies which increase the return to savings, education and work.

These policies will increase average incomes; however, it is not clear what effect increases in demands for labor and capital will have on the shape of the distribution. Again the result depends on the form of the policies. For example, incentives to increase the rate of capital formation may increase both growth and poverty. The increased demand for capital will be accompanied by an increase in demand for high-skilled workers and a decrease in demand for low-skilled workers if capital is complementary with high-skilled workers and substitutable for low-skilled workers. Poverty will increase unless the labour-upgrading response to the resulting increase in the wages for high-skilled workers more than offsets the decreased wages for those who remain unskilled.

Williamson and Lindert (1980) review the evidence offered by US economic history. They show that the correlation between economic growth and inequality is weak. The nineteenth century was marked by rapid increases in output and in inequality. However, in the first half of the twentieth century a similarly rapid growth in output was accompanied by a trend toward income equalization. This demonstrates that simultaneous increases in output and inequality are more than a theoretical possibility, even in an industrialized country. In fact, some authors have suggested that the increased employment in 'high-tech' industries in recent years has had similar effects.

There are at least two other factors which currently limit the inequality-reducing effects of economic growth in the United States. The first, the demographic composition of households, is likely to have similar effects in other advanced economies. The second arises from the fact the US poverty line is fixed in real terms, so that the line falls as a percentage of real income as income grows.

Demographic Factors

While an improvement in macro-conditions can raise the earnings of poor households with an able-bodied head, it alone cannot raise incomes or eliminate poverty for households whose heads have weak attachments to the labor force. There are simply two many low-income households that cannot benefit directly from improved labour market conditions.

For example in 1979, the last cyclical peak, almost two-thirds of households defined as poor by the official definition were headed by a person who was elderly, a student, disabled, or a woman with a child under six years of age. Given today's social norms, these heads of household can be classified as not expected to work. Indeed, almost all of them did not work during this year of relatively low unemployment. While those families will not gain directly from growth, they may benefit indirectly if a portion of the increased tax revenues resulting from growth are distributed through anti-poverty programmes.

The proportion of poor households not expected to benefit from economic expansion is not only large, but growing. In 1939, when poverty rates were much higher, less than one-third of poor household heads were classified as not expected to work by this definition. From a purely demographic standpoint, it was easier to reduce poverty through growth of the economy in the 1940s and 1950s than it is today.[1]

Non-linear Relationship Between Growth and Poverty

Another factor limiting the impact of growth on poverty is that poverty, as officially measured in the United States, is simply the cumulative distribution of income up to a fixed line. As long as this poverty line falls to the left of the mode (the location of the most frequently occurring values) of the income distribution, fewer and fewer people will be taken out of poverty as the distribution shifts to the right. This results from the decreasing density of the distribution as one moves away from the mode. For example, the poverty line for a family of four was almost 80 per cent of mean family income in 1949, but only about 40 per cent in 1985. Suppose that all incomes increased by 2 per cent a year for several years. All those households with incomes within 2 per cent of the poverty line would rise above the poverty line in each successive year, but the number leaving poverty would diminish each year. Thus, even if there were no changes in the demographic composition of the poor or in the shape of the income distribution, there would still be diminishing returns to economic growth. Of course, measures of relative poverty and inequality are not affected by this factor.

In summary, the debate over the role of economic growth in reducing poverty has tended to lump all forms of increased economic activity together. We argue that the source of increased economic activity is crucial. Decreased cyclical unemployment unambiguously decreases poverty, but pure economic growth has an ambiguous impact. Since theory leaves us with this ambiguity, we now turn to some empirical tests.

4. EMPIRICAL PATTERNS

Secular Growth[2]

Using data from the Census of Population over the period 1950–80 inclusive, we first review the relationship between poverty and the location and shape of the income distribution. Since the effects of cyclical swings become less important over these ten-year periods, we interpret these changes in poverty as reflecting secular changes. Because 1969 and 1979 were both cyclical peaks, this interpretation is particularly appropriate for the last decade covered.

We analyse data for households headed by men aged 25–64 years. Relative to other households, they have the strongest attachment to the labour force and the smallest reliance on government transfers. They are, therefore, the group most likely to benefit directly from economic growth.

*Table 5.3   Secular growth and the trend in the official (post-transfer)
poverty rates for households headed by men aged 25–64,
selected years, 1949–79*

	Year			
	1949	1959	1969	1979
1. Mean income/needs[a]	1.600	2.408	3.330	3.789
2. Variance ln (income/needs)[a]	.738	.771	.627	.730
3. Poverty rate	33.1%	16.2%	7.7%	7.1%
Change in poverty rate due to:[b]				
4. Change in mean	—	− 13.8%	− 6.1%	− 1.3%
5. Change in shape (inequality of income)	—	− 3.1%	− 2.4%	+ 0.7%
6. Percentage-point decline in poverty due to a one percent increase in the mean, holding inequality constant[c]	− 0.77	− 0.28	− 0.12	− 0.09

Notes:
a.   Because the poverty lines are adjusted for changes in the Consumer Price Index (CPI), income/needs ratios are fixed in real terms. Poverty in 1949 is derived by adjusting the official lines back from 1959 using the CPI in the same way that they have been brought forward to the present.
b.   The percentage-point difference between the poverty rates over any decade equals the sum of rows 4 and 5 in the column of the latter year.
c.   Defined as the percentage point difference between the actual poverty rate in each year and a rate that results from increasing each household's income: needs ratio in the base year by 1 per cent.

Source:
Computations by authors from computer tapes of the 1950, 1960, 1970 and 1980 Censuses of Population.

A focus on prime-aged men also provides a rough correction for demographic change by excluding households headed by women, who have above-average poverty rates and represent an increasing proportion of all households.

Because the poverty line varies with family size, poverty will fall if family size declines, even if household income is constant, *ceteris paribus*. To control for the decline in family size that has occurred, we analyze the ratio of a household's income to its poverty line (the income:needs ratio).

The first three rows of Table 5.3 show the mean and log variance of the income/needs ratio and the official poverty rate in each of the Census years. The log variance is an inequality measure which is sensitive to changes in the lower tail of the distribution. Note, however, that it measures only one aspect of change in the shape of the distribution, since it does not reflect changes in other moments.

Rows 3 and 1 show that poverty declined when the mean increased and that the declines in poverty and the increases in the mean became successively smaller with each passing decade. At this superficial level, it seems that a rising tide was indeed lifting all boats. Such bivariate relationships do not, however, hold other factors constant.

The observed change in poverty over each decade is decomposed into one component associated with shifts in the mean (row 4), and another with changes in the shape (row 5). The following thought experiment illustrates this decomposition. First, suppose that every household experienced the average increase in income in relation to needs. There would be no change in inequality and, as the distribution shifted to the right, poverty would drop. The difference between the initial-year poverty rate and this simulated rate gives the change in poverty when inequality is held constant.

Second, the effects of changes in inequality are obtained by comparing this simulated distribution to the actual distribution in the later year. By construction, the means of the two distributions are the same. However, if the actual distribution is less equal than the simulated distribution, changes in the shape will have increased poverty. By definition, the actual change in poverty over the decade is the sum of these two partial effects.

Row 4 of Table 5.3 shows how poverty rates would have changed if all households had experienced the average growth in the income/needs ratio. A rising mean was the primary cause of the reduction in poverty over the thirty years. However, the anti-poverty effect of growth in the mean decreased in each successive decade (row 4), primarily because of the falling rate of secular growth (row 1).

In addition, the anti-poverty effect of growth declined because of the non-linear relationship between growth and poverty. Row 6 shows the percentage-point decline in the poverty rate associated with a 1 per cent increase in the mean, holding inequality constant. As poverty declined from 33.1 to 7.1 per cent between 1949 and 1979, this measure of the anti-poverty effect declined from −0.77 to −0.09 percentage points. Thus, a given percentage increase in the mean removed a much smaller number of households from poverty as the poverty rate declined.[3]

Row 5 shows the impact of changes in inequality, holding the mean constant. The changes in poverty due to changes in inequality were much smaller than those due to growth in the mean (compare rows 4 and 5). However, between 1969 and 1979, two years of comparable unemployment rates, the change in the shape of the distribution was poverty-increasing, and offset roughly half of the poverty-decreasing effect of the rising mean.

Table 5.4   Simulated percentage-point change in pre-transfer poverty rate due to changes in the mean and shape of the distribution of income/needs,[a] male household heads, ages 25–64

| | Whites | | | Blacks | | |
| | | Change in Poverty Due to Changes in:[c] | | | Change in Poverty Due to Changes in:[c] | |
Region	Growth of Mean[b] (1)	Mean (2)	Shape (3)	Growth of Mean[b] (4)	Mean (5)	Shape (6)
North-east						
1969–73	8.7%	− 0.59%	+ 0.80%	6.5%	− 0.90%	+ 0.37%
1973–79	2.3	− 0.19	+ 1.75	− 1.8	+ 0.68	+ 6.89
1979–84	4.5	− 0.36	+ 2.51	4.5	− 0.34	+ 1.31
Total, 1969–84	16.3	− 1.14	+ 5.06	9.3	− 0.60	+ 8.57
North-Central						
1969–73	10.2	− 0.91	+ 0.99	21.0	− 3.09	+ 3.20
1973–79	2.8	− 0.17	+ 0.98	2.3	− 0.40	− 0.38
1979–84	− 5.6	+ 0.57	+ 3.51	− 5.9	+ 1.51	+ 9.43
Total, 1969–84	6.9	− 0.51	+ 5.48	16.5	− 1.98	+ 12.25
South						
1969–73	13.3	− 1.71	+ 1.02	18.6	− 6.43	+ 1.69
1973–79	1.3	− 0.11	+ 1.53	17.3	− 6.01	+ 0.74
1979–84	5.3	− 0.77	+ 2.28	3.2	− 0.50	+ 1.78
Total, 1969–84	20.9	− 2.59	+ 4.83	43.5	− 12.94	+ 4.21
West						
1969–73	6.7	− 0.66	+ 1.49	2.6	− 0.82	+ 5.96
1973–79	3.5	− 0.26	+ 0.47	11.3	− 0.98	+ 3.00
1979–84	− 0.3	+ 0.08	+ 2.57	− 8.5	+ 0.54	− 0.65
Total, 1969–84	10.1	− 0.84	+ 4.53	4.5	− 1.26	+ 8.31

Notes:
[a] The percentage-point difference in the actual poverty rate over any period equals the sum of the columns 'change in mean' and 'change in shape'.
[b] Defined as 100 times the later year mean of income/needs less initial year mean divided by initial year mean. Because the base is different for each subperiod, the total change for 1969–84 does not equal the sum of the changes for the three sub-periods.
[c] The actual changes in poverty between 1969 and 1984 by race and region were as follows. For whites, poverty increased from 4.91 to 8.83 per cent in the Northeast; from 5.34 to 10.31 per cent in the North-Central region; from 9.58 to 11.82 per cent in the South; and from 6.94 to 10.63 per cent in the West. For blacks, poverty increased from 11.82 to 19.77 per cent, from 12.39 to 22.66 per cent, declined from 31.90 to 23.16 per cent, and increased from 10.95 to 18 per cent in these four regions.

Differences by Race and Region

What has happened in recent years? To answer this question, Table 5.4 presents a similar analysis using Current Population Survey data for the period 1969–84 for households headed by white and black males in each of the four Census regions. In this table, poverty is measured prior to the receipt of government transfers. During this period there were some very large mean income increases in some regions in some subperiods, as well as some income declines (see columns 1 and 4). For example, between 1969 and 1973, the mean income/needs ratio for blacks grew by almost 20 per cent in the North–Central and Southern regions, while the mean grew very slowly for blacks in the West. Between 1979 and 1984, real income declined significantly for whites and blacks in the North–Central region and for blacks in the West.

The results of the thirty-year period are confirmed: when growth of the mean is rapid, *ceteris paribus*, poverty falls rapidly (columns 2 and 5). But in almost all cases, poverty-increasing changes in the shape of the distribution after 1969 were greater than the poverty-reducing changes in the mean. The only exception is for blacks in the South. Over the 1969–79 period, income growth was so rapid there that it offset the poverty-increasing changes in the shape. Note also that all 16 rows for whites (column 3) and 14 of 16 rows for blacks (column 6) have positive signs, indicating poverty-increasing changes in the shape. Again, this is in stark contrast to the poverty-reducing changes in the shape that characterized the 1949–69 period (see row 5 of Table 5.3).

Black poverty has been somewhat more responsive to changes in the mean than has poverty among all persons because black poverty is at a higher level (i.e. because of the non-linear relationship between growth and poverty) and because black incomes have grown somewhat faster than average.

Differences by Race and Sex

While the results in Tables 5.3 and 5.4 are based on a simulation methodology, Table 5.5 uses a more complex methodology to disentangle the anti-poverty effects of market income and transfer income. The methodology, fully described in Gottschalk and Danziger (1985), focuses directly on the relationship between changes in poverty and changes in the joint distribution of market income and transfer income. Poverty is viewed as changing because of shifts in the level and distribution of each income source. These shifts can be described by changes in the means, variances, covariances and higher-level moments of the distribution of market and government transfer income.

For expositional simplicity, changes in poverty for non-aged families with children are attributed in Table 5.5 to three factors: changes in mean market income, changes in mean transfer income, and changes in the

Table 5.5   Decomposition of official poverty rate for non-aged white and non-white heads of households with children, 1968 to 1983

| | Persons living in households Where head is: | | | |
| | Non-white | | White | |
	Male (1)	Female (2)	Male (3)	Female (4)
1. Actual percentage-point change in poverty[a]	− 2.8	− 2.5	3.8	3.6
Percentage-point change in poverty due to change in:				
2. Mean market income	− 8.0	− 6.7	− 1.5	− 0.5
3. Mean transfer income	− 2.1	2.9	− 0.5	2.7
4. Shape (inequality of income)	7.3	1.3	5.8	1.4

Notes:
In each column, the sum of rows 2, 3, and 4 equals the actual percentage-point change. The actual percentage-point change is the difference between the 1983 and 1968 poverty rates for each demographic group.

[a] Between 1968 and 1983, the official poverty rate declined from 23.4 to 20.6 per cent for non-white males and from 65.8 to 63.3 per cent for non-white females; the rate increased from 6.6 to 10.4 per cent for white males and from 39.6 to 43.2 per cent for white females.

Source:
Computations by authors. See Gottschalk and Danziger (1985) for discussion of methodology.

shape of the distribution. The first row shows the actual percentage-point changes between 1968 and 1983 in poverty rates for the four family types. During this period poverty declined for nonwhites, but rose for whites.

Row 2 shows the impact of changes in mean market income on the poverty rate of each sub-group. Increases in mean market income were much more important for non-whites – the poverty rates for non-white males and females would have decreased by 8.0 and 6.7 points, respectively, as a result of changes in mean market income. The corresponding figures for whites are only 1.5 and 0.5 points.

Row 3 shows the impact of income transfers. For females, the anti-poverty effect of changes in transfers during this period is similar among whites and non-whites. Both would have experienced an almost 3 percentage-point increase in poverty solely as a result of their reduced real cash transfers. For males, transfers rose over this period. The poverty-reducing impact of increased transfers is considerably higher for nonwhites (− 2.1 points) than for whites (− 0.5 points).

Row 4 shows the importance of increased inequality of income within each demographic group. Consistent with the results in Tables 5.3 and 5.4, these data show that increased inequality was important for all groups, but especially important among both non-white and white men. Since income transfer growth for the non-elderly has been virtually halted in the United States by the budgetary retrenchment of the 1980s, it is unlikely that transfers can offset the tendency toward inequality that has accompanied the slower economic growth of recent years.

5. EXPLAINING INCREASES IN INEQUALITY: WHAT WE KNOW AND WHAT WE DON'T

The preceding sections have shown that the increase in inequality since the early 1970s has been large and has had a substantial impact on poverty. Whereas the driving force behind poverty reduction during the 1950s and 1960s was rapid economic growth, that situation has changed. As a result, slow growth in mean income and increased inequality have contributed significantly to the rising poverty rates of the late 1970s and early 1980s.

These facts are clear. What is much less well understood is why inequality has increased. In this section we review several alternative explanations which have been offered. Unfortunately, while each has some merit, none can fully explain the observed trend. And no research to date has systematically decomposed the trend into components due to these or other factors.

Cyclical Changes

It is well known that inequality is cyclically sensitive (see Blinder and Esaki, 1978; Blank and Blinder, 1986). During recessions people in the lower tail of the distibution experience disproportionately large declines in income and people in the middle-income group are more likely to experience income losses than are high-income people. The result is a counter-cyclical pattern in inequality.

The 1970s and 1980s have been a period of unusually large cyclical swings. How much of the increased inequality reflects nothing more than the expected response to the cycle? The data suggest that we are experiencing something more profound.

First, poverty increased between the cyclical peaks of 1973 and 1979 (Danziger and Gottschalk, 1986). Furthermore, in 1987, after four years of economic recovery and with median family income above its previous cyclical peak, the poverty rate remained 2.4 percentage points above its historic low of 11.1 per cent, which occurred in 1973.

Second, the fastest-growing regions, which experienced relatively modest cyclical changes during the recent recessions, still had large increases in inequality. As shown in Table 5.4, the mean income of males in the South grew by 5.3 per cent for whites and 3.2 per cent for blacks between 1979 and 1984, while inequality grew among both groups. Since inequality increased both over time and space when income levels rose, something other then cyclical swings must account for the change.

Changes in Cohort Size

The second explanation focuses on demographic changes associated with the baby boom, followed by the baby bust. This view emphasizes the fact that the groups which grew the fastest were the young and old, whose mean incomes tend to be at the two extremes of the earnings distribution. Such a demographic shift would increase inequality among all workers. Furthermore, the variance of income within age groups also tends to be highest for the young and old, again contributing to increased inequality.

The problem with this explanation is that inequality has also increased within experience groups – the young do have an above-average degree of inequality in any year, but inequality among them has increased over the recent period. In fact, Dooley and Gottschalk (1984) find that inequality grew even after controlling for experience, education, unemployment and a variable measuring a possible behavioural response to increases in cohort size. One can thus only explain some of the increased inequality by demographic changes.

Changes in Female Headship

It is well known that families headed by non-married women have considerably lower incomes than their male counterparts and that female headship has grown substantially over the past two decades. By itself, this demographic change would lower mean income and increase inequality among all families. But because inequality has also increased within both married couple families and female-headed familes, this factor, like cohort size, offers only a partial explanation.

Changes in Government Income Transfers

An alternative explanation focuses on adverse behavioural responses to government income transfers. This view, popularized by Murray (1984), argues that increased benefits, especially in income-tested welfare programmes, had such large work-disincentive effects that the total incomes of the poor actually fell.

Elsewhere (Danziger and Gottschalk, 1985b) we have shown that trends in welfare spending are inconsistent with this view. Historically, the real value of welfare benefits increased most between 1960 and the mid-1970s, but fell thereafter. Although this rise provides the basis for the increased negative family and work effects attributed to social programmes, there were no reversals in the trends of either family composition or work effort after real benefits began to fall.

While such time-series data are suggestive, they do not resolve the debate about the relative importance of poor economic performance or the disincentive effects of transfers in explaining the trend in poverty. There is, however, an extensive experimental literature (see Burtless, 1986) that shows that the magnitudes of the labour supply and family structure effects of transfers are much smaller than those required to confirm Murray's hypothesis.

Changes in Industrial Structure

Bluestone and Harrison (1986) and others have attributed increased inequality to changes in industrial structure. It is claimed that the loss of manufacturing jobs and the increased service sector employment have reduced the percentage of high-paying production-line jobs and increased the percentage of low-wage service jobs.

The problem with this explanation is that it can be tailored to fit the facts. If industries and occupations are defined sufficiently narrowly, then each person is his/her own unique group and all changes in inequality are attributable to changes in industrial structure by definition. However, if industries and occupations are defined broadly, then this explanation is incomplete because inequality has also increased within various sectors (see Beach, 1988, for a review). Without a theoretical construct to guide decisions about the appropriate level of aggregation, discussions about the role of deindustrialization remain problematic.

In sum, inequality has increased over time and within various demographic, geographic, and sectoral groups during the 1970s and 1980s. These inequality increases have been well documented, but their causes have not been fully explained.

NOTES

*   Sheldon Danziger is Professor of Social Work and Public Policy and Faculty Associate at the Population Studies Center at the University of Michigan. Peter Gottschalk is

Professor of Economics at Boston College. Both are Research Affiliates of the Institute for Research on Poverty at the University of Wisconsin-Madison.

Support from the Graduate School Research Committee of the University of Wisconsin, the Russell Sage Foundation, and the Assistant Secretary for Planning and Evaluation at the US Department of Health and Human Services is gratefully acknowledged. Any opinions expressed are those of the authors alone and not of the sponsoring institutions.

1. This discussion is based on the assumption that demographic changes are exogenous. But if some portion of the demographic change is endogneous, then these conclusions must be modified. For example, some part of the increased tendency of the elderly to head their own households is due to their rapid income increases. Thus, rapid growth reduced poverty and inequality directly by raising incomes, but also led to offsetting changes that operated through increases in the total number of households. Similarly, slow growth in the recent period has contributed to rising poverty and inequality, but its effects have been mitigated by the increased labor force participation of wives and their resulting fertility declines, which were undoubtedly partially caused by the reduction in economic growth.
2. This section is drawn from Danziger and Gottschalk (1986).
3. If a distribution is unimodal, a constant absolute increase in the mean will by definition yield a declining percentage point change in poverty. Row 6 shows that a constant percentage increase in the mean also has a declining impact. In fact, the elasticity – the percentage decline in poverty with respect to a constant percentage increase in the mean – also declines (data not shown).

REFERENCES

Beach, Charles, 'The "Vanishing" Middle Class?: Evidence and Explanations', Institute for Research on Poverty, Discussion Paper, 1988.

Blank, Rebecca and Blinder, Alan, 'Macroeconomics, Income Distribution and Poverty', in Sheldon Danziger and Daniel Weinberg (eds), *Fighting Poverty: What Works and What Doesn't*, Cambridge, Mass.: Harvard University Press, 1986, pp. 180–208.

Blinder, Alan and Esaki, Howard, 'Macroeconomic Activity and Income Distribution in the Post-War United States', *Review of Economics and Statistics*, 60, 1978, pp. 604–9.

Bluestone, Barry and Harrison, Bennett, 'The Great American Job Machine: The Proliferation of Low Wage Employment in the U.S. Economy', Joint Economic Committee of the US Congress, 1986.

Bradbury, Katherine L., 'The Shrinking Middle Class', *New England Economic Review*, September/October 1986, pp. 41–55.

Brady, Dorothy S., 'Research on the Size Distribution of Income', in *Conference on Research in Income and Wealth*, 1951, pp. 2–55. National Bureau of Economic Research Studies in Income and Wealth, vol. 13. New York: National Bureau of Economic Research.

Browning, Edgar, 'How Much More Equality Can We Afford?', *Public Interest*, 1976, No. 43, pp. 90–110.

Burtless, Gary, 'The Work Response to a Guaranteed Income: A Survey of Experimental Evidence', in Alicia Munnell (ed.), *Lessons from the Income Maintenance Experiments*, Boston, Mass.: Federal Reserve Bank of Boston, 1986.

Danziger, Sheldon, and Gottschalk, Peter, 'The Impact of Budget Cuts and

Economic Conditions on Poverty', *Journal of Policy Analysis and Management*, 4, Summer 1985a, pp. 586-93.

Danziger, Sheldon and Gottschalk, Peter, 'The Poverty of *Losing Ground*', *Challenge*, 28, May/June 1985b, pp. 32-8.

Danziger, Sheldon, and Gottschalk, Peter, 'Do Rising Tides Lift All Boats? The Impact of Secular and Cyclical Changes on Poverty', *American Economic Review*, May 1986, pp. 405-10.

Dooley, Martin, and Gottschalk, Peter, 'Earnings Inequality among Males in the United States: Trends and the Effect of labor Force Growth', *Journal of Political Economy*, January 1984, pp. 59-89.

Gottschalk, Peter, and Danziger, Sheldon, 'A Framework for Evaluating the Effects of Economic Growth and Transfers on Poverty', *American Economic Review*, 74 March 1985, pp. 153-61.

Kuznets, Simon, 'Economic Growth and Income Inequality', *American Economic Review*, 45 March 1955, pp. 1-28.

Murray, Charles, *Losing Ground: American Social Policy 1950-1980*, New York: Basic Books, 1984.

Plotnick, Robert, and Skidmore, Felicity, *Progress against Poverty: A Review of the 1964-1974 Decade*, New York: Academic Press, 1975.

Reynolds, Morgan, and Smolensky, Eugene, 'The Fading Effect of Government on Inequality', *Challenge*, July/August, 1978.

Thurow, Lester, 'A Surge in Inequality', *Scientific American*, 256 1987, pp. 30-7.

Williamson, Jeffrey and Lindert, Peter, *American Inequality: A Macroeconomic History*, New York: Academic Press, 1980.

Wilson, William Julius, 'Cycles of Deprivation and the Underclass Debate', *Social Service Review*, 59, December 1985, pp. 541-59.

6. Poverty, Affluence and the Income Costs of Children: Cross-National Evidence from The Luxembourg Income Study (LIS)*

Timothy M. Smeeding

1. INTRODUCTION

Have children become economic liabilities instead of assets? Would a 'modern' woman want children? Joan Huber (1985) suggests a very pessimistic answer to the declining fertility rates in the USA in particular, and in modern Western society in general:

> First, the direct costs of child-rearing continue to rise, exceeding £175,000 for the first child. Second, the psychic costs of having children increase as parents face friends, peers and professional advice contradicting their beliefs. [Huber points to studies showing mothers at home with preschoolers to be the most unhappy group in the population.] Third, the economic rewards of childbearing decline as Social Security wipes out the economic bonds of parents to children. Fourth, as women's education level and job opportunities rise, the cost of staying home also increases. Fifth, husbands have become primary advocates of working wives, having learned (as did husbands in the Soviet Union) that the added income, in practice, costs them almost nothing in terms of extra housework. And sixth, the dramatic rise in the divorce rate since 1965 has suppressed the desire for children, by increasing women's risks of being saddled with the children alone.

The purpose of this chapter is to look into the economic condition of families with children – their place in the size distribution of income – in the US and in nine other industrial nations around the turn of the decade. In particular, we shall compare the economic status of childless couples to that of both single- and two-parent families with children. The next section describes the Luxembourg Income Study database which allows this comparison. The third section explains the basis of the choices of analytic perspective which we make in examining the well-being of families with children. The next section presents the results of these

98

analyses while the final section discusses the policy implications of our findings.

The implicit perspective espoused here is that having enough children to maintain a steady-state country population (i.e. 'replacement' or 'zero population-growth' levels of fertility) is a desirable end for public policy, and further, that once children are born into society, their well-being becomes a public, social and moral as well as a private, personal and family obligation. In other words, the long-term economic well-being of a society is dependent to some extent upon the quality and quantity of its offspring, and children are therefore not merely the private consumption goods of the family that beget them.

The total fertility rates of women (age-specific birth-rates weighted by the share of the population within the reproductive lifespan) among the countries studied here sets the stage for our discussion. A replacement fertility rate of 2.1 babies per woman is a rough guide to a stable long-run population for a country, excluding any significant immigration or emigration. Among the countries studied here, we find that only Israel has a total fertility rate above replacement (roughly 2.6, we estimate). Among the other countries studied, Australia at 1.9 has the highest and Germany and Netherlands at 1.5 have the lowest total fertility rates.[1] The United States, United Kingdom, and Canada approach 1.8, while Norway, Sweden and Switzerland are at about 1.7 (Teitelbaum and Winter, 1985, Appendix). Should these 'baby bust' fertility trends continue, or even if they modestly increase and are not offset by net population immigration, each of these countries (excluding Israel) will see a slowing of the growth of their populations and possibly even an absolute decline early in the twenty-first century. As a result, each of these countries will experience a significant rise in the median age of the population (Teitelbaum and Winter, 1985, pp. 144–5), and with it, the concomitant social expenditure pressures of an increasingly ageing and retired population (Office of Economic Cooperation and Development (OECD), 1988).

Viewed from one perspective, this paper should not be interpreted as alarmist. To quote the title of an excellent book on this topic, the fear of population decline (Teitelbaum and Winter, 1985) need be seen in a much longer and broader context than that presented here. We only seek to document the relative economic status of families with children at one point in time, and to compare the economic status of the childless with the people with children at the turn of the decade. Other social, political and economic futures might reverse or change the findings of this paper. But fears of population ageing, baby busts and the implicit social costs of an ageing society are of major international policy concern. The topic is in large part at the base of the 'generational equity' debate that in the United

States, has generated a great deal of political interest and policy analysis (e.g. Preston, 1984; Kingson, Hirshorn and Cornman, 1986; Longman, 1987). While we are among a group that believes that a more careful consideration of the facts is in order before jumping to radical policy conclusions (see e.g. Palmer, Smeeding and Torrey, 1988), and while this chapter is designed to add to this factual base, the results of our analyses, should they prove robust, do provide some cause for policy concern.

2.   LUXEMBOURG INCOME STUDY (LIS)

Under the sponsorship of the government of Luxembourg, the LIS experiment was instigated in summer 1983. The purpose of the project was to gather in one central location, the Centre for Population, Poverty and Policy Studies, and International Networks for Studies in Technology, Environment Alternatives and Development (CEPS/INSTEAD) in Luxembourg, sophisticated micro-data sets which contain comprehensive measures of income and economic well-being for a set of modern industrialized welfare states. Because of the breadth and flexibility afforded by the LIS microdata, researchers are free to make several choices of perspective: identification of unit (family, household, etc.); measure of income; and population to be studied; e.g. younger and elderly households or families with and without children – the groups which we compare here – within the same research paper. This truly comparable micro-data creates a potentially rich resource for cross-national policy research.

The LIS databank currently covers ten countries – Australia, Canada, Israel, Netherlands, Norway, Sweden, Switzerland, United Kingdom, United States and West Germany – with data for 1979, 1981, 1982 or 1983. The basic procedure used to prepare the datasets is contained in Smeeding et al. (1985), while the basic description of the dataset can be found in the 'LIS Information Guide' (Buhmann et al., 1988a).[2] Table 6.1 contains an overview of these datasets: country, dataset name and size, income year, data sampling frame and representativeness of the population.

The LIS database which emerged from this procedure consists of country income microdata sets prepared to a common plan, based on common definitions of income sources (including several sources of taxes and transfers) and family and household characteristics. Already the LIS database has been used to study income poverty, the relative economic status of one-parent families and of the elderly, and the overall distribution of government cash transfers vs. direct taxes (Smeeding, O'Higgins and Rainwater, 1988; Smeeding, Torrey and Rein, 1988).

Table 6.1   *An overview of LIS datasets*

Country	Dataset name, income year (and size)[1]	Population coverage[3]	Basis of household sampling frame[8]
Australia	Income and Housing Survey 1981–82 (17,000)	97.5[4]	Dicennial Census
Canada	*Survey of Consumer Finances*, 1981 (37,900)	97.5[4]	Dicennial Census
Germany	*Transfer Survey*, 1981[2] (2,800)	91.5[7]	Electoral Register and Census
Israel	*Family Expenditure Survey*, 1979 (2,300)	89.0[5]	Electoral Register
Netherlands	*Survey of Income & Program Users* 1983 (4,833)	99.2	Address Register of the Postal & Telephone Cos.
Norway	*Norwegian Tax Files*, 1979 (10,400)	98.5[4]	Tax Records
Sweden	*Swedish Income Distribution Survey*, 1981 (9,600)	98.0[4]	Population Register
Switzerland	*Income and Wealth Survey*, 1982 (7,036)	95.5[9]	Electoral Register & Central Register for Foreigners
UK	*Family Expenditure Survey*,[2] 1979 (6,800)	96.5[6]	Electoral Register
USA	*Current Population Survey*, 1979 (65,000)	97.5[4]	Dicennial Census

Notes:
[1] Dataset size is the number of actual household units surveyed.
[2] The UK and German surveys collect sub-annual income data which is normalized to annual income levels.
[3] As a percentage of total national population.
[4] Excludes institutionalized and homeless populations. Also some far northern rural residents (Inuits, Eskimos, Lapps, etc.) may be under-sampled.
[5] Excludes rural population (those living in places of 2000 or less), institutionalized, homeless, people in kibbutzim, and guest workers.
[6] Excludes those not on the electoral register, the homeless, and the institutionalized.
[7] Excludes foreign-born heads of households, the institutionalized, and the homeless.
[8] Sampling frame indicates the overall base from which the relevant household population sample was drawn. Actual sample may be drawn on a stratified probability basis, e.g. by area or age.
[9] Excludes non-resident foreigners but includes foreign residents and the institutionalized.

Through funding initially from the Government of Luxembourg and from the Ford Foundation, and subsequently through an international jointly financed consortium of science foundations from member countries, LIS has now moved beyond the initial experimental stage to provide a databank which can be perpetually updated and expanded to include the most recent data available for any and all nations with high quality income microdata sets which choose to participate. Additional country datasets from Finland, France, Luxembourg and Italy are expected to be added to LIS over the next year, while negotiations to include Japan, Hungary and other countries remain in the planning stages. The entire LIS dataset will be updated during 1989 at which time income year 1985 and 1986 datasets will be added for most current LIS countries and those listed above.

3.   MEASURING THE ECONOMIC WELL-BEING OF FAMILIES WITH CHILDREN

Because of the availability of the LIS micro-data, researchers are allowed a wide degree of breadth in selecting measures of income, demographic unit of aggregation, and perspectives for comparison across and within countries. The unit of aggregation chosen here is the family – all persons living together and related by blood, marriage or adoption. In this chapter we have selected disposable family income adjusted by an adult equivalence scale or 'adjusted income' as our measure of economic well-being. Disposable income includes all forms of cash and near-cash income[3] including earnings, realized capital income and government transfers, net of income and payroll taxes. This is the most commonly accepted measure of net ability to consume goods and services. It differs from the US Census money income definition used to measure family income and poverty in the US since 1947 (e.g. US Bureau of the Census, 1987, 1987a) in that we subtract direct taxes and include food stamps as near-cash income. Hence, direct comparisons between the US estimates in Table 6.2 and the rest of the estimates in the subsequent tables should be made with caution.[4] Adjusted income makes allowance for the differential needs of different size families by using the median value of the equivalence scales implicit in the poverty lines of eight of the ten countries studied to adjust disposable income for family size.[5] This adjustment is made by dividing the income of a given size unit by the relative number of equivalent adults normalized to a family of size three. Hence, a childless couple's income is divided by .83, a couple with one child (or a single parent with two children) has its disposable income divided by 1.0, and a family of four by 1.24, five by 1.42, etc.

Our reasoning for using adjusted income can be explained by considering Table 6.2. Here we find official US Bureau of the Census estimates of poverty among families in the US and adjusted and unadjusted Census family income for 1985. Estimates are presented for married couples, for married couples with from one to six or more children, for all married couples with children and for all female-headed single-parent families with children.

The first noteworthy item is the official US estimates of poverty. Overall in 1985, only 4.8 per cent of childless couples were poor as compared to 8.9 per cent of couples with children and 45.4 per cent of

Table 6.2   *Poverty rate, unadjusted and adjusted family income in the United States in 1985. Married couples vs. married couple families with children*

Row	Type of family	Poverty rate[1]	Unadjusted income level	As per cent row 1	Adjusted income level[2]	As per cent row 1	Per Capita income level	As per cent row 1
1.	Married couple no children	4.8	$29,387	(100)	34,985	(100)	14,694	(100)
	Married couple plus:							
2.	One child	6.1	34,009	(116)	34,009	(97)	11,336	(79)
3.	Two children	8.3	32,582	(111)	25,455	(73)	8,146	(55)
4.	Three children	13.5	30,310	(103)	19,941	(57)	6,122	(42)
5.	Four children	20.5	27,216	(93)	15,916	(45)	4,536	(31)
6.	Five children	33.6	24,185	(82)	13,002	(37)	3,455	(24)
7.	Six or more children[3]	44.6	24,814	(84)	11,930	(34)	2,919	(20)
8.	All married couple families with children	8.9	32,631	(111)	27,048	(77)	11,380	(77)
9.	All single-parent families with children	45.4	13,660	(46)	11,412	(33)	4,844	(33)

Notes:
1. Poverty rate is percentage of families of each type who are poor.
2. Income is adjusted using the US poverty line equivalence scale normalized to the income of the modal family, a couple with one child.
3. The average family size is 6.48 persons in families with six or more children.

Source:
US Bureau of the Census, 1987, Table 18; 1987a, Tables 3, 14.

single-parent families headed by a female. Hence, couples with children are at nearly twice the risk of poverty as are childless couples. Single-parent females with children were roughly ten times as likely to be poor in 1985. Among families with children the poverty rate increases continuously and dramatically going from 6.1 per cent for couples with one child to 44.6 per cent for families of six or more. While these figures are based on US Census income definitions using the official poverty line for 1985, and are hence not directly comparable to those which have been calculated from LIS, the same general pattern is found in the 1979 LIS data for the United States (Smeeding and Torrey, 1988). Moreover, the official rate of poverty among married couple families with children grew from 6.1 per cent in 1979 (the year of the LIS data) to 8.9 per cent in 1985, nearly a 50 per cent increase.

Coupling this trend with the continuing high rates of poverty among single-parent females with children and their high numbers in the US, poverty rates for all families with children in the US rose from 12.6 to 16.7

per cent in 1985 (US Bureau of the Census, 1987a, Table 3). The increase in poverty among single-mother families over this same period was from 39.6 to 45.4 per cent. Of the 5.6 million poor families with children in the US in 1985, 3.1 million or 55 per cent of them were single-mother families.

Table 6.2 also presents three different measures of income for families in 1985: unadjusted (Census) income, income adjusted using the US poverty line equivalence scale, and per capita income. These three measures represent three different philosophies of looking at the economic well-being of families with children. Unadjusted income implicitly assumes that children are consumption goods, that the decision to have children is a completely rational economic decision. No adjustments for family size or costs of additional children are made; nor, according to this point of view, should such adjustments be made.

Equivalence adjusted income takes account of the extra consumption needs due to having children. It assumes that well-being is measured by income relative to needs, and that these needs should be counted in judging the economic status of families with children regardless of the rationality of deciding to have (or not have) children. The US poverty line equivalence scales used in Table 6.2 to make this adjustment have been criticized elsewhere (e.g. Jencks and Mayer, 1987) as being too generous, i.e. over-adjusting for family size. Yet in the world of equivalence scales, the size of these allowances for extra children are not so great as those used by those concerned with family budgets, e.g. OECD and the US Bureau of Labor Statistics (Buhmann et al., 1988, Table 2). Finally, the elasticity of the US poverty line equivalence scale with respect to family size is .56, nearly identical to the .55 mean elasticity of the equivalence scales used to measure low income in eight of the ten countries examined here.[6]

The final perspective, that of per capita income, ignores all economies of scale in providing consumption goods to additional children and implicitly assumes that each person's well-being is measured by their share of household income. From a 'needs-adjusted' perspective, per capita income adjusts most fully for family size, the exact counterpoint to disposable income which makes no such adjustment. While disposable income makes no adjustment for needs, per capita income over-adjusts because it fails to recognize economies of scale in producing household goods and services such as food, living space, and heat. Equivalence adjusted income, our choice of perspective, falls somewhere in the middle of the two.

The philosophical basis of the comparisons in Table 6.2 is to present the income (or well-being) of a couple without children and, at a point in time, to compare it to that of families with one, two, three, etc., children. The unadjusted income estimates in Table 6.2 indicate that in 1985 married couple families with one, two or three children had higher incomes than those who had none. Beyond three children, however, family income fell below that of couples. Unadjusted income increases and then decreases with family size (as measured by additional children in married couple families at a point in time). However, the equivalence adjusted and per capita income estimates both indicate that family economic well-being, as measured by income relative to needs, consistently declines as the number of children increase. That is, married couple families with children have lower income to needs ratios than married couples without children, and this ratio continuously declines as additional children are added to the couple. For instance, the average person in a married couple family with two children is only 73 per cent as well off as a person in a childless couple family according to equivalence adjusted income, and only 55 per cent as well off on a per capita basis. In general, married couple families and single-parent families with children have only 77 and 33 per cent the adjusted incomes of married couples, respectively.

Granting all of the measurement problems posed by such comparisons as these, if money income relative to needs adjusted by a reasonable equivalence scale is an acceptable measure of family economic well-being, there appears to be a substantial economic sacrifice involved in having children. Moreover, Table 6.2 indicates that the greater that number of children, the greater the sacrifice, in the United States. How the US situation compares with that in other countries, and how these comparisons vary over the income spectrum is the topic of the next section.

4.   RESULTS: WELL-BEING OF FAMILIES WITH CHILDREN ACROSS TEN COUNTRIES

This section presents estimates of the relative economic status of families with children across the ten LIS countries. Ranking families by the adjusted income concept to find the median family we have divided the population according to the cumulative percentage of persons living in families below or above given fractions of median income in each country. We have selected three fractions of median income and have constructed a table (Table 6.3) which presents estimates for five groupings of persons in families: all persons in families or total families including the elderly; and four groups with heads age 60 or less: childless couples, couples with one child, couples with two or more children, and single parents living with their children.[7] Estimates are presented for the ten country average of each measure as well.

The three levels of well-being which we have chosen to focus on in Table

Table 6.3   *Income position of persons in various types of families ranked*
            by adjusted income

Country	Couples no children	Couples with one child	Couples with two + children	Single women with children	Total all families
1. Percentage poor (below half median income)					
Australia	2.7	6.2	10.3	55.0	12.3
Canada	4.0	5.1	12.0	48.5	13.2
Germany	2.2	1.7	3.4	–b–	5.2
Israel	2.9	2.9	11.4	–b–	12.1
Netherlands	6.1	8.5	7.4	–b–	8.0
Norway	4.1	2.1	3.1	18.3	5.1
Sweden	2.6	3.1	4.7	10.6	5.4
Switzerland	2.0	2.2	6.2	21.4	8.5
United Kingdom	1.7	1.9	6.7	28.5	11.4
United States	4.2	5.4	13.0	55.2	18.1
Average	3.3	3.9	7.8	33.9	10.1
2. Percentage not quite upper middle class (below 100 per cent median income)					
Australia	15.4	32.4	59.6	85.2	50.0
Canada	21.8	33.3	61.2	86.8	50.9
Germany	25.2	46.2	63.3	–b–	50.8
Israel	25.7	25.7	56.2	–b–	50.7
Netherlands	23.4	49.5	65.5	–b–	50.8
Norway	18.0	31.3	54.6	80.8	51.2
Sweden	17.8	31.1	51.6	79.9	50.9
Switzerland	20.1	38.5	64.3	72.7	50.6
United Kingdom	16.7	36.4	57.9	73.9	51.6
United States	18.9	32.1	55.6	87.6	50.1
Average	20.3	35.8	59.0	81.0	50.8
3. Percentage affluent (above 150 per cent median income)					
Australia	59.4	30.9	10.5	3.5	22.1
Canada	50.5	25.5	9.8	8.1	19.4
Germany	35.0	13.2	8.7	–b–	17.0
Israel	47.4	40.3	18.2	–b–	23.6
Netherlands	48.6	22.5	10.3	–b–	22.8
Norway	46.3	17.9	7.7	5.2	13.1
Sweden	35.3	14.2	6.0	0.8	10.1
Switzerland	37.8	16.7	7.4	12.4	16.9
United Kingdom	47.8	24.8	9.6	2.1	19.8
United States	49.3	30.1	12.5	1.7	28.3
Average	45.8	23.6	10.1	4.8	19.3

Note:
Families weighted by number of persons; income adjusted using eight country average poverty line equivalence scale; total includes all types of families: one person families, elderly units as well as those shown above. Averages are the simple mean of the estimate over all countries with estimates. Couple families include families with parents living together regardless of marital status; single women with children are families with only one adult and children under 18 in the household.

(–b–) = less than 3 per cent of all persons.

Source:
LIS database.

6.3 are percentage below half median (adjusted) income, percentage below median income, and percentage above 150 percent of median income. The first and last of these groups can roughly be interpreted dividing the poor and the affluent, respectively. Those living in families with adjusted incomes below the median for all families presents a measure of how many persons in such families are not quite middle class. The analysis will be conducted by considering each of the three living standard indicators in turn.

Poverty

The largest variance across countries and groups is found in the estimate of the percentage of persons in families with adjusted incomes below half the median. Because of the widely differing tax and transfer policies in these ten countries, this should come as no surprise to those who have studied cross-national social policy. However, the specific results should surprise most analysts.

With respect to overall poverty in general, and child poverty in particular, the countries fall into roughly four groups: The Scandinavians (Norway, Sweden) and Germany with the lowest poverty rates, near 5 per cent overall, and lower for couples with children. These are followed by the Swiss and Dutch in the 8 per cent range but still below the overall average rate of 10.1 per cent. Slightly above average are the third group: the Canadians, Israelis, Australians and UK, all in the 11–13 per cent range. The US has by far the highest overall rate at 18.1 per cent, forming a group of one at the bottom of the heap.

In all countries, childless couples and couples with children do better than average.[8] In fact, if we only look at couples with children, the UK joins the below-average group while the Dutch move closer to the group average. In families with two or more children, four countries have double-digit poverty rates, with the US again highest, but more closely followed by Canada, Australia and Israel than in the overall figures. Countries with large geographic boundaries and with diverse economic conditions across the fiscal subjurisdictions of those boundaries (e.g. US, Canada, Australia) are more likely to have high poverty rates than smaller, more homogeneous countries like those in Scandinavia and Europe.

In general, and as expected, persons in single-parent families with children have relative poverty rates which are at least twice as high and up to 8–10 times as high, as persons living in married couple families. On average, a third of persons in single-parent families are poor, compared to rates of less than 8 per cent for two-parent families with children. While single parenthood creates a severe economic burden on the persons involved, some countries cope better with poverty and single parenthood than do others. For instance, consider the US, Canada and Australia with rates near or above 50 per cent. They do measurably less well than the United Kingdom or Switzerland which are below average but still in the 20–30 per cent range. The Scandinavian countries do best, with Norway and Sweden at 18.3 and 10.6 per cent respectively. This result is in large part due to differences in the social protection systems and in the labour force behaviour of single parents across these countries (Smeeding and Torrey, 1988).

Looking across family types more closely, the decision to have one child appears only slightly to increase the poverty rate for couples, from 3.3 to 3.9 per cent on average. However, the decision to have two or more children exactly doubles the chances of poverty to 7.8 per cent (compared to the one-child family). Explanations for poverty among large families are numerous. Among married couple families with children, economic conditions in labour markets, i.e. unemployment, relative wage levels and the like, are liable to influence low income as much as tax and transfer policy. One factor to consider is labour force participation. The earnings levels of married women in LIS drop precipitously in virtually all countries when two or more children are present, hence reducing family income levels. While we have no evidence on trends in husband vs. family earnings in other countries, Levy (1987) has recently documented the falling relative wages of husbands and the necessity of having two-earner families to maintain a 'middle-class' standard of living. While the figures in Table 6.3 suggest that such a pattern may extend to poverty as well in the US, we have no similar studies for the other countries involved. Still countries with stronger union involvement, countries which may be said to be more concerned with the 'family wage' and hence having more equal wage structures (e.g. Germany and Scandinavia), tend to have the lowest poverty rates among larger families. Another factor is the depth and breadth of the social insurance and income transfer systems. For instance, the only countries studied which do not have a child allowance as a part of their income transfer policies are the US and Switzerland. Among poor families with children, the US has by far the lowest percentage of families receiving social insurance transfers such as unemployment compensation (Smeeding and Torrey, 1988).

Middle Class and Affluence

While one must take careful note of the variance in poverty rates across family types and countries and their explanation, the patterns of living standards for various family types as measured by percentage below median and percentage above 150 per cent of the median are much more consistent, with a much smaller range across countries. Looking first at the percentage of persons in families with adjusted incomes below the median,[9] only 20 per cent of childless couples fall into this group. The range across countries for this group is only from 15.4 per cent in Australia to 25.7 per cent in Israel. Having one child increases one's chances of falling below the median to nearly 36 per cent, with the range from 25.7 in Israel to 41.2 in Germany and 49.5 in Netherlands – but with all other countries within the 31–6 per cent range.

Having two or more children increases the chances of being below the median to nearly 60 per cent. *All* countries have a greater percentage of larger couple families with children below the overall median than the percentage of persons in all types of families combined below the median (last column of Table 6.3). In all countries the chances of falling into this 'not quite middle-class' group increase consistently and substantially as we move from childless couples to couples with one, then two or more children and finally to single parents. In this latter group, one's chances of being below the median average more than 80 per cent. In virtually all countries the chances of being below the median at least double and on average triple when we compare a childless couple to a family of two or more.

The final panel is in many ways the obverse side of the other two, relative affluence and not relative poverty or middle-class standing is the issue here. Only in Sweden and Norway, where overall levels of inequality are very low, do we find less than 17 per cent of persons being above 150 per cent of the median. The United States – which has the greatest degree of inequality among the countries studied (Buhmann et al., 1988) – has 28.3 per cent of the population living in relative affluence. On average about 20 per cent of all persons in the countries studied are affluent by this measure. But almost half, 45.8 per cent, of childless couples are in this position. Only Germany, Sweden and Switzerland pull the average down.

Perhaps most apparent is the affluence cost of having large families in these countries. As expected, single parents have a very small chance of being affluent, less than 5 per cent. Only in Switzerland, where child support and alimony payments are both high and strictly enforced, do we find a figure above 10 per cent (Smeeding, Torrey and Rein, 1988). For couples with children, the average odds of affluence fall from 46 to 24 per cent with one child and all the way to 10 per cent if two or more children are present. Again, the pattern is continuous and consistent across each of the countries studied. Excluding the outliers – Israel, due to its high birth rate an anomolous country to begin with, and Sweden, where equality is the norm – the percentage of large two-parent families which are affluent varies only from 7.4 to 12.5 per cent across the remaining eight countries. In short, having children in general, and large families in particular, severely reduces one's ability to live in relative affluence in modern societies such as those studied here.

5. IMPLICATIONS

In a recent paper, we have used the LIS data to show that poverty and low income among families with children can be largely offset by effective social policy (Smeeding and Torrey, 1988). Among the countries shown here, the risk of poverty among families with children can be greatly reduced via government tax and transfer policy. While in some countries, e.g. the US, Canada and Australia, the fear of becoming a poor single parent may be a real deterrent to the decision to have children, this is not universally the case. A single parent with children in Sweden is less likely to be poor by our definition than is a married couple with two or more children in the US, Canada or Israel. Most well-developed Western welfare states, those in Europe and Scandinavia, have well-targeted child allowances and other tax-transfer benefits which reduce the risk of poverty to large families. But the evidence presented here suggests that perhaps the low fertility rate among adults in the countries studied has more to do with reduced chances of affluence than with increased risk of poverty.

US feminists are said to argue that 'modern' women want it all: job, family, status and income. But recently Dr Joyce Brothers (1988) argued that while perhaps 'you can have it all, you cannot have it all, all of the time.' The evidence suggests that indeed you cannot have it all, all of the time. It suggests that the low birthrate in modern Western societies correlates well with the universal and strong inverse relationship between having children and being affluent. Recalling the quote which began this chapter, the quest for affluence and societal status appears to be at odds with having children in general and with large families in particular. In Israel, the country with the largest percentage of affluent families with two or more children, the high birthrate may be better explained by national security arguments than by socioeconomic choices. Unlike the other countries studied here, the desire for state and religious survival (i.e. national defence) provides a strong impetus to have children in Israel. Among the others studied, the comfortable material status and affluence of DINKS (Double Income No KidS) family units seem clearly influenced by the material cost of children. If the suggestions in this paper are borne

Table 6.4   *Persons in families with and without children as a percentage of total persons*

| Country (1) | Married couples no children (2) | Couples | | Total (5 = 3 + 4) | Single parents | | Total (8 = 6 + 7) | Total, families with children (9 = 5 + 8) |
		one child (3)	two + children (4)		one child (6)	two + children (7)		
Australia	14.5	13.1	41.8	54.9	2.2	3.1	5.3	60.2
Canada	15.0	16.1	37.0	53.1	2.0	3.4	5.5	58.6
Germany	12.2	11.0	34.1	45.1	1.4	1.5	2.9	48.0
Israel	16.4	19.4	30.0	49.4	1.2	1.2	2.4	51.8
Netherlands	8.9	12.3	54.7	67.0	2.0	0.6	2.6	69.6
Norway	18.5	17.0	37.0	54.0	1.4	1.6	3.0	57.0
Sweden	6.0	11.7	44.4	56.1	2.7	2.3	5.0	61.1
Switzerland	12.1	12.9	27.5	40.4	2.6	2.5	5.1	45.5
United Kingdom	14.8	14.9	38.4	53.3	1.4	3.0	4.4	57.7
United States	13.3	14.8	33.6	48.4	3.1	6.3	9.4	57.8

Source: LIS Datafile

out by additional research on this topic,[10] universal child allowances, better social safety net systems and other 'pro-natalist' policies such as those now firmly entrenched in Western Europe (e.g. see Teitelbaum and Winter) may prevent poverty among large families. Surely there is need for such policies in the US given its inordinately high rate of child poverty. But if the trade-off between material affluence, job status and children is really at the heart of low birthrates in Western societies, the emerging proclivity not to have children will not be much affected by such measures. Despite their liberal policies for subsidized childcare and parental leave for childbirth, Western European and Scandinavian countries have large family incomes which follow the same relative pattern of declining affluence as do those in the US, Canada and Australia. These countries also have the lowest fertility rates of those studied here.

Should these trends towards low birthrates continue, the high social cost of an ageing society will loom large in all of these countries within a quarter of a century (OECD, 1988). To the extent that fewer working adults and dwindling payroll tax revenues early next century will force governments to target better their social retirement benefits to those with little else in the way of resources, the incentive not to have children, but instead to have greater affluence in middle age so that one can save for older age will increase, further exacerbating the income patterns apparent in Table 6.3. If broad payroll tax support for social retirement is a major goal of Western society, greater reliance on immigration to provide younger workers and taxpayers may be required by major Western societies.

NOTES

*   The author thanks the Alfred P. Sloan Foundation for their financial support, the LIS country sponsors for financial support and use of their data, and Brigitte Buhmann, Ryan Smeeding, and John Coder for their assistance with data preparation. All errors of omission, commission, theory and fact are assumed by the author.

1.   These estimates are taken from Teitelbaum and Winter (1985), Appendix A. The Israeli total fertility rate is estimated using the Teitelbaum and Winter estimates for other countries and average numbers of children per country as reported in the LIS data.

2.   Copies of the 'LIS Information Guide' can be obtained by writing to LIS at CEPS/ INSTEAD; BP No. 65; L–7201 Walferdange, Luxembourg.

3.   Near-cash income is that which is nominally in-kind income but which has a cash equivalent value that is identical to its market value. For instance, 'food stamps' in the US and 'housing allowances' in Sweden and the UK are included here.

4.   For instance, the official US estimate of the percentage of families with children below the official US poverty line in 1979 is 12.6 per cent; the comparable LIS disposable income estimate for 1979 is 13.8 per cent.

5.   These include all countries but Israel and Norway which do not have national estimates of poverty lines or low income cut-offs.

6.   Other equivalence scales could and have been used and the results shown below may be

somewhat sensitive to this choice. For more on this topic the reader should consult Buhmann et al., 1988.

7. This latter group is referred to as single women with children because 90 per cent or more of this group are mothers living alone with their children. Because of sample size problems in some of the smaller datasets this category is further limited to only those countries with at least 3 per cent of the population living in such units (see Appendix A-1).

8. In the US families with children (including single-parent families) have had above-average poverty rates since 1973, but this is largely due to the high rates among female single parents as shown in Table 6.2.

9. The careful reader will note that after adjustment for needs the percentage of persons in families below adjusted median income is slightly above 50 per cent. The figure would only be exactly 50 per cent (as in Australia) if equal numbers of larger and smaller families were above and below the family median so that 50 per cent of persons were in each family group.

10. Future extensions of this type of research will include updating these data to 1985, further exploring the labour force participation and earnings of female spouses and single parents in each type of family, and further breaking down the age groupings of couples and families with children. While the average age of heads in childless couples is not much different from that of heads in families with children, the age distribution of heads in the former may be different from that of the latter. However, these refinements are not expected to change the basic trends evident in Table 6.3.

REFERENCES

Brothers, Joyce 'Having it All', *Tennessean*, Sunday, 10 July 1988.

Buhmann, B., L. Rainwater, G. Schmaus and T. Smeeding, 'Equivalence Scales, Well-Being, Inequality and Poverty: Sensitivity Estimates Across Ten Countries Using the LIS Database, *Review of Income and Wealth*, June 1988, pp. 115–42.

Buhmann, B., L. Rainwater, G. Schmaus, and T. Smeeding, 'Information Guide to LIS', LIS-CEPS Working Paper No.7 (Walferdange, Luxembourg: LIS at CEPS/INSTEAD), April 1988a.

Huber, Joan, 'Will U.S. Fertility Decline Toward Zero?', mimeo, University of Illinois, Urbana, 1985.

Jencks, C. and S. Mayer, 'Poverty and Hardship: How We Made Progress While Convincing Ourselves that We Were Losing Ground', interim report to the Ford Foundation, mimeo, Northwestern University, January 1987.

Kingson, E., B. A. Hirshorn and J. M. Cornman, *Ties That Bind*, Washington, D.C.: Seven Locks Press, 1986.

Levy, F., *Dollars and Dreams*, New York: Russell Sage Foundation/Basic Books, 1987.

Longman, P., *Born to Pay, The New Politics of Aging in America*, Boston, Mass.: Houghton-Mifflin, 1987.

Office of Economic Cooperation and Development (OECD), *Aging Populations: The Social Policy Implication*, Paris: OECD, July 1988.

Palmer, J., T. Smeeding and B. Torrey (eds), *The Vulnerable*, Washington, D.C.: Urban Institute Press, September 1988.

Preston, S., 'Children and the Elderly in the U.S.', *Scientific American*. Volume 251, No.6, December 1984, pp. 44–9.

Smeeding, T., G. Schmaus and S. Allegrezza, 'Introduction to LIS', LIS-CEPS

Working Paper No. 1 (Walferdange, Luxembourg: LIS at CEPS/INSTEAD) July 1985.

Smeeding, T., M. O'Higgins and L. Rainwater (eds), *Poverty, Inequality and Income Distribution in International Perspective*, London: Wheatsheaf Books, 1988.

Smeeding, T., B. Torrey and M. Rein, 'Levels of Well-Being and Poverty Among the Elderly and Children in the U.S. and Other Major Countries', in J. Palmer, T. Smeeding and B. Torrey (eds), *op. cit.*

Smeeding, T. and B. Torrey, 'Poor Children in Rich Countries', *Science*, 11 November 1988.

Teitelbaum, M. and J. Winter *The Fear of Population Decline*, New York: Academic Press, 1985.

US Bureau of the Census, 'Money Income of Households, Families and Persons in the U.S., 1985, *Current Population Reports*, Series P-60, No. 156, US Government Printing Office, Washington D.C., 1987.

US Bureau of the Census, 'Poverty in the United States', *Current Population Reports*, Series P-60, No. 158, US Government Printing Office, Washington D.C., 1987a.

7. Macroeconomic Conditions and the Size Distribution of Income: Evidence from the UK

Brian Nolan

1. INTRODUCTION

In order to understand observed changes over time in the size distribution of personal income, the influence of macroeconomic conditions must be explored. Only by tracing these shorter-term influences can we distinguish the longer-term structural factors which are also at work in altering the distribution. In addition, it is of crucial importance in the assessment of macroeconomic policy to know how the costs and benefits of macroeconomic developments and alternative policy responses are distributed.

This chapter presents an analysis of the main factors linking macroeconomic conditions and the size distribution of income, based on data for the United Kingdom. This proves to be a particularly appropriate case for study, with dramatic changes in both the macroeconomy and the size distribution in recent years, and also with a database which permits a variety of approaches to the problem.

The chapter begins by outlining the major channels whereby changes in the macroeconomy are likely to feed through to the size distribution of income, and the approaches which have been taken in previous analyses of this relationship – almost all based on US data. Section 3 looks at one of these approaches, the analysis of time-series data on macroeconomic aggregates and the income distribution, and presents results for the UK corresponding to those for the US produced by Blinder and Esaki (1978). Section 4 outlines an alternative approach based on micro-data, and describes the relevant database for the UK and the way in which such an approach can be implemented. Section 5 presents the results of a simulation-type analysis of the impact of changes in unemployment on the size distribution of income in the UK. Section 6 relates these findings to recent changes in the UK size distribution. Finally, Section 7 summarizes the conclusions of the analysis.

2.   THE MACROECONOMY AND THE SIZE DISTRIBUTION

In suggesting that changes in macroeconomic conditions have an impact on the size distribution of personal income – a hypothesis which appears to be widely accepted – three major channels of influence have been seen as significant.

1.   The changes in factor income shares which are associated with fluctuations in the level of economic activity over time;
2.   changes in the level of unemployment;
3.   changes in the rate of inflation.

As far as factor income shares are concerned, since upper-income groups tend to receive a relatively high proportion of their income from investment income it would be generally assumed that an increase in the share of profits in factor income would increase the share of these groups. The links in this chain are, however, increasingly complex, as we shall explore.

It would also be generally assumed that an increase in the level of unemployment affects those towards the bottom of the income distribution disproportionately, leading to an increase in inequality. With inflation, there may be no such clear expectation of the pattern of effects on the size distribution, with considerable variation possible depending on how income from particular sources is affected in particular instances: much attention has however traditionally been paid to certain low-income groups that may suffer as inflation rises – those on non-indexed pensions, for example.[1]

Three distinct approaches to analysing the relationship between these macroeconomic variables and the size distribution have been adopted in the literature, almost all of which has dealt with the US, and these will be discussed briefly in turn.

Time-series Approaches

Using time-series data, this approach attempts to relate actual changes in the size distribution over time to various macroeconomic variables. Schultz (1969), Metcalf (1969, 1972) and Thurow (1970) summarized the changes in the income distribution through the Gini coefficient (Schultz) or the parameters of a particular functional form fitted to the data (a 'displaced lognormal' in the case of Metcalf, whereas Thurow used a beta distribution). Beach used the actual quintile income levels for the distribution as endogenous variables in an 'indirect quantile approach'. It was only with Blinder and Esaki (1978) that the direct method of relating changes in quintile shares to macroeconomic variables was implemented. A variety of macroeconomic variables, measured in different ways, were used as explanatory variables in these studies.

The results of these studies – with the exception of Schultz's based on the Gini coefficient only[2] – did indicate some significant influence of macroeconomic changes on the US size distribution, but with a somewhat variable pattern. The most consistent result was the significant disequalizing effect of increases in unemployment on the distribution. Results for both inflation and factor shares, where included among the explanatory variables, were much less consistent. Thurow and Blinder/Esaki suggested that increases in the inflation rate might have an equalizing effect, whereas Metcalf found an adverse effect on some lower-income groups. The difficulty of identifying the opposite effects of falling unemployment and increasing profits share, which tend to take place at the same time, were noted by a number of the studies.

The general problem with such time-series studies is clearly that many different influences – structural and cyclical – are producing the relatively small observed changes in the size distribution from year to year. Even if we had greater confidence in the actual distribution time-series, the separation of the various effects would be fraught with difficulty.

Simulation Approaches

An alternative approach, using cross-section data as the basis for 'simulation' of the effects of different macroeconomic changes on the size distribution, thus has obvious appeal. Budd and Whiteman (1978), for example, simulated the effects of increased unemployment on the distribution of earnings based on the 1967 Survey of Economic Opportunity. Budd and Seiders (1971), Palmer (1973), Nordhaus (1973) and Minarik (1979) looked at the effects of inflation on different income groups using the same type of approach. The most comprehensive of these was Minarik and showed inflation having little effect on the distribution of money income. When a more comprehensive income concept including capital gains, pension rights and imputed rent was used, though, those at the top of the distribution were seen to be adversely affected by increased inflation because of the decline in market values of long-term assets and transfers from creditors to debtors.

Panel Data

A third approach would be actually to examine changes in the distribution of income in a sample over time. The increasing availability of panel data has made this possible in recent years, though teasing out exactly what is bringing about the observed changes in the distribution and relating these to macroeconomic conditions remains an analytic challenge. Mirer (1973a, b) used data from the Michigan Panel Study of Income Dynamics for 1967–70 to compare the actual distribution in 1970 with that which he estimates would have been produced if there had been no recession that year. He found middle rather than bottom income groups to be the main losers. Gramlich (1974) looked at the impact of increased unemployment on the annual incomes of families in the Michigan panel for the years 1967–72. With families ranked by 'permanent economic well-being' – income averaged over a number of years and adjusted for differences in family composition – the effects tended to be regressive for families headed by men, though not those headed by women. Neither study related these effects to the resulting size distribution of income, the focus of the present paper.

Having surveyed briefly the main channels whereby macroeconomic conditions are thought to influence the size distribution and the approaches adopted to analysing this relationship, we now turn to the implementation of the time-series approach to UK data.

3.   EVIDENCE FROM THE UK TIME-SERIES

The Data

The most comprehensive source of information on the distribution of personal income in the UK is the Blue Book distribution, the official series compiled by the CSO.[3] This series covers 1949, 1954, 1959 and each of the years 1961 to 1978/79. It was then decided to produce the figures only at three/four-year intervals, since when estimates for 1981/2 and 1984/5 have been published.[4] The series is thus a relatively long one in terms of total coverage, but a continuous annual series is only available from 1961 to 1978/79. Even here changes in definition and coverage affect the consistency of the series, so that a reasonably consistent run of data only goes up to 1975/6.

The figures are compiled mainly on the basis of income tax statistics from the Inland Revenue's *Survey of Personal Incomes*, but supplemented by information from administrative social security records and the annual *Family Expenditure Survey* (FES). There is also a separate series available from 1957 based purely on the FES, but this is thought to be less reliable as the basis for changes over time since it is subject to sampling variation. In addition, the FES suffers from problems of differential response which may lead to inadequate coverage of high incomes. Although the Blue Book series is more comprehensive, it still has a number of deficiencies, analysed in detail in the reports of the Royal Commission on the Distribution of Income and Wealth.[5]

The analysis of the Blue Book series in this section will concentrate on the period for which an annual series is available, 1961 to 1978/79. The shares of selected income groups in pre-tax income for these years, together with the single years 1949, 1954 and 1959 for comparison, are shown in Table 7.1. Key shares are graphed in Figure 7.1. The figures refer to pre-tax income distributed among tax units (broadly equivalent to the nuclear family). Figures for 1976/7 to 1978/9 are on a broader income definition including, in particular, mortgage interest payments (which had previously been excluded because they are tax-deductible). Data are shown on both 'old' and 'new' basis for 1975/76, allowing the effects of the change in definition to be gauged.[6]

The major change in the distribution over the period from 1949 to 1978/79 was the steady and substantial decline in the share of the top 1 per cent. The bottom of the distribution has shown no strong trend. The fall in the share going to the very top has been balanced by an increase in that of the 10–50 per cent group, i.e. those in the top half but not the top decile of the distribution.

The Model

In analysing the influence of macroeconomic factors on the UK size distribution over the relatively short period for which we have a continuous annual series, the straightforward approach applied by Blinder and Esaki (1978) to US data is used. Taking the quintile shares of the US time-series on the personal distribution (from the Current Population Census), they estimated the model

$$S_{it} = \alpha_i + \beta_i U_t + \gamma_i \pi_t + \delta_i T_t + \epsilon_{it}$$

where:
   S_{it} is the share of the ith quintile in total income in year t;
   U_t is the unemployment rate;
   π_t is the rate of inflation;
   T is a linear time trend.

The time trend is included in order to try to separate secular trends in the distribution from cyclical influences. Estimation is by OLS, which automatically imposes the cross-equation restrictions.

Table 7.1   Distribution of income in the UK, 1949-1978/79: Blue Book Series. Pre-tax income among tax units

	Top 1%	Top 5%	Top 10%	Top 20%	Share of Fourth quintile	Third quintile	Second quintile	Bottom 20%	Bottom 10%	Gini Coefficient
1949	11.2	23.8	33.2	47.3	20.8	n.a.	n.a.	n.a.	n.a.	0.411
							} 31.9			
1954	9.3	20.8	30.1	45.2	22.9	16.3	n.a.	n.a.	n.a.	0.403
							} 15.6			
1959	8.4	19.9	29.4	44.5	23.3	16.6	10.3	5.3	n.a.	0.398
1961	8.1	19.2	28.9	43.7	23.3	17.1	10.6	5.4	n.a.	0.388
1962	8.3	19.5	29.2	44.4	23.5	16.8	10.4	5.1	n.a.	0.397
1963	8.0	19.2	28.9	44.3	23.5	16.6	10.3	5.3	n.a.	0.395
1964	8.2	19.5	29.1	44.6	23.5	16.6	10.1	5.2	n.a.	0.399
1965	8.1	19.6	29.0	44.2	23.2	16.8	10.3	5.6	n.a.	0.390
1966	7.7	18.8	28.5	43.7	23.5	16.5	10.7	5.6	2.2	0.386
1967	7.4	18.4	28.0	43.2	23.7	16.8	10.8	5.6	2.2	0.382
1968/69	7.1	17.8	27.1	42.5	23.9	17.0	10.9	5.7	2.3	0.374
1969/70	7.0	17.8	27.2	42.7	24.0	17.0	10.8	5.5	2.2	0.380
1970/71	6.6	17.7	27.5	43.4	24.1	16.4	10.5	5.6	2.5	0.385
1971/72	6.5	17.5	27.3	43.2	24.2	16.6	10.4	5.6	2.3	0.383
1972/73	6.4	17.2	26.9	42.7	24.1	16.7	10.7	5.8	n.a.	0.374
1973/74	6.5	17.1	26.8	42.4	24.1	16.8	10.5	6.2	2.7	0.370
1974/75	6.2	16.8	26.6	42.4	24.1	16.9	10.4	6.2	2.6	0.371
1975/76[a]	5.6	16.0	25.8	41.9	24.5	16.9	10.5	6.2	2.6	0.366
1975/76[b]	5.7	16.4	26.2	42.3	24.7	16.7	10.3	6.0	2.5	0.373
1976/77	5.5	16.3	26.2	42.4	24.4	16.5	10.5	6.2	2.5	0.372
1977/78	5.5	16.1	26.2	42.5	24.4	16.4	10.5	6.1	2.5	0.372
1978/79	5.3	16.0	26.1	42.6	24.7	16.5	10.3	5.9	2.4	0.375

Notes:
[a] 1975/76 and previous years on the 'old' basis, i.e. excluding mortgage interest repayments, etc.
[b] 1975/76 and following years on the 'new' basis, i.e. including mortgage interest repayments, etc.

Sources:
RCDIW Report No. 7, Table A1.   *Economic Trends*, February 1981, p. 82, Table A.   *Economic Trends*, July 1984, p. 97, Table A.

*Figure 7.1   Shares of selected quantile groups in the Blue Book
distribution (pre-tax income), 1949–1978/79*

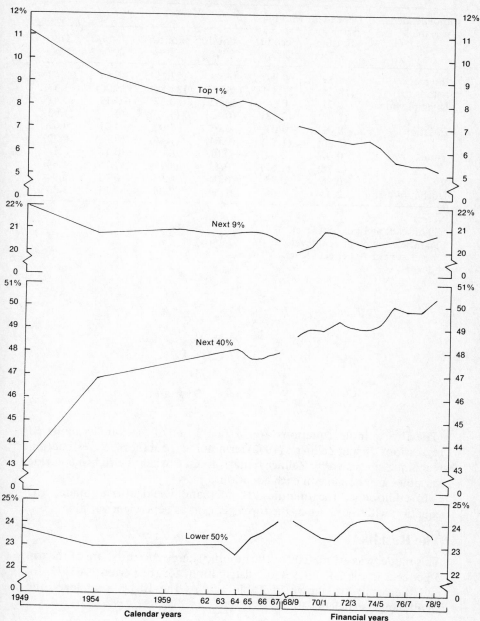

*Table 7.2   Estimation results for quintiles and top 5 per cent.
Using Data for 1961 to 1975/76*

Independent variable	Dependent variable					
	Bottom 20%	Second 20%	Third 20%	Fourth 20%	Top 20%	Top 5%
Intercept	4.59[a]	9.89[a]	16.94[a]	22.29[a]	46.54[a]	22.40[a]
t-statistic	(18.36)	(27.45)	(45.46)	(134.84)	(58.00)	(43.37)
Unemployment	− 0.21[c]	0.04	− 0.02	0.32[a]	− 0.13	− 0.41[c]
	(2.03)	(0.28)	(0.12)	(4.58)	(0.38)	(1.93)
Inflation	0.02[a]	− 0.03[c]	0.01	− 0.01	− 0.01	− 0.01
	(1.80)	(1.80)	(0.64)	(1.46)	(0.34)	(0.32)
Time	0.07[a]	0.04	− 0.01	0.05[a]	− 0.16[b]	− 0.18[a]
	(3.78)	(1.57)	(0.43)	(4.17)	(2.76)	(4.64)
R^2	0.86	0.28	0.04	0.95	0.75	0.94
Durbin–Watson	2.33	1.06	1.59	2.39	1.05	1.34

Notes:
[a] Significant at 1 per cent level.
[b] Significant at 5 per cent level.
[c] Significant at 10 per cent level.

$$\sum_{i=1}^{5} \alpha_i = 1$$

$$\sum_{i=1}^{5} \beta_i = \sum_{i=1}^{5} \gamma_i = \sum_{i=1}^{5} \epsilon_i = 0$$

$$\sum_{i=1}^{5} \epsilon_{it} = 0 \text{ for all t.}$$

(The five quintile equations are in fact a set of 'seemingly-unrelated regressions', using Zellner's (1962) terminology, but the SURE estimation technique suggested by Zellner reduces to OLS when the right-hand side variables are the same in each equation.)

In addition to the quintiles, Blinder and Esaki also estimated the equation with the share of the top 5 per cent as dependent variable.

The Results

This model was estimated for the quintile shares and the share of the top 5 per cent in the UK Blue Book distribution, for the period 1961–75/76, and the result are shown in Table 7.2. At the 10 per cent level, the significant coefficients are:

unemployment:	negative for the bottom quintile and the top 5 per cent, positive for the fourth quintile from the bottom;
inflation:	negative for the bottom quintile, positive for the second;
time trend:	positive for the bottom and fourth quintile, negative for the top quintile and top 5 per cent.

These results are based on the relatively consistent series up to 1975/76 which provides only fifteen observations. When data up to 1978/79 are included with a dummy variable to pick up the effects of the change in definition, the results are very similar. The independent variables were measured by the overall unemployment rate (including school leavers) and the GDP deflator, and using alternative measures again made little difference to the results.[7]

The unemployment and inflation coefficients found to be significant are compared with Blinder and Esaki's results for the US (using data from 1947 to 1974) in Table 7.3. Both for the UK and the US, unemployment was seen to have a negative effect on the share of the bottom quintile (and this was also found in a study applying this approach to Canadian data: Buse, 1982). Blinder and Esaki also found a negative effect on the second quintile, balanced by an increase in the share of the top quintile, whereas for the UK we find a positive unemployment coefficient for the share of the fourth quintile rather than the top one.

Both also saw inflation having a positive effect on the bottom group, though with much smaller coefficients. (Blinder and Esaki's results were not robust in this respect, however, when more reliable data for a shorter period only were used.)

The surprising feature of the UK results, whether contrasted with those of the US or with *a priori* expectations, is the estimated *negative* effect on the unemployment variable for the share of the top 5 per cent. To explore

Table 7.3 Comparison of UK and US (Blinder and Easki) time series results

	Coefficient on			
	unemployment		inflation	
	UK	US	UK	US
Bottom quintile	− 0.21	− 0.13	+ 0.02	+ 0.03
Second quintile		− 0.14	− 0.03	
Third quintile				
Fourth quintile	+ 0.32			− 0.03
Top quintile		+ 0.27		
Top 5%	− 0.41			

this further, the equation was also estimated with each of the shares of the top 1 per cent, 2–5 per cent, 6–10 per cent and 11–20 per cent as dependent variables. The results showed the expected significant positive effect of unemployment only for the 11–20 per cent group, i.e. the second decile from the top. The coefficient for the top 1 per cent, by contrast, was significant negative and, at −0.33, quite large.

Since we would obviously not expect an increase in unemployment *per se* to reduce the share of the top 1 per cent, an explanation may be sought in other variables which are likely to affect the very top of the distribution and may be highly correlated with unemployment. For example, the share of investment income in total income may be inversely related to unemployment and forms a large part of the income of the top 1 per cent. A number of such possible explanations were explored using the limited data available, but failed to produce a convincing conclusion. Both a substantial downward trend in the share of investment income in total income and a narrowing in the dispersion of employment income contributed to the decline in the share of the top 1 per cent over the period, but a relationship between these and movements in the unemployment rate which would lead to the latter acting as 'proxy' was not confirmed. The short period, lack of full and consistent data, and multicollinearity between the variables prevented any strong conclusions however.[8]

It is unsurprising that such aggregate data over a short time-period do not permit robust conclusions on the relationship between macroeconomic variables and the size distribution. By their nature, they also cannot reveal much about the way in which these influences on the distribution made themselves felt through individuals and families. In order to explore the way in which changes in the distribution are brought about, we now turn to the use of micro-data.

4.   A SIMULATION APPROACH

The Data-base

The micro-data base which has the most comprehensive information on incomes for the UK is the *Family Expenditure Survey* (FES). This is primarily focused on gathering expenditure data to provide weights for the Consumer Price Index, but also obtains detailed information on income from various sources. The survey covers about 7000 households, interviewing each adult, and is held annually. In addition to the published reports, the data-tapes are made available to researchers. Comparisons with other data sources such as the Census, the National Accounts, the

Revenue tax-based data and the *New Earnings Survey* do reveal certain deficiencies – notably at the very top of the income distribution – but in general lead to a reasonably high degree of confidence in the representativeness of the survey.[9]

The income data in the survey refer for the most part to current income, that is income received last week/month – from employment, pensions, social security. For the particularly variable income types self-employment and investment income a twelve-month period is used instead.[10] In analysing the impact of macroeconomic conditions on the income distribution, though, particularly the effect of increased unemployment, we may be more interested in annual than current incomes. In the first place, it is the size distribution of annual incomes that is usually measured in official series such as the Blue Book one for the UK. The underlying structure, abstracting from very short-term fluctuations, is the primary focus of interest – and the tax data on which such series are often based obviously refer to annual incomes. Secondly, in looking at the effects of changes in the level of unemployment, the importance of changes in *duration* of unemployment means that looking only at current weekly incomes would not adequately reflect the impact on different individuals.

In order to use the FES as the base, therefore, it was first necessary to estimate the annual income of each individual in the sample. This was done using additional information gathered in the survey together with certain assumptions. (The procedure is described in detail in the Appendix to Nolan (1986) and in Nolan (1987b Appendix 4.) The most important information was the length of time in the previous year spent in receipt of certain social security benefits, and the number of weeks in the current spell out of work for those currently away from work. These allowed the number of weeks in the past year spent in work, unemployed and sick to be estimated. Annual income from employment and from social security could then be estimated, while investment and self-employment income was already on a twelve-month basis.[11]

Annual incomes were estimated in this way for the individuals in the 1977 FES, the base for our micro-data analysis. It is usually assumed that annual income will be more equally distributed than current weekly income as short-term fluctuations are evened out. This turns out to be the case when estimated annual original (i.e. pre-transfer) and gross incomes of families in this sample are compared with the standard FES current income distribution, shown in Table 7.4. (The family, rather than the broader household unit which is the unit of analysis in the published FES reports, is used here for ease of comparison with the Blue Book distribution series.)

It is also of interest to compare the estimated unemployment exper-

Table 7.4   Decile shares in current and annual income for families: original and gross income, 1977 FES

Decile	Current original	Annual original	Current gross	Annual gross
	%	%	%	%
1	0	0	1.90	2.12
2	0.39	0.72	3.30	3.41
3	2.17	2.77	4.40	4.56
4	4.98	5.32	5.79	5.94
5	7.57	7.61	7.54	7.66
6	10.01	9.98	9.41	9.48
7	12.48	12.40	11.48	11.47
8	15.15	14.99	13.76	13.72
9	18.61	18.31	16.76	16.56
10	28.65	27.90	25.66	25.08

Table 7.5   Concentration of unemployment experience in the 1977 FES

Duration of unemployment during year (wks)	No. of cases	% of cases who experienced unemployment	% of workforce	% of total weeks of unemployment
> 26 ≤ 52	255	29.18	2.62	65.83
> 13 ≤ 52	413	47.26	4.24	84.87
> 8 ≤ 52	520	59.40	5.34	91.86
> 4 ≤ 52	654	74.83	6.72	97.01
> 2 ≤ 52	748	85.59	7.68	98.94
All	874	100.00	8.98	100.00

ienced over the previous year by respondents with the more usual length of spell for those currently unemployed. A total of 406 individuals, 4.2 per cent of the workforce, were currently unemployed when sampled, whereas (of those currently in the workforce) 874 or 9 per cent experienced unemployment during the year. When the spread of individuals currently unemployed by length of current spell is compared with the spread of all those who experienced unemployment by duration of unemployment during the past year. The latter are more concentrated in lower duration categories: this is because those who are currently employed but with some unemployment during the year are more heavily concentrated there.

It is of considerable interest to use these estimates to look at the overall concentration of unemployment experienced during the year. Table 7.5 shows the spread of the total weeks of unemployment experienced among (a) those who experienced them, and (b) the workforce as a whole, and

Figure 7.2 *Lorenz curves for the distribution of total weeks of unemployment among (a) those experiencing it and (b) the workforce*

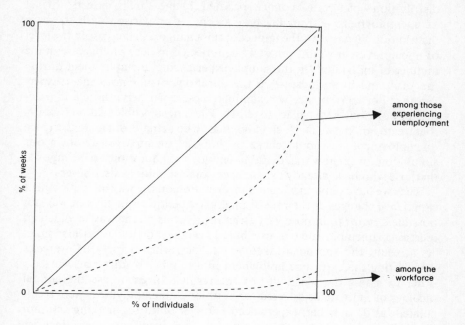

Lorenz curves for these distributions are shown in Figure 7.2. This shows, for example, that 47 per cent of those who experienced unemployment – 4 per cent of the workforce – had 85 per cent of the weeks of unemployment. A similar degree of concentration has been shown in studies such as Clark and Summers (1979) and Bowers (1980) using US data.[12]

The Simulation Approach

In analysing the impact of macroeconomic conditions on the UK size distribution using the 1977 FES as the base, we focus in this paper on one of the three main channels of influence noted earlier – unemployment. The second, factor shares, was also analysed in Nolan (1987a, b) and we make reference to the results below, but for reasons of space the analysis will not be described in the present chapter. The third, inflation, will not be dealt with because it has already been the topic of a number of comprehensive simulation-type studies using US data (notably Minarik, 1979), and because the FES does not contain the detailed data on asset-holdings which would allow such an approach to be properly applied.

In essence, the simulation approach seeks to construct a hypothetical distribution which reflects only a specified change – in this case in the level of unemployment – from the base sample. Comparison with the base distribution then reveals the impact of this change. An increase in the level of unemployment would generally be reflected in both an increase in the number of individuals in the sample experiencing unemployment during the year, and in an increase in the durations of unemployment experienced.[13] For convenience we examined these separately, though in practice they obviously take place together. The central problem in each case is that we do not know (1) which individuals who actually did not experience unemployment we should chose to 'impose' unemployment on in our simulation, or (2) how the 'extra' unemployment durations to be imposed on those who have already experienced some should be distributed.

Since we have only very limited information on the way unemployment experience changes as the rate of unemployment rises or falls, it was not possible *a priori* to impose very strict restrictions on the way in which an increase in unemployment is distributed over the individuals in the sample. As a result, the approach taken was to perform a variety of exercises distributing the extra unemployment in a number of different ways, in order to assess the sensitivity of the results. In each case the annual incomes of individuals selected for additional unemployment were recalculated 'as if' they had experienced a longer duration, making assumptions about the incomes they would have received from social security during that period and the loss of employment income. The overall size of the increase imposed in these exercises was a rise in the unemployment rate of about 1 percentage point. It is important to emphasize that no behavioural responses to the rise in unemployment – for example through labour supply decisions of other family members – are incorporated, the exercises may thus be regarded as focusing purely on 'first round' effects.

5.   THE RESULTS OF THE SIMULATION EXERCISES

The increase in the level of unemployment was thus reflected in two ways in the simulation exercises imposed on the 1977 FES sample:

1.   Most of the additional weeks of unemployment 'required' to bring the overall unemployment rate up by 1 percentage point took the form of increased durations for those who already experienced some unemployment, using a variety of allocation procedures.[14]

2. A further increase was brought about by raising the number experiencing unemployment by 25 per cent. This (separate) exercise used those who had actually experienced only relatively short durations of unemployment as 'proxies' for the type of individuals who would be likely to become newly unemployed, and imposed a reasonable pattern of increased total unemployment durations on these individuals.

The results of these exercises showed that the particular allocation procedure used to 'distribute' extra unemployment over the sample did influence the precise results obtained but not the broad pattern. This pattern – taking (1) and (2) above together – was that the increase in unemployment led to the following shift in the size distribution of gross income among families:

- the share of the bottom quintile fell by about 0.1;
- the share of the bottom half fell by 0.2–0.3;
- the share of the top decile rose by about 0.15;
- each of the bottom 6 deciles had a reduction in share, so there was an unambiguous shift away for these groups towards the top four (but particularly top 1) deciles.

How do we assess whether these are 'large' or 'small' effects? Compared with the actual base levels of the shares of the different groups, they would represent movements of only about $\frac{1}{2}$–2 per cent of these levels. However, the more interesting and relevant comparison, in the context of relating changes in macroeconomic conditions to movements in the size distribution, is with the actual changes from year to year in these shares. If we use the Blue Book official series as a benchmark, the mean absolute year-to-year changes over the period 1961–75/76 for these groups were

0.14 for the bottom quintile,
0.3 for the bottom half,
0.35 for the top decile.

Compared with these, the estimated effects of the increase in unemployment are quite large. It may also be noted that an increase in the unemployment rate of 1 per cent, the basis for these results, would have been substantial when compared with actual experience during the period in question.[15]

Despite this, the effects may not be as large, or as concentrated at the bottom of the distribution, as might have been expected. A number of interesting factors at work were identified which contribute to explaining the relatively diffuse nature of the impact of higher unemployment on the size distribution.

1. The results refer to annual rather than current incomes, so even where an individual's current income was substantially reduced by unemployment this might have a much smaller effect on annual income where the unemployment was only for part of the year.

2. Because of this, but also, more importantly, because of the presence of other earners in families/households containing an unemployed person, these recipient units are not all concentrated at the bottom of the income distribution. For the narrower family unit on which we have focused in this chapter, 35 per cent of these affected by unemployment during the year were in the top half of the size distribution of annual gross income, and only 30 per cent were in the bottom quintile.[16]

Two important points should be kept in mind in interpreting the results. First, they refer to the shape of the overall income distribution, not to the shares of particular groups of households – there may obviously be considerable re-ranking as unemployment rises, in addition to the changes in decile/quintile shares. Secondly, the incomes of the families in the sample have not been adjusted to take difference in size and composition, and thus in needs, into account. When such an adjustment is made, those affected by unemployment are more heavily concentrated towards the bottom than in the unadjusted distribution.[17] Here though, our primary focus is on the latter and the way it changes over time.

Before turning to the actual changes in the size distribution in recent years, the results of the simulation analysis dealing with the impact of factor shares on the size distribution referred to above may be very briefly noted. Having attempted to distinguish cyclical changes in factor shares from longer-term structural trends, the impact of the former on the size distribution was explored, also using the 1977 FES as base. Restrictive assumptions were required about the way in which different income groups are affected – essentially assuming that changes in the shares of income from a particular source affect recipients in direct proportion to their receipt of that income type. The results showed that a shift in factor income shares associated with a substantial upturn in the macroeconomy would, through increasing the share of profits and therefore investment (and self-employment) income, increase the share of upper income groups. The top decile gains at the expense of the remainder of the distribution, its share increasing by about 0.1. The size of this effect is

Table 7.6   Percentage shares of income, before tax, 1978/79, 1981/82 and 1984/85, United Kingdom (Blue Book series)

Quantile group		Percentages[1]		
		1978/79	1981/82	1984/85
Top 1	percent	5.3	6.0	6.4
2–5	percent	10.7	11.6	12.1
6–10	percent	10.1	10.7	10.9
Top 10	percent	26.1	28.3	29.5
11–20	percent	16.5	16.7	16.8
21–30	percent	13.5	13.2	13.0
31–40	percent	11.2	10.7	10.3
41–50	percent	9.2	8.6	8.2
51–60	percent	7.3	7.0	6.6
61–70	percent	5.8	5.8	5.4
71–80	percent	4.5	4.4	4.4
81–90	percent	3.5	3.5	3.5
91–100	percent	2.4	2.0	2.3
Median income: £		3,370	4,720	5,480
Mean income: £		4,110	6,050	7,520
Gini (percent)		37	40	41

Note:
[1]The figures in this table are rounded and may therefore not sum to 100.
Source:
Economic Trends nos. 409, November 1987, Table A, p. 94.

quite small, though again when compared with actual changes in the size distribution over time it assumes greater significance.[18]

6.   RECENT CHANGES IN THE UK DISTRIBUTION

The continuous annual time-series on the UK size distribution, discussed in section 3, was discontinued after 1978/79. Our results so far, based on either that time-series or on the 1977 FES micro-data, can now be used to elucidate what has happened to the size distribution since the late 1970s. For the Blue Book series, estimates have been published of the distribution in 1981/82 and 1984/85. These are compared with 1978/79 in Table 7.6, and are particularly interesting given the dramatic changes in the macroeconomy which took place over these years.

Looking first at the size distribution between 1978/79 and 1981/82, a very substantial shift in favour of the top of the distribution took place over this relatively short period. The share of the top 1 per cent rose by 0.7, and that of the top decile by 1.5. This was quite unprecedented for the entire period from 1949 for which we have data. The 'losers' were the second and third quintile from the top, and the bottom decile which saw its share fall by 0.4 per cent of total income. The changes represent a shift from the bottom 80 per cent to the top 20 per cent, the Lorenz curve for 1981/82 is unambiguously outside that for 1978/79, and the Gini coefficient increased markedly from 0.375 to 0.4 – a level not previously seen since the mid 1950s (see Table 7.1).

At the time these shifts in the distribution were taking place, there were very significant changes in the macroeconomic environment. The unemployment rate almost doubled, rising from about 5.5 per cent to 10 per cent. The inflation rate, while falling, was only marginally lower in the later year – 10.6 per cent compared with 11.7 per cent. There was also a substantial change in the importance of different income types in total household income, with the share of investment income rising from 4.5 per cent in 1978 to about 7 per cent.[19]

Given that there was little difference in inflation rates between the two years, and its estimated effects on the size distribution from our time-series analysis were in any case small, this factor may have had little impact. However, the sharp rise in unemployment would, according to both the time-series and cross-section results, have had a significant effect in bringing about a transfer towards upper-income groups. For the bottom quintile the cross-section results would predict that such an increase in unemployment would reduce the share by about 0.3–0.4, which is close to the fall that actually took place. (The time-series results would suggest a bigger reduction, but the cross-section approach suggests this may be overstated.) It appears plausible, then, that the sharp increase in unemployment played a major part in the fall in the share of the bottom groups, as well as some part in that of the rest of the bottom 50 per cent. This is supported by analysis of the FES samples for these years, showing a sharp increase in the number of households affected by unemployment among those towards the bottom of the distribution (see O'Higgins, 1987).

As far as the top of the distribution is concerned, the cross-section analysis would predict that the decline in the share of lower groups as a result of the increase in unemployment would be balanced by an increase of about 0.75 in the share of the top decile. This would contribute to, but by no means fully explain, the actual increase of 2.2 in the share of this decile between the two years in question. To explain the remainder we may turn to the increase in the share of investment income in total income.

Since the top 10 per cent receive a larger share of their income from this source than other income groups, such an increase will tend to be reflected in a rising share for the top decile, *ceteris paribus*. The limited information available on the decomposition of the income going to different groups in the Blue Book distribution shows that top groups actually gained even more than this would suggest from the increased importance of investment income – that is, their share in total investment income also rose.[20] Taken together, this would appear to be the dominant influence on the rising share of the top groups between 1978/79 and 1981/82.

Turning now to the most recent data, for 1984/85, these show that the increase in the share of top groups has continued. The share of the top decile rose by a further 1.2 per cent of total income compared with 1981/82. At the bottom, by contrast, there has been some recovery in the share of the bottom decile. The 'losers' have been the middle of the distribution, with each of the deciles from the third to the seventh (from the top) having a decline in share. The Gini coefficient rose further, from 0.40 to 0.41 – much less than the increase between 1978/79 and 1981/82.

The macroeconomic background against which these changes took place saw:

1. the unemployment rate, after a very rapid increase from the late 1970s, reaching a plateau at about 11.75, about 1.5 per cent higher than in 1981/82;
2. the inflation rate was significantly lower, at about 6 per cent compared with about 10.5 per cent in 1981/82;
3. self-employment income had grown much more rapidly than employment income, increasing its share of total income (as allocated to households in the size distribution estimates) from 6 per cent to 8 per cent, while the share of employment income fell from 68 per cent to 64 per cent. Occupational pensions also grew relatively rapidly.[21]

The continued trend towards increased income shares for top groups between the two years is consistent with both the further rise in unemployment and the increased importance of self-employment income. A surprising feature against this background, though, is the recovery in the share of the bottom decile. With the limited data available it is only possible partially to decompose and explore this development, but one interesting feature does emerge. The relatively rapid growth in pensions relative to employment income, together with an increase in the dispersion of the latter – i.e. increased inequality in the earnings distribution – has brought about a significant change in the composition of the bottom income groups. Those on low earnings have become more important, replacing some pensioners who have moved up the distribution. Any effect of higher unemployment on the bottom income groups may therefore have been masked by such changes – and the effects of unemployment would in any case be spread over the distribution rather than purely concentrated at the bottom, as we have seen. This highlights the difficulties in attempting directly to interpret actual shifts in the time-series on the size distribution, due to the level of aggregation and the variety of factors – structural and cyclical – at work simultaneously.

7. CONCLUSIONS

The major channels through which changes in macroeconomic conditions may be expected to influence the size distribution of income among persons are unemployment, inflation and factor income shares. A direct approach to analysing these effects is through relating observed changes in the size distribution over time to particular macroeconomic variables. This was done with US data, using the quintile shares in the size distribution as dependent variables, by Blinder and Esaki (1978). When the same approach is applied to the official income distribution data series for the UK, significant macroeconomic effects broadly corresponding with the US results are found.

Both these particular results and the general approach give rise to reservations, though – it being very difficult to disentangle the many factors at work in bringing about what are generally quite small changes from year to year in the size distribution. An alternative approach is to simulate the effects of specified macroeconomic developments on the size distribution using data on individual families as the base. This was done for the UK using the *Family Expenditure Survey* for 1977. The results of 'imposing' an increase in unemployment on the distribution of gross income in this sample showed the effects to be dispersed over the distribution rather than purely concentrated at the bottom, though bottom groups did lose. The effects were significant in size relative to the year-to-year changes in the distribution. The dispersion of the impact of rising unemployment was influenced by the fact that not only were many individuals only out of work for part of the year (the results being based on annual incomes), but in many cases there were other economically active family members.

Since the late 1970s the UK size distribution has been changing dramatically. The share of top income groups has risen in a way which is unprecedented since the late 1940s. This has been for the most part at the expense not of the very bottom income groups, but of the middle of the distribution. The macroeconomic environment in which these changes took place, of rapidly rising unemployment and an increase in the relative importance of investment and self-employment vis-a-vis employment income, appears to have been a major influence on the distribution.

NOTES

1. The description of inflation as the 'the cruellest tax', arising from concern with this group, has been cited by Tobin (1972) as an example of the 'facile generalizations' on this topic.
2. Schultz did however find some significant macroeconomic influences on the Gini coefficient when he applied the same approach to data for the Netherlands.
3. For a description of the series, see *Economic Trends*, No. 262, August 1975 and Royal Commission on the Distribution of Income and Wealth Report No. 5, Appendix C.
4. The 1981/82 figures were published in *Economic Trends*, No. 369, July 1984, and those for 1984/85 in *Economic Trends*, No. 409, November 1987.
5. See Royal Commission on the Distribution of Income and Wealth, Report No. 5, ch. 3 and Appendix C.
6. The changes in the coverage of the income concept used from 1975/76 are described in *Economic Trends*, No. 295, May 1978.
7. For unemployment, both excluding school leavers and focusing purely on unemployment among males – which is thought to be more reliably measured – were alternative measures used. For inflation, the Retail Price Index was tried as an alternative to the GDP deflator.
8. For a full discussion of the data available and the analysis of the relationship between these variables and the share of the top 1 per cent, see Nolan (1987b, ch. 2).
9. For a description of the *Family Expenditure Survey*, see Kemsley, Redpath and Holmes (1980). For an analysis of differential response based on a comparison with the Census see Redpath (1986). For other aspects of the representativeness of the Survey, see Atkinson, Micklewright and Stern (1981 and 1982), Atkinson and Micklewright (1983) and Hope (1988).
10. For investment income, this is the twelve months prior to the date of sampling, but for self-employment income it is the most recent 12-month period for which figures are available.
11. Income from pensions was estimated on the basis of current receipts plus number of weeks retired.
12. Bowers, for example, found that in 1978 42 per cent of the weeks of unemployment were experienced by 2.3 per cent of the labour force. This may be compared to 2.6 per cent of the labour force having 66 per cent of the weeks in our estimates in Table 7.5.
13. Recent labour market studies have emphasized the role of increasing durations rather than increasing inflows into unemployment as a primary force in producing increases in the stock of unemployed – e.g. Nickell (1979), Owen (1978), Bowers (1980).
14. The three basic allocation procedures used were (a) equal increases for all, (b) increases varying in proportion to actual unemployment experienced, and (c) varying increases in duration allocated over the individuals at random.
15. Changes in the unemployment rate from one year to the next of about that size, but no more, did take place over the period: these were associated with relatively substantial shifts in the level of activity in the economy.
16. This pattern is considerably more pronounced for the wider household unit – the more usual basis for analysis of the FES – where only 11 per cent of households affected by unemployment were in the bottom quintile and 46 per cent were in the bottom half of the distribution. As a result, the impact of increased unemployment on the household distribution is more diffuse, with little reduction in the share of the bottom 10 per cent – 20 per cent.

17. The effect of adjusting for household size and composition on the location in the distribution of those who experienced unemployment is analysed in Nolan (1987b, ch. 7).
18. See Nolan (1987a; 1987b, chs 3 and 4) for details of this exercise.
19. This refers to the share of investment income in total income allocated in the size distribution. This will not correspond exactly to the income of the household sector in the National Accounts, since not all of this income is actually allocated in the distribution estimates.
20. This conclusion is based on the analysis of changes in the composition of the income of the top 1 per cent and 25 per cent of the distribution, together with that of total income in the distribution, given in Table D and Appendix 4 Table 2, *Economic Trends*, July 1984, pp. 99 and 104, respectively.
21. See *Economic Trends*, November 1987, Table D, and Appendix 4, Table 2, pp. 97 and 104, respectively.

REFERENCES

Atkinson, A. B. and J. Micklewright, 'On the Reliability of Income Data in the Family Expenditure Survey 1970–77, *Journal of the Royal Statistical Society*, series A, vol. 146, 1983, pp. 33–61.

Atkinson, A. B., J. Micklewright and N. H. Stern, 'A Comparison of the Family Expenditure Survey and the New Earnings Survey 1971–77: Part I: Characteristics of the Sample', *Taxation, Incentives and the Distribution of Income Discussion Paper 27*, London School of Economics, 1981.

Atkinson, A. B., J. Micklewright and N. H. Stern, 'A Comparison of the Family Expenditure Survey and the New Earnings Survey 1971–77: Part II: Earnings of Men and Women', *Taxation, Incentives and the Distribution of Income Discussion Paper 32*, London School of Economics, 1982.

Beach, C. M., 'Cyclical Sensitivity of Aggregate Income Inequality', *Review of Economics and Statistics*, LIX (1), February 1977, pp. 56–66.

Blinder, A. and H. Esaki, 'Macroeconomic Activity and Income Distribution in the Postwar United States', *Review of Economics and Statistics*, LX (4), November 1978, pp. 604–9.

Bowers, N., 'Probing the Issues of Unemployment Duration', *Monthly Labour Review*, July 1980, pp. 23–32.

Budd, E. C. and D. F. Seiders, 'The Impact of Inflation on the Distribution of Income and Wealth', *American Economic Review, Paper and Proceedings*, 61, May 1971, pp. 128–38.

Budd, E. C. and T. C. Whiteman, 'Macroeconomic Fluctuation and the Size Distribution of Income and Earnings in the US', in Griliches, Z., Krelle, W., Krupp, H-J and Kyn, O. (ed), *Income Distribution and Economic Inequality*, New York: Campus-Verlag, 1978.

Buse, A., 'The Cyclical Behaviour of the Size Distribution of Income in Canada 1947–78', *Canadian Journal of Economics*, 15 (2), May 1982, pp. 189–204.

Clarke, K. B. and J. H. Summers, 'Labour Market Dynamics and Unemployment: a Reconsideration', *Brookings Papers on Economic Activity*, 1, 1979, pp. 13–72.

Gramlich, E. M. 'The Distributional Effects of Higher Unemployment', *Brookings Papers on Economic Activity*, 2, 1974, pp. 293–342.

Hope, S., 'Validation of Tax-Benefit Models', *Taxation, Incentives and the*

Distribution of Income Discussion Paper 115, London School of Economics, 1988.

Kemsley, W. F. F., R. Redpath and M. Holmes, *Family Expenditure Survey Handbook*, London: HMSO, 1980.

Metcalf, C. E., 'The Size Distribution of Personal Income During the Business Cycle', *American Economic Review*, 59, September 1969, pp. 657–67.

Metcalf, C. E. *An Econometric Model of the Income Distribution*, Institute for Research on Poverty, Monograph Series, Chicago: Markham, 1972.

Minarik, J. J., 'The Size Distribution of Income During Inflation', *Review of Income and Wealth*, Series 25 No. 4, December 1979, pp. 377–92.

Mirer, T., 'The Distributional Impact of the 1970 Recession', *Review of Economics and Statistics*, May 1973a, pp. 214–24.

Mirer, T., 'The Effects of Macroeconomic Fluctuations on the Distribution of Income', *Review of Income and Wealth*, Series 19 No. 4, December 1973b, pp. 385–405.

Nickell, S., 'The Effect of Unemployment and Related Benefits on the Duration of Unemployment', *Economic Journal*, 84, March 1979, pp. 34–49.

Nolan, B., 'Unemployment and the Size Distribution of Income', *Economica*, 53, November 1986, pp. 421–45.

Nolan, B., 'Cyclical Fluctuations in Factor Shares and the Size Distribution of Income', *Review of Income and Wealth*, Series 33 no. 2, June 1987a, pp. 193–210.

Nolan, B., *Income Distribution and the Macroeconomy*, Cambridge: Cambridge University Press, 1987b.

Nordhaus, W. D., 'The Effects of Inflation on the Distribution of Economic Welfare', *Journal of Money, Credit and Banking*, 5 (1) part II, February 1973, pp. 465–504.

O'Higgins, M. 'Inequality, Redistribution and Recession: The British Experience, 1976–1982', *Journal of Social Policy*, 14, 3, 1987, pp. 279–307.

Owen, S., 'The Inequality of Male Unemployment and Sickness', mimeo, University College of Cardiff, April 1978.

Palmer, J. L., *Inflation, Unemployment and Poverty*, Lexington M.A.: D. C. Heath, 1973.

Redpath, R., 'A Second Study of Differential Response comparing Census Characteristics of FES Respondents and Non-Respondents', *Statistical News*, No. 72, February 1986.

Royal Commission on the Distribution of Income and Wealth, *Report No. 5, Third Report on the Standing Reference*, London: HMSO (Cmnd 6999).

Schultz, T. P., 'Secular Trends and Cyclical Behaviour of Income Distribution in the United States 1944–65', in Soltow, L. (ed.) *Six Papers on the Size Distribution of Wealth and Income*, New York: Columbia University Press, 1969.

Thurow, L., 'Analysing the American Income Distribution', *American Economic Review*, Papers and Proceedings, 60, 1970, pp. 261–9.

Tobin, J., 'Inflation and Unemployment', *American Economic Review*, 62, March 1972, pp. 1–18.

Zellner, A., 'An Efficient Method for Estimating Seemingly Unrelated Regressions and Tests for Aggregation Bias', *Journal of the American Statistical Association*, 57, 1962, pp. 346–68.

8. The Welfare State in a Programme of Economic Recovery

John Cornwall

1. INTRODUCTION

Cross-country Comparisons

Following a period of rapid and sustained growth, developed capitalist economies have for over a decade and a half experienced high rates of inflation and high and rising rates of unemployment. Table 8.1 details the records for 18 OECD economies allowing a comparison of the decade preceding the breakdown with the period after 1973. The pronounced upward trend in unemployment rates is universal. The widespread failure of inflation rates to return to their pre-1974 levels is also clear.

But Table 8.1 also reveals substantial differences in the unemployment and inflation performances between countries as well as in the misery index, i. e. the sum of unemployment and inflation rates. Some economies performed well in both periods (e.g. Japan, Sweden and Switzerland), some performed poorly in both periods (e.g. Canada and the United States) while others did well before the early 1970s but relatively badly later (e.g. Belgium and Denmark).

Many valuable studies are now available to explain why growth rates differ between countries. Less familiar to economists are studies that explain cross-country differences in unemployment and inflation rates. It is the contention of this chapter that something even more useful and basic emerges from studies of why unemployment and inflation rates have differed among the capitalist economies in the postwar period. That 'something' includes the proper policy response to the current economic breakdown.

Some Earlier Studies

Consider the following. Studies by political scientists argue that 'party control matters' in explaining differences in unemployment rates. On this

Table 8.1   *Annual average standarized unemployment rates (U), rates of inflation of consumer prices (p) and misery indices (MI) in 18 OECD countries*

Low unemployment economies	1963–73			1974–79			1980–86		
	U %	p %	MI %	U %	p %	MI %	U %	p %	MI %
Austria	1.7	4.2	5.9	1.8	6.3	8.1	3.2[a]	4.6	7.8
Japan	1.3	6.2	7.5	1.9	10.2	12.1	2.5	3.1	5.6
New Zealand	0.2	5.3	5.5	0.9	13.8	14.7	4.3[a]	12.9	17.2
Norway	1.8	5.3	7.1	1.8	8.7	10.5	2.5	9.0	11.5
Sweden	1.9	4.9	6.8	1.9	9.8	11.7	2.8	9.0	11.8
Switzerland	0.0	4.5	4.5	0.4	4.0	4.4	0.6[a]	3.7	4.3
Average	1.2	5.1	6.3	1.5	8.8	10.3	2.7	7.1	9.8
High unemployment Economies									
Canada	4.7	3.7	8.4	7.2	9.2	16.4	9.8	7.3	17.1
Ireland	5.3	6.4	11.7	6.8	15.1	21.9	11.6[a]	13.4[a]	25.0[a]
Italy	5.3	4.9	10.2	6.6	16.1	22.7	9.2[a]	13.6	22.8
United States	4.5	3.6	8.1	6.7	8.6	15.3	7.8	6.1	13.9
Average	5.0	4.7	9.7	6.8	12.3	19.1	9.6	10.1	19.7
low-high unemployment economies									
Australia	2.0	4.0	6.0	5.0	12.2	17.2	7.7	8.7	16.4
Belgium	2.3	4.0	6.3	6.3	8.5	14.8	11.3	6.1	17.4
Denmark	1.2	6.3	7.5	6.0	10.8	16.8	9.5[a]	7.9	17.4
Finland	2.2	6.2	8.4	4.5	12.9	17.4	5.1	8.1	13.2
France	2.1	4.7	6.8	4.5	10.7	15.2	8.6	9.1	17.7
Germany	0.8	3.5	4.3	3.2	4.7	7.9	6.2	3.5	9.6
Netherlands	1.6	5.7	7.3	5.0	7.2	12.2	10.0	3.9	13.9
United Kingdom	3.2	5.3	8.5	5.3	15.7	19.0	10.6	8.1	18.7
Average	1.9	5.0	6.9	5.0	10.1	15.1	7.5	6.9	14.4
Overall average	2.3	4.9	7.2	4.2	10.2	14.4	6.8	7.7	14.5

Note:
[a] 1980–85.

Sources:
Economic Outlook, OECD Paris, June 1987, Tables R10 and R12; *Historical Statistics, 1960–1986*. OECD, Paris, 1988, Table 8.11; *The Revised OECD Data Set*, Centre for Labour Economics, London School of Economics. All averages are unweighted.

reading low (high) rates of unemployment in some country are due to control of government by left-wing (right-wing) parties.[1] In order to reduce inflationary pressures at full employment (FE), it is further argued that left-wing parties when in power extend the welfare state and redistribute income through progressive taxes in exchange for wage restraint.[2]

More recently a diametrically opposed hypothesis has been expressed under the title 'Eurosclerosis'. According to this view heavily unionized countries with extensive welfare programmes and left-wing governments are more prone to rigidities, especially in the labour market. In such economies there are strong tendencies for the real wage to be pushed above its market-clearing level by unions causing classical unemployment, i.e. unemployment that does not respond to stimulative aggregate demand policies. These rigidities are seen also to lead to reduced profits, investment and productivity growth as well as the kind of high unemployment experienced today in Europe. Recovery can be achieved only if drastic reforms are introduced. These include reducing the power of labour and the size of the welfare state and a shift in the distribution of income towards profits.[3]

Even more recently, the argument has been advance that superior employment performance is not to be understood in terms of the presence or absence of the welfare state, but is largely to be explained in terms of the structure of the trade union movement. Both economies in which collective bargaining is highly centralized (e.g. Sweden) and economies with highly decentralized, firm-level bargaining (e.g. the United States) are alleged to perform better than those in which collective bargaining is conducted at the industry or regional level (e.g. West Germany).[4]

The Argument to be Made

While there is an element of truth in the party control and structure of the trade union explanations of performance, the Eurosclerosis theory is incorrect as analysis and in its policy implications. What is to be argued is that differences in the unemployment and inflation dimensions of macroeconomics performance can be explained largely in terms of the ability of important economic and political interest groups to strike some kind of a social bargain or cooperative solution to a potential form of market failure. This form of market failure is one of unacceptable rates of inflation at low rates of unemployment, a malfunctioning which has and will continue to induce restrictive policies and mass unemployment. The policy implications of the argument to be made require that the welfare state be maintained and even expanded in many countries in any recovery programme.

The particular bargain is an agreement between capital, labour and government to coordinate wage settlements in labour markets with some overall national goal expressed in terms of a wage norm, i.e. a voluntary incomes policy. In return, labour is promised (as a minimum) full employment (i.e. job security) and a fair distribution of the national product. In addition, and as a beneficial side-effect, labour receives a more rapid improvement in per capita incomes and, in some countries, the benefits of an extensive welfare state.[5]

The argument is advanced in the following manner. Cross-country comparisons of the OECD economies in the period following the war but before the breakdown will be discussed first, as events in this period provide useful information about the institutional prerequisites for reaching a successful bargain. During this period there existed an environment in which the success or failure to achieve a bargain was primarily dependent upon the existence or non-existence of conditions internal to the country desiring to work out a bargain. Events since 1973 have created external conditions that are hostile to the success of domestic policies aimed at wage restraint under FE in most countries, including many who were successful before 1974. A similar cross-country analysis is then made of these economies in this less favourable environment. In both periods, cross-section regressions with unemployment rates and the misery index as dependent variables are utilized to illustrate and support the arguments. While most of the chapter can be properly described as analysis, the policy implications are apparent throughout.

2.   CROSS-COUNTRY PERFORMANCES BEFORE THE BREAKDOWN

Figure 8.1 shows annual average rates of unemployment and price inflation for 18 OECD countries during the postwar period until 1974. The scatter of points indicates that the sample of countries can be divided into two groups depending upon the unemployment policy pursued during the 1963 – 73 period. There are the high unemployment countries – i.e. Canada, Ireland, Italy, and the United States. The remaining countries qualify as low unemployment countries, although the United Kingdom raises some difficulties.[6].

The party control or demand-determined theory of policy determination argues that aggregate demand (AD) policies and, therefore, unemployment rates will vary inversely with forces such as the strength of the trade union movement and the 'leftist' composition of government. Figure 8.1 reveals that strongly unionized countries with left-wing governments and extensive welfare programmes such as Austria, Norway and Sweden experienced low rates of unemployment while countries with weak

*Figure 8.1   Average rate of increase of consumer prices (p) and standar-
dized unemployment rates (U), 1963–73, for 18 countries*

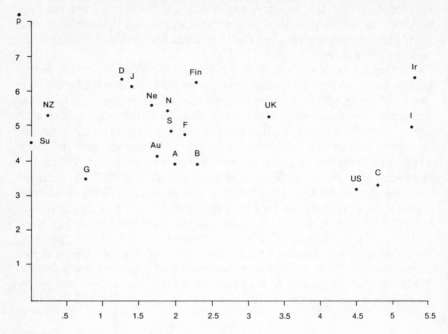

Notes:
A = Australia, Au = Austria, B = Belgium, C = Canada, D = Denmark,
Fin = Finland, F = France, G = Germany, Ir = Ireland, I = Italy, J = Japan,
Ne = Netherlands, NZ = New Zealand, No = Norway, Su = Switzerland,
S = Sweden, UK = United Kingdom, US = United States.

Source:
The Revised OECD Data Set, Centre for Labour Economics, London School of
Economics.

union movements, restricted welfare programmes and right-wing governments such as Canada, Italy and the United States experienced high unemployment. To this extent the 1963–73 unemployment performances lend
support to the party control theory and further indicate that, if there is truth
to the Eurosclerosis argument, it can only be so for the post-1973 period.

But the Japanese and Swiss records are particularly hard to reconcile
with the demand-determined explanation of unemployment policy. Both
countries had limited welfare programmes, weak trade union movements
and right-of-centre, pro-business governments, yet they experienced some
of the lowest unemployment rates in the sample of countries. Clearly

strong union movements, a developed welfare state and left-of-centre governments are, at best, only sufficient conditions for full employment policies. Obviously other influences are at work here.

Consider next the impact of union strength on rates of inflation. Those economies with high union densities did not experience higher rates of inflation than those with weak union movements, as a comparison of the Scandinavian countries with, say, the North American ones reveals. Yet the stronger bargaining power of labour in the countries with high union density would lead one to expect more explosive cost–push mechanisms to be at work, other things being equal. This suggests the ability in countries like Norway and Sweden to obtain the cooperation of labour and business in restraining wages and prices in spite of strong labour (and booming demand conditions). It also suggests a need to introduce other factors and to distinguish between potential and actual inflationary pressures.

All of these considerations are reflected in Figure 8.1 in the lack of any cross-country trade-off between unemployment and inflation rates during this period.[7] What Figure 8.1 also depicts are appreciable differences in the 'misery' or 'discomfort' index, i.e. the sum of the average rates of unemployment and inflation, between countries. Higher unemployment only brought greater misery, not reduced rates of inflation. Since differences in the misery index are primarily due to differences in unemployment rates, the main task is to explain the lack of cross-country correlation between inflation and unemployment rates in the light of substantial differences in union power and political control.

The discussion therefore shifts to the determination of those institutional features of an economy that contain potentially strong inflationary forces at low rates of unemployment. These same features go far to explain why there was no correlation across countries between unemployment and inflation rates.

3. WHY PHILLIPS CURVES DIFFER

Beyond the Phillips Curve

The appreciable differences in unemployment rates and discomfort indices shown in Figure 8.1 would be 'explained' by many economists as simply due to differences in Phillips curves, each country observation in Figure 8.1 representing one point on the country's Phillips curve. Countries with high rates of unemployment have been forced to restrict AD in order to keep inflation rates down to rates experienced by countries faced with a more favourably placed Phillips curve, etc. Unfortunately, this explanation is of little help to policy-makers intent upon improving the performance of the economy.

Rather, the emphasis here is on why Phillips curves varied across countries and to explain these differences in terms of the relative success of a social bargain. Clearly, labour market behaviour must be modified if inflationary pressures at FE are to be reduced, and this leads straight to an analysis of what policies, rewards and punishments and institutional frameworks have supported and enforced a more social form of conduct.

A Rejection of *Laissez-faire* Policies

First and foremost, it will be proposed that only in those economies in which it has been widely understood and accepted by government, labour and employers that unrestricted collective bargaining is incompatible with FE and politically acceptable rates of inflation has it been possible to realize these latter two goals (as well as external equilibria) simultaneously for any period of time. Rejection of a belief in the creative powers of 'market forces', 'countervailing powers' or 'invisible hands' has been a necessary condition for superior macro-performance. For only in these economies has it been clear that a constant effort on the part of government and others is necessary to make individual wage settlements consistent with some national goal of wage (and price) stability, i.e. to implement a permanent income policy.

Two Kinds of Social Bargains

A rejection of *laissez-faire* as an approach to policy is but a first step in specifying the institutions found necessary for superior performance. Also important for success has been the continuous functioning in the labour market of some kind of bargain, both implicit and explicit, embodied in convention and law, outlining the rewards and punishments for compliance with some wage goal or target. For example, labour would have the right to expect FE and welfare benefits if they restrain their wage demands and would face restrictive AD measures if they fail to live up to their obligations.

The nature of the bargain and other relevant institutions need not be, and were not, identical during this post-war period. It is helpful to think of all bargains falling into one or the other of two types. On the one hand, there were those countries in which the labour movement was so strong that pro-labour governments were able to gain power for an appreciable part of the time. In these economies the bargain struck involved FE, the introduction of welfare programmes to enhance the 'social wage' of labour, together with tax schemes that greatly reduce the distribution of after-tax incomes.

The main elements of such bargains were first, to lead a centralized labour movement, because of its 'encompassing' nature, to internalize the inflation costs of its wage demands; and second, to transfer the distributional conflicts of the society from the labour market to the political arena.

On the other hand, there were those economies in which the trade union movement had never been strong, the welfare state was never extensively developed, although the tax structure acted to redistribute the after-tax distribution of incomes towards equality, and pro-labour parties never governed alone at the national level. Nevertheless a bargain with labour was struck so that wage settlements were very much influenced by their impact on, for example, export success or the profitability of the firm. As a result, relative moderate wage and price developments at the firm level aggregated into respectable overall inflation performances. In exchange for so restraining their wage demands, workers received various rewards, e.g. bonus payments, good working conditions, acceptable grievance procedures, a share of productivity gains and continuous employment.

The two kinds of bargain had several things in common. First, in both cases they took place within an industrial relations system that could be characterized as cooperative; labour and management started from a position of trust and cooperation, believing that there are always important areas of common agreement that must be preserved by continuous compromise and consultation. Second, in both cases there was common agreement that the key to wage and price stability was wage stability. This was based on realization that many prices cannot be influenced directly by policy (e.g. imports), whereas most wages are set in domestic markets. In addition, the tendency of firms to price on a relatively stable per cent mark-up allowed for a relatively predictable indirect control of prices through an influences on wages. Third, in both cases governments were prepared in one form or another to provide the kinds of leadership needed to bring wage and price settings into line with national goals, i.e. a form of policy-making usually designated as 'corporatist'. But in neither case was government prepared to reduce the power of labour. Fourth, both kinds of bargains were structured to convince labour that restraint was in their long-run self-interest. Fifth, pronounced differences in after-tax incomes were prevented, at least compared to those economies unable to work out a social bargain.

The main thrust of this chapter is that those economies in which a bargain could not be struck faced much stronger inflationary pressures at every rate of unemployment. The result was higher rates of unemployment.

4. CORPORATISM

Corporatist Policy-making

The structures of policy-making that was operative during the 1963–73 period (and to some extent today) enabling both relatively low rates of inflation and low rates of unemployment need elaboration. The term 'corporatism' has meant different things to different people but in the present context it is most usefully referred to as an insitutionalized pattern of (economic) policy-making. Large interest group organizations cooperate with each other and with public authorities, not only in the discussion of policies, in this case how to restrain wages and prices under FE conditions, but also in their implementation and monitoring. The term necessarily implies an ideology of social and political partnership (rather than class politics) that in varying degrees guides routine politics and industrial relations. In many cases the partnership and cooperation involves representatives of large highly centralized organizations ('peak organizations') which are encouraged by the state, granting the private groups a representational monopoly in decision-making. But in all cases the cooperative partnership element is seen as an important feature affecting behaviour in the labour market.

As already revealed in the discussion of two types of bargains, corporatist policy-making operates with different kinds of institutional frameworks, depending upon such critical factors as: (a) the coalitions that control the government, e.g. whether dominated by business or labour groups; and (b) the nature of the political institutions and channels of influence available to the state and private groups. In particular, these 'policy networks' will determine the degree to which representatives of unions, employers and other organized interest groups are integrated into and cooperate with government agencies. As a result, (c) the social bargain or system of rewards and punishments for compliance with general goals vary.

5. PREDICTORS OF SUCCESS

Social scientists (including more recently economists) have become interested in forms of policy that stress bargains because they appear to lead to more successful economic performance, e.g. a lower rate of inflation at some unemployment rate and a reduction of industrial disputes as indicated by some measure of strike activity. To further establish this connection, indices of corporatism have been developed that allow a ranking of capitalist economies in terms of their degree of corporatism variously measured.[8] A cross-country comparison is then made between the index and various measures of macro-performance to establish the relationship.

The problem is one of selecting and quantifying those features of an economy thought to be important prerequisites for containing potentially strong inflationary forces. Previous studies stress the importance of wage-setting and the manner in which it is carried out. For example, the distinguishing feature of Calmfors's and Driffill's approach is to relate performance to the structure of the union movement. Both strong centralization and decentralization are seen to lead to favourable records while intermediate degrees of centralization lead to bad performance.[9]

More in keeping with the views expressed here are those of Crouch.[10] Crouch singles out four characteristics of an industrial relations system as critical:

1. How centralized is the union side in collective bargaining?
2. How centralized is the employers' association?
3. How much rank-and-file autonomy is allowed in collective bargaining decisions?
4. How widespread are institutions of codetermination or cooperation throughout the industrial relations system?

Trade union movements with highly centralized collective bargaining structures facing centralized employers' associations receive two points in his 'corporatist' index with additional points obtained if there is little rank-and-file autonomy and if institutions of codetermination are widespread. Maximum values of 4 are achieved by Austria, Germany, the Netherlands, Norway and Sweden.

There is much to applaud in this heroic effort to abstract from the institutional framework a few key features critical for success. This index rightly stresses the importance of encompassing organizations for market participants internalising social costs, and it implicitly rejects the notion of an invisible hand and instead values the need for a spirit of cooperation in the labour market. It does not include a measure of the size of the welfare state, efforts to redistribute income through progressive taxation or the importance of party control. However, since left-wing governments, highly progressive tax systems and large developed welfare states tend to coexist in countries with highly centralized trade union movements, these former influences are picked up in the index.

What the index fails to account for are other types of social bargains that, according to the earlier analysis, also lead to superior macro-performance. To put it otherwise, what the earlier remarks emphasize is that there are other configurations of institutions that are and have been conductive to wage restraint under FE conditions. Basic is an industrial relations system characterized by trust and cooperation between capital and labour. Thus, even without highly centralized 'peak' organizations, it is clear that economies have been able to reach a bargain in which labour seeks its fair share of output through means other than maximum exertion of its market power, i.e. seeking the maximum short-run increase in money wages that the market will bear. In order to allow for two distinct kinds of social bargains and two quite different systems of industrial relations, proxy variables reflecting the 'labour market climate' or the degree of cooperativeness within the industrial relations system must be used. Some measure of strike activity has been used in other studies and is adopted here.

The general rationale of the approach has been outlined by McCallum.[11] First, strikes are a manifestation of conflict in the labour market between capital and labour. Those economies with high levels of strike activity will also be subject to relatively high levels of money wage demands and settlements at any level of unemployment but especially at FE.

Second, in a world of uncertainty labour at the firm level must rely largely on the information provided by management with regards to the economic condition of the firm, especially its current and future competitiveness. Most important is the alleged size of wage increases consistent with the preservation of the firm including jobs. The greater is the degree of trust on the part of the workers in response to such pronouncements by management, the less likely will the aims of the two sides diverge in a wage dispute and the less likely therefore will there be excessive wage settlements and strikes. If this carries over to the national level, then again the level of strike activity national wide will reflect a labour market climate leading to success or failure. For example, according to the view advocated here, the higher is strike activity in a country, other things being equal, the higher will be the rate of wage and, therefore, price inflation at any level of unemployment. The higher would, therefore, be the rate of unemployment permitted by the authorities, other things being equal.[12]

6.   SOME SIMPLE CORRELATIONS

As a preliminary to more elaborate multiple regression analysis, Table 8.2 presents correlation coefficients for the average volume or the log of the

Table 8.2 *Simple correlations between unemployment rates/misery indices (U/MI) and average volume of strike activity (S), selected periods*

	(U/MI) 1963–73	(U/MI) 1974–79	(U/MI) 1980–84
S 1955–62	.68/.47	—	—
S 1955–73	.82/.66	—	—
S 1963–73	.87/.74	—	—
S 1963–79	—	.70/.80	.51/.71
S 1974–79	—	.64/.78	.50/.70
S 1974–84	—	—	.46/.70
S 1980–84	—	—	.38/.69
log S 1950–69	.70/.67	—	—
log S 1950–78	—	.70/.82	.56/.68

average volume of strike activity and average rates of unemployment and values of the misery index for selected periods. Account is taken of the possibility that the relevant years determining the 'climate' of the labour market may sometimes precede as well as correspond to the performance period.

In all three periods, but especially the first two, the simple correlations between both the unemployment rates and the misery index and the average volume of strikes are high. For example, average strike volume in 1963–73 correlates highly with unemployment and the misery index 1963–73 ($r = .87$ for the former and .74 for the latter). The relationship is maintained in the 1974–79 period with the volume of strikes 1963–79, 1974–79 and the logarithm of strike volume 1950–78 all correlated with performance in 1974–79 at a highly significant level.[13] By the 1980s the relationship has weakened somewhat but still remains high.

While no *a priori* justification for the use of any particular measure of the strike variable is available, the mere fact that a number of measures of the proxy for successful bargains are significantly correlated with performance is supportive of the approach adopted here and in other studies. The regressions further support this conclusion.

7. UNEMPLOYMENT RATES AND THE MISERY INDEX, 1963–73

Cross-country regressions of the unemployment rates and the sum of the rates of unemployment and price inflation, the misery index, were run for 18 OECD countries covering the period when standardized unemployment rates were available in the LSE data set. This period was then divided into three periods: 1963–1973, 1974–1979 and 1980–1984. The three periods represent, respectively, an extended period of boom, the period after the first oil shock but before the main impact of the second, and the period encompassing most of the second oil shock up to the last year for which data was available.

For the 1963–73 period, the dependent variables were regressed against various political and economic institutional variables as well as more conventional economic ones, applying OLS techniques. Proxies used to measure the presence or absence of those institutional features leading to FE at acceptable rates of inflation included Crouch's corporatist index, C_j, and the average volume of strike activity, S_j, in a country for either 1955–62, 1955–73, 1963–73 or the logarithm of strike volume 1950–69.[14] Additional predetermined variables included the average rate of price inflation in a previous period and the rate of growth of productivity during the period. Neither were ever significant.

Table 8.3 summarizes the results. What stands out clearly in the regressions was the importance of the strike variable in explaining differences in unemployment across countries and its superiority to the corporatist variable. This was true whatever strike measure was used, indicating the robustness of the variable as already discussed. Both the corporatist and strike variables were used as measures of the degree of cooperation between employers and workers, not merely with respect to shop-floor activities, but also cooperation between these two and government in furthering wage and price stability.[15] Therefore, both variables were hypothesized to influence the position of the Phillips curve and, therefore, the inflation costs of any unemployment rate. For example, the higher is the volume of strike activity or the lower the degree of corporatism, the greater the degree of conflict in the labour market over the distribution of income. Therefore, it was hypothesized the higher would be the misery index, the rate of inflation and the rate of unemployment.

As seen in regressions (1) and (2) in Table 8.3, each variable when entered separately had the correct sign but the R-square was substantially higher for the regressions with the strike variable. The R-square varied from .46 to .77 (with the average strike volume in 1963–73 giving the best result). When they appeared together in the same regression, the corporatist variable was non-significant.

Regressions were also run that included as independent variables measures of the distribution of political power. The political or party control variables tried were votes for left-of-centre parties in any country on average for 1946–76, the share of cabinet posts held by left-of-centre parties 1965–81 and the average per cent of the labour force unionized in 1946–76. It was hypothesized that if two countries had similar strike

Table 8.3   *Cross-country regressions for unemployment rates (U) and misery indices (MI), 1963–73 in 18 OECD countries*

							R^2
(1)	U_j	=	$.94$ $(.22)$	$+$	$6.05S_j$ $(.73)$		$.77$
(2)	U_j	=	3.68 $(.47)$	$-$	$.71C_j$ $(.20)$		$.33$
(3)	U_j	=	2.00 $(.62)$	$+$	$5.32S_j -$ $(.79)$	$.03L_j$ $(.02)$	$.80$
(4)	U_j	=	4.86 $(.74)$	$-$	$.53C_j -$ $(.22)$	$.05L_j$ $(.03)$	$.46$
(5)	U_j	=	2.28 $(.66)$	$+$	$5.94S_j -$ $(.99)$	$.04L_j$ $(.02)$	$.75$
(6)	U_j	=	$.86$ (1.1)	$+$	$.72S_j -$ $(.16)$	$.07L_j$ $(.02)$	$.65$
(7)	MI_j	=	5.83 $(.29)$	$+$	$6.40S_j$ $(.99)$		$.62$
(8)	MI_j	=	2.88 (1.3)	$+$	$.90S_j$ $(.25)$		$.42$

Notes:
The dependent variables, U, and MI are the average rates of unemployment and the sum of the rates of price inflation and unemployment, the misery index, for 1963–73, respectively; S is a measure of strike volume. In regressions (1), (3) and (7) average strike volume 1963–73 is used. Regressions (6) and (8) use the log of strike volume 1950–68, and regression (5) uses the volume of strikes 1955–62. L is the percent of left votes, 1946–76 and C is Crouchs index of corporatism.

The data for the dependent variables are taken from the LSE data bank; the strike and corporatist data has been constructed from ILO sources or are taken from McCallum, 'Inflation and Social Consensus . . .'; *op. cit.* The voting data is from Korpi, *The Democratic Class . . ., op. cit.*, p. 38.

Figures in parentheses are standard errors. The R-squares are corrected for degrees of freedom.

records (and, therefore, similar inflation rates at any unemployment rate), the country with the strongest 'leftist' vote would have the lower unemployment record. These variables representing the demand for FE were meant to test whether a prolonged period of, say, pro-left voting sentiments or strong union power generated a political environment which was conducive to a low unemployment policy.[16]

The per cent of votes for left-of-centre parties, L_j, always gave better statistical results than the per cent of the labour force unionized or the share of leftist cabinet posts and neither of the latter were significant when either variable was used in the same regression equation as the leftist vote variable.

The inclusion of a 'demand' for FE variable with either a strike or corporation variable very much increased the R-square (whatever strike variable was used) although it was not significant at the 5 per cent level when included with the corporatism variable, equation (4), or the average volume of strikes 1963–73, equation (3). It did prove to be significant when the strike measure used was the logarithm of the volume of strikes 1950–68, equation (6), and the volume of strikes 1955–62, equation (5).

Finally, several regressions using the misery index were tried. Regressions (7) and (8) set out typical results with the volume of strikes 1963–73 and the log of strike volume 1950–69, respectively, highly significant. Regression (7), especially, reveals how powerful a predictor strike activity is of macro-performance. For example, according to regression (7) an increase in the average volume of strikes of 100 man-days per 1000 workers increases the misery index by .64 ($= .1 \times 6.4$) per cent.

8.   CONTINUITY IN PERFORMANCE

Low rates of unemployment and low values for the misery index were strongly correlated with the degree of industrial conflict as measured by strike volume in the 1963–73 period. As a result, variations across countries in strike volume explained a high per cent of the variance in unemployment rates and the misery index. Since the rise of unemployment rates in the early 1970s, a number of writers have fostered the Eurosclerosis argument as noted earlier by which more strongly unionized economies with more extensive welfare states can be expected to have more serious unemployment problems. In varying degrees, depending upon the writer, the prolonged period of mass unemployment since the early 1970s can be attributed to an unwillingness of labour to permit the reduced rate of growth of real wages that would allow the labour market to clear and eliminate most of unemployment.

It should be clear that whatever the impact of strong unionization and extensive welfare states, these did not lead to real wage problems in the period before 1974. Among the low unemployment countries of this period were Austria, Belgium, Denmark, Sweden, countries with union densities of 50 per cent or over and the extensive welfare states as well.[17]

There is strong evidence disputing the Eurosclerosis thesis in more recent periods as well. Table 8.4 records correlation coefficients between cross-country unemployment rates (and misery indices) from one sub-period of the postwar period to the next. What Table 8.4 indicates is that

*Table 8.4   Intertemporal correlations between unemployment rates (U),
inflation rates (p) and misery indices (MI), 1963–73 and
1974–79 and 1974–79 and 1980–84, for 18 OECD economies*

		1963–73	1974–79
U/MI	1974–79	.80/.82	
	1980/84		.90/.92

from 1963–73 to 1974–79 and from 1974–79 to 1980–84 not only did the
rankings of economies according to their unemployment and misery index
records change little but the deviations of the various countries performances from the mean of all 18 countries depicted a (positive) linear
relation over time. This is illustrated by the correlation coefficients for
cross-country unemployment rates and for the misery indices in the 18
OECD countries between 1963–73 and 1974–79 of .80 and .82, respectively and the even stronger correlations between the 1974–79 and 1980–84
periods for both variables.[18] Whatever are the forces determining relative
performances, they have not changed appreciably over time and have had
little to do with unionization and the size of the welfare state.

9.   REGRESSION ANALYSIS – UNEMPLOYMENT AND MISERY INDICES SINCE 1973

With these points in mind, consider the period since 1973. Regression
analysis was undertaken for the 1974–79 period between the two oil shocks
and the period since the second oil shock until 1984.

Table 8.5 indicates that strike activity played an important explanatory
role in explaining cross-country unemployment rates and misery indices in
the two post-1973 sub-periods as well as in 1963–73. For the 1974–79
period, unemployment rates were regressed on different measures of
strike volume, and then with political control variables and several
economic variables as well. Regressions with the logarithm of strike
volume 1950–78 gave the best result in the simple regressions, regression
(1), and also when entered with the per cent of leftist votes 1961–80 as the
only other independent variable, regression (2). When a lagged value for
price inflation (p_{jt-1} = the average rate of inflation 1969–73) was added,
the coefficients for the strike and party control variable were little
changed, the inflation variable was significant and the R-square improved
as seen in regression (3). The negative sign can be attributed to a
willingness to live with inflation once it has set in.[19]

Regressions of the misery index on the logarithm of strike volume

Table 8.5   Cross-country regressions for unemployment rates (U) and misery indices (MI), 1974–79 and 1980–84, in 18 OECD countries

1974–79					R^2
(1) U_j =	1.65 (1.4)	+ $1.19S_j$ $(.28)$			.46
(2) U_j =	2.28 (1.6)	+ $1.11S_j$ $(.20)$	− $.09L_j$ $(.03)$		.65
(3) U_j =	5.81 (1.9)	+ $1.11S_j$ $(.17)$	− $.11L_j$ $(.02)$	− $.48p_{jt-1}$ $(.22)$	.71
(4) MI_j =	$.20$ (2.0)	+ $2.88S_j$ $(.40)$			.75
(5) MI_j =	10.4 $(.57)$	+ $16.1S_j$ (1.8)			.76
1980–84					
(6) U_j =	7.84 (2.6)	+ $1.22S_j$ (3.2)	− $.18L_j$ (0.4)		.54
(7) U_j =	9.53 (2.3)	+ $1.77S_j$ $(.38)$	− $.20L_j$ $(.04)$	− $.38p_{jt-1}$ $(.18)$	.62
(8) MI_j =	10.6 (1.1)	+ $23.74S_j$ (4.3)			.58
(9) MI_j =	11.4 (1.1)	+ $16.65S_j$ (3.3)			.56

Notes:
The strike variable, S, used is the logarithm of strike volume 1950–78 in regressions (1)-(4), (6) and (7), the volume of strikes 1963–79 in regression (5), the volume of strikes 1980–84 in regressions (8) and (12) and the volume of strikes 1974–84 in regression (9). L is the percent of left-of-centre voters 1961–80 and p_{t-1} the average rate of price inflation 1969–73 in regression (3) and the average rate of price inflation 1974–79 in regression (7).

Figures in parentheses are standard errors. The R-squares are adjusted for degrees of freedom.

1950–78 and volume of strikes, 1963–79 are shown by regression (4) and (5) respectively. The R-squares are very high and the coefficients highly significant. Comparing regression (5) of Table 8.5 with regression (7) in Table 8.3, it is clear that the importance of industrial conflict for performance has much increased.[20]

As revealed in Table 8.2, the strike variables would explain a smaller part of the variance of unemployment rates in the 1980–84 period. Regression (6) and (7) in Table 8.5 record the best results where S_j is the logarithm of strike volume, 1950–78, L_j the per cent of leftist votes,

1961–80 and p_{jt-1} the average rate of inflation 1974–79. Comparing the similar regression for the 1974–79 period, regression (2), with regression (6) the most notable differences are the larger coefficients in the later period and the reduced R-square. The greatly increased constant term in the 1980–84 regression suggests the omission of one or more important variables.

As in the other two periods, the strike variable explain a large part of the variance of the misery index for 1980–84. Regressions (8) and (9) give the simple regression results when average volume of strikes 1980–84 and 1974–84, respectively, are used.

10. CONCLUSIONS

Admittedly the statistical results of this study are not as strong as would be liked and the data used are often crude. The chief difficulty is that so little is known about the way in which to introduce and measure the relative demand and supply forces underlying AD policies and unemployment and inflation outcomes. For example, the political control variables by necessity are averages over a number of years and strive to pick up the political climate or centre and outer limits of the political spectrum. Yet very little is known about the correct number of years over which to average the political control variables in order to determine this climate. Further refinement of the political variables is clearly required, yet ignorance in this regard is massive.

The same can be said for the impact of institutions on the position of the Phillips curve. There is ample evidence by now that strike activity strongly reflects important characteristics of a country's industrial relations system, characteristics that very much influence the likelihood of wage restraint under FE conditions. But again, the correct time-interval over which to average strike activity in order to best represent these characteristics is not well known.

There are some things, however, to be said in favour of the approach. At the very least, the attempt at quantifying the influence of institutional forces on economic outcomes can be seen as an advance over the more common approach in applied econometrics which falls back on dummy variables to pick up such influences. In addition, the results appear to be largely insensitive to different contending definitions of the institutional variables suggesting that while the appropriate variables may not be known with great precision, the importance of the institutional influence is clear. Third, the results of this study do not compare unfavourably with other similar studies.

With this in mind, the following conclusions are in order. Much of the first part of this chapter was given over to a study of the crucial institutions fostering high levels of employment and acceptable rates of inflation. Without too much simplification it was argued that during this period two kinds of social bargains were struck in some of the OECD economies that allowed superior macro-performances. One of these bargains, the one that has received so much attention in the literature, involved the exchange of FE and generous welfare provisions for wage restraint on the part of highly centralized, powerful trade union movements.

This kind of interpretation of success has come under attack in recent times in the form of the 'Eurosclerosis' thesis according to which strong trade unions and an extended welfare state, far from fostering a favourable macro-record, are now held to be chiefly responsible for high unemployment and inflation. The remedy is to reduce the power of the unions, cut back on the welfare state and shift the distribution of income towards profits.

The second part of the chapter subjected this analysis and its policy prescriptions to some rather rudimentary but relevant statistical tests. These tests strongly supported the conclusions drawn from the earlier sections in which it was argued that a generous welfare state and strong unions can be supportive of favourable performance. Such institutions are not necessary for a superior record, as the Japanese and Swiss experiences show. But this finding in no way lessens the truth of the argument. It merely indicates that common to all successful performances has been a cooperative arrangement between government, capital and labour. The policy implications of the institutional analysis and the statistical results are quite different from those of the Eurosclerosis view.

If nothing more, the statistical analysis consistently shows how important harmony is for a well-functioning economy. Not only does this lead to the obvious results of low levels of strike activity and losses of output. More important, such harmony is associated with favourable combinations of unemployment and inflation, i.e. the misery index, and low unemployment rates.

At a minimum these results should suggest caution on the part of those who wish to dismantle the institutions that have been instrumental in fostering the 'social democratic' bargain. According to the view adopted here, programmes of reducing the power of labour and cutting back the welfare state will only make it impossible to achieve FE and low rates of inflation because no social bargain would then be possible. Inflation will, therefore, have to be contained by the only other way possible – by creating more unemployment.

It is true that while relative performances were largely unchanged, beginning in 1974 macro-performances deteriorated most everywhere. But this is another story and it is most unlikely that an explanation of, say, the rise of the average rate of unemployment in the OECD countries over time can be well accounted for by the kinds of influences considered here.

NOTES

I wish to thank the Social Sciences and Humanities Research Council of Canada for financial support.

1. E. Tufte, *Political Control of the Economy*, Princeton University Press, 1978.
2. See D. Hibbs, 'Political Parties and Macroeconomic Policy', *The American Political Science Review*, December 1977.
3. For a typical example, see A. Lindbeck and D. Snower, 'Union Activity, Unemployment Persistence and Wage-Employment Rachets', *European Economic Review*, Feb./Mar. 1987.
4. See L. Calmfors and J. Driffill, 'Bargaining Structure, Corporatism and Macroeconomic Performance', *Economic Policy*, April 1988.
5. The need for a social bargain as a requisite for satisfactory macro-performance is a post-World War II development. It emerged from the simultaneous occurrence of four important developments; the universal extension of the franchise, the rise of an egalitarian ethos, prolonged period of FE and the rise of the power of labour in general and the trade unions in particular. These developments were largely responsible for two additional influences; growing per capita incomes and the extension of the welfare state in many economies. Together these developments have greatly affected the wage determination process making capitalist economies potentially inflation prone.
6. The dividing line between high and low unemployment rates is somewhat arbitrary since unemployment rates in the United Kingdom never fell below 3 per cent after 1966 and averaged 3.6 per cent from 1966 to 1973. The sample mean and standard deviation for average rates of inflation are 4.9 and .95, respectively. The same statistics for unemployment rates are 2.3 and 2.3, respectively.
7. The correlation between average rates of inflation and unemployment is $r = -.06$. The correlation between average rates of inflation and unemployment for the same countries 1951–73 is $r = -.25$.
8. See C. Crouch, 'The Conditions for Trade Union Wage Restraint', in *The Politics of Inflation and Economic Stagnation*, L. Lindberg and C. Maier (eds), The Brookings Institution, Washington, 1985.
9. Calmfors and Driffill, *op. cit.*, p. 5.
10. *Op. cit.*
11. J. McCallum, 'Inflation and Social Consensus in the Seventies', *Economic Journal*, December 1983. See also M. Paldam, 'Industrial Conflict and Economic Conditions', *European Economic Review*, 1983; and D. Hibbs, *The Political Economy of Industrial Democracies*, Harvard University Press, Cambridge, Mass., 1987, Chapter 3.
12. Note that the emphasis of the text is on causation running from strikes to inflation. There is a theory that reverses this causation arguing that it is inflation that causes strikes. However work by Paldam strongly supports the position that conflict or strikes lead the wage-price increases. See Paldam, ibid.
13. McCallum (*op. cit.*), obtained a highly significant correlation between the logarithm of strike volume, 1950–78 and the misery index, 1974–83.
14. At this stage it was not considered feasible to experiment with other time-periods for the simple reason that so little theoretical work has been done that would suggest the appropriate intervals to use.
15. They are highly correlated with $r = -.74$.
16. See K. Rothschild, ' "Left" and "Right" in "Federal Europe",' *Kyklos*, No. 3, 1986. This approach overcomes problems associated with lags, while cross-section analysis also holds constant external influences on policy outcomes.

17. See W. Korpi, *The Democratic Class Struggle*, Routledge and Kegan Paul, London 1983, p. 31, for data on union density.
18. Calmfors and Driffill chose the changes in unemployment rather than the level of unemployment as the one of the important performance variables to study. It is difficult to see a justification for this. Table 8.1 reveals an increase in unemployment rates of only 3.3 in the United States from 1963–73 to 1980–86 while unemployment, increased from by 5.4 per cent in Germany between these periods. This is hardly grounds for assigning higher marks to the American performance. The fact remains that only 95.5 and 92.2 per cent of the American labour force was employed in the 1963–73 and 1980–86 periods while the corresponding figures for Germany were 99.2 and 93.8 per cent. See Calmfors and Driffill, *op. cit.*, Table 2.
19. See McCallum, *op. cit.*
20. A measure of party control was also introduced in the regression but it was never significant.

9. The Terms of Trade from the Long View*

William Darity Jr

1. INTRODUCTION

In an important conference paper, Ronald Findlay (1981) undertook an extensive examination of the 'fundamental determinants' of the terms of trade – fundamental in the sense that these are real factors in dynamic equilibrium, governing the relative price at which commodities exchange in interregional trade. While Findlay (1981, pp. 442–4) also explored short-run factors influencing the terms of trade when they function to clear trade balances, the more intriguing aspects of his paper concern the long-run factors. Findlay sought not just to identify the short-run direction of change of the terms of trade but looked for the central value towards which they must ultimately gravitate.

To identify the long-run value of the terms of trade, Findlay followed the structuralist tradition of investigating their determinants in the context of a North–South trade model. Here the North is the more affluent industrial region, while the South is the poorer, predominantly agrarian region. The North exports manufactures and the South exports primary products, establishing an asymmetry between the regions via the international pattern of specialization.

One can presume that the pattern arises from old-fashioned comparative advantage. However, the dynamic effects of such a pattern of specialization need not be salutary for Southern growth rates nor for the Southern terms of trade. Prebisch (1959) and Singer (1950) both theorized that the South typically would experience slower growth and deteriorating terms of trade given such an international pattern of specialization. Moreover, for Prebisch and Singer declining terms of trade served as a virtual index of divergent growth between South and North.

But Findlay endeavoured, instead, to find the 'resting point' for the terms of trade. The short-run or secular trends might have an eventual position of equilibrium, an equilibrium whose characteristics can inform us about the 'fundamental determinants' of the terms of trade. The short-run factors that have the terms of trade equilibrating the trade balance are more ephemeral, in part because the interaction of supply and demand from a classical perspective only offers a value consistent with market-clearing (a 'temporary' equilibrium) but not a long-run or long-period position (or dynamic equilibrium).

In what follows fundamental or dynamic equilibrium analyses of the terms of trade are examined in four sections: (1) a review of the Lewis theory of the terms of trade, (2) a review of Findlay's own explanation of the long-*run* terms of trade, (3) a Findlay-style explanation of the long-*run* terms of trade with less than full employment in the North, and (4) a long-*period* explanation of the terms of trade. The distinction between the long run (or uniform growth rate condition) and the long period (or uniform profitability condition) will be explained in greater detail below. The third and fourth sections also present and explore an interesting and seemingly paradoxical relationship between mark-up pricing and the terms of trade.

1.   THE LEWIS THEORY OF THE NORTH–SOUTH TERMS OF TRADE

Arthur Lewis's (1969, pp. 17–22) Wicksell lectures provide the *locus classicus* of his analysis of the factors governing the terms of trade. However, the model of the Wicksell lectures is exactly the same as the model of trade between the temperate zone and the tropics near the end of Lewis's (1954, pp. 182–4) justifiably famous paper on growth with surplus labour.

The North, or the temperate zone, produces two goods – steel and food. The South, or the tropics, produces two goods also – coffee and food. Each region consumes all three goods. The North exports steel and the South exports coffee. Labour is the solitary factor of production, with fixed technical coefficients for production of each good in each country. Findlay (1981, pp. 431–3) incorporated import demand elasticity effects into the model, but these are not in Lewis's original version, giving the original an altogether Ricardian resonance. Currency differences and monetary factors are assumed away.

The key to the model is that both countries produce a common good: food. Since the good is the same in both countries, food must exchange one for one internationally. However, food is cheaper to produce in the North than the South. The North has more productive agriculture and hence lower unit labour requirements in food-making.

In the North one unit of labour can produce three units of food or three units of steel. In the South, however, Lewis assumes that one unit of labour can produce only one unit of food or can produce one unit of coffee. Again, note that food must exchange one for one internationally. But internally in the North, one food equals one steel while internally in the South one food exchanges for one coffee. This means that the commodity terms of trade set one unit of coffee equivalent to one unit of steel, but the factoral terms of trade favour Northern labour since one Northern wage equals three Southern wages due to the Northern edge in food productivity.

Lewis's approach can be treated a bit more formally by assuming that there is no surplus above wage payments, i.e. a zero 'profit' condition. With positive profits and the same periods of production in both regions (in this one-factor model) all the same results will carry through if the long *period* assumption (more on this below) is maintained that rates of profit are uniform everywhere.

Cost-determined food pricing implies:

$$P_F^N = w_F^N 1_F^N \tag{1a}$$

$$P_F^S = w_F^S 1_F^S \tag{1b}$$

where P_F^i is the price of food, w_F^i is the wage rate, and 1_F^i is the inverse of productivity in each region ($i = N, S$). The law of one price dictates

$$P_F^N = P_F^S \tag{2}$$

so that, by implication,

$$w_F^N / w_F^S = 1_F^S / 1_F^N \tag{3}$$

Because $1_F^S > 1_F^N$ due to a higher labour–output ratio in the South, the wage rate in the North must necessarily be higher. If we read causation from right to left, the productivity gap in agriculture dictates the international wage differential. This could be due to a surplus labour assumption for both regions where average agricultural productivity establishes the customary wage, or in a more directly Ricardian manner, the differential reflects the relative 'natural' price of labour.

What about the commodity terms of trade? Each commodity price also is cost-determined:

$$P_s = w_s^N 1_s^N \tag{4}$$

$$P_c = w_c^S 1_c^S \tag{5}$$

In (4), P_s is the price of steel, w_s^N is the Northern wage in steel production, and 1_s^N is the inverse of productivity in steel-making in the North. In (5), P_c is the price of coffee, w_c^s is the Southern wage for coffee workers, and 1_c^s is the labour–output ratio in coffee production.

We can assume that $w_s^N = w_F^N$ and $w_c^s = w_F^s$. Or we can assume that w_s^N and w_c^s are higher than the corresponding wage for food workers in their respective regions by the same mark-up. As long as the ratio (w_s^N/w_c^s) is the same as the ratio (w_F^N/w_F^s), Lewis' conclusions will be self-evident from the following expression for the commodity terms of trade derived using (3)

$$\theta^* = \frac{w_c^s 1_c^s}{w_s^N 1_s^N} = \frac{w_F^s 1_c^s}{w_F^N 1_s^N} = \frac{1_F^N 1_c^s}{1_F^s 1_s^N} \tag{6}$$

$$\theta = p_c/P_s$$

above.

In Lewis's numerical example $\theta^* = 1$ because $1_F^N/1_F^s = \frac{1}{3}$ and $1_F^s/1_s^N = 3$. θ^* is a determinant equilibrium expression for the terms of trade if all prices are at their classical 'natural' levels. Here we have a direct link between productivities in each region and the relative price of the exported goods.

If productivities and the pattern of specialization are stable this is the end of the story for Lewis. If productivities are changing but the pattern of specialization is stable, then Prebisch–Singer results can follow. Lewis (1969; also see Findlay, 1981, p. 433) asserts that empirically productivity has risen fastest in developed country agriculture, next fastest in developed country manufacturing, slower in developing country primary product-making, with virtually no technical progress in developing country agriculture.[1] In percentage rates of change, equation (6) becomes:

$$\hat{\theta}^* = (\hat{1}_F^N - \hat{1}_F^s) + (\hat{1}_c^s - \hat{1}_s^N) \tag{7}$$

With $\hat{1}_F^s \cong 0$ and $\hat{1}_F^N$ strongly negative the differential in rates of change in agricultural productivity could be sufficient to sustain a secular deterioration in Southern terms of trade. As Findlay (1981, p. 433) notes, 'It is difficult to conceive of a more elegant and economical theory from which to derive the implication of an adverse secular trend in the terms of trade of the developing countries.' Ironically, productivity improvements in Southern coffee production only serve to aggravate the downswing in Southern terms of trade by reducing costs in the export sector. The South must raise its wage to improve its terms of trade, and it can do so only by raising agricultural productivity. The South will remain poorer in relative wages as long as it is poorer in its ability to grow food.

Lewis offers up 'real' determinants of the terms of trade – real costs of production in each region. But how 'long run' is this tale? It is only as 'long run' as the posited pattern of specialization remains intact. As Lewis (1969, p. 22) observed, 'the terms of trade are tied rigidly by productivities only for so long as it pays both countries to produce both food and one other commodity. As soon as productivities move outside these limits, the terms of trade cease to be tied rigidly.' Andre Burgstaller (1987) has recently provided a clever speculative history (and forecast?) of how the terms of trade might unfold under various scenarios as the pattern of specialization alters between 'England' and 'India'. In Burgstaller's long run, India becomes the industrial centre and England an agrarian nation, reversing their initial roles. Of course, the terms of trade continuously will move against the 'South', but here the South formerly was the North![2]

2. FINDLAY'S LONG-RUN TERMS OF TRADE

The Findlay (1981, pp. 439–54) explanation for the long-run terms of trade is derived from his version of a North–South trade model. Findlay postulates that the North, producing a manufacturing export that serves as an investment good for both regions, is growing neoclassically in smooth Solow fashion. The South, in contrast, is a Lewis unlimited labour economy producing a primary product. Aggregate production functions are characteristically neoclassical in both regions with well-defined marginal products in both labour and capital.

After Solow, Findlay assumes perfect price flexibility in the North provides continuous full employment growth, or the North grows at its 'natural' rate. After Lewis, Findlay assumes a fixed real wage in the South results in a perpetual surplus of labour there. The South grows at the rate dictated by its savings activity. Southern growth is savings-driven since all investment is derived in one-for-one fashion from savings. In short, there is no financial intermediation in Findlay's world, no investment 'financed' independently of a new act of savings.

Findlay also makes the extreme Kaleckian (1971) assumption in the South: All savings are from profits; all wages are consumed. The propensity to save out of profits in the South is positive (and large); the propensity to save out of wages in the South is zero.

The Southern profit rate, ρ_s, is defined as:

$$\rho_s = \theta\pi'(k_s) \tag{8}$$

where θ is the terms of trade again, the ratio of primary products price to manufacturers price. $\pi'(k_s)$ is the marginal product of capital where the function π is the intensive form of the South's aggregate production function and k_s is the capital–employment ratio in the South.

If σ is the savings rate out of profits in the South, under the extreme Kaleckian assumption, the growth rate, g_s, there will be:

$$g_s = \sigma\theta\pi'(k_s) \tag{9}$$

The Northern growth rate, g_N, given Solow steady state growth must be at the natural rate, n_N:

$$g_N = n_N \tag{10}$$

Now Findlay (1981, pp. 441–2) identifies the *long run* as a condition where the two region's growth rates become the same, or for 'steady state equilibrium in the world economy':

$$g_s = g_N \tag{11}$$

which constrains the South to save (and accumulate) at the North's natural rate of growth. This means, in turn, that:

$$\sigma\theta\pi'(k_s) = n_N \tag{12}$$

Solving for θ yields Findlay's expression for the long-run terms of trade:

$$\theta* = \frac{n_N}{\sigma\theta\pi'(k_s)} \tag{13}$$

This is a very compact and interesting result. Findlay's equation for the terms of trade under balanced growth worldwide has it that the terms of trade are governed by the natural rate of growth in the North, the savings rate out of profit income in the South, and technical conditions in the South's export sector. As Findlay (1981, p. 442) observes, the provocative feature of this result is that the terms of trade '[are] completely independent of [the] production function and [the] propensity to save of the North and of the demand for imports in the two regions.'

One interpretation is that the terms of trade serves as the relative price that adjusts to bring about balanced growth. An alternative interpretation is, if and when balanced growth obtains, the terms of trade must take the value given under (13) for consistency. The first interpretation allows us to ask questions in 'comparative dynamics', like how will the terms of trade adjust if the natural growth rate rises in the North or the profit-saving rate falls in the South. The second interpretation requires us to ask what value θ^* *must* take, instead, if we get into balanced growth in the world economy.

3. LONG-RUN TERMS OF TRADE SANS FULL EMPLOYMENT

It is Findlay's assumption of full employment growth in the North that eliminates Northern savings behaviour and technology from being determinants of the long-run terms of trade. With unemployed labour in both regions matters will change sharply, although demand elasticities will remain irrelevant. Note also in what follows, similar to Findlay, Laursen-Metzler (1950) effects are ignored – so that savings rates in both regions do not depend upon the terms of trade. In fact, savings rates are assumed fixed and immutable in both North and South for posterity. They are average long-term savings propensities.

Now if the North does not grow at its full employment rate, its growth will be dictated by its savings activity also. Findlay's use of the Solow model for the North introduces an additional asymmetry beyond the dichotomy in specialization. In the South, all savings is out of profits, while in the Solow model of the North, now growing with surplus labour as well, savings come out of total income. This means that while the Southern growth rate still is given by equation (9), Northern growth is specified as:

$$g_N = sa(k_N) \tag{14}$$

where s is the propensity to save in the North, $a(k_N)$ is the average product of capital in the North, and k_N is the capital-employment ratio in the North.

Under steady-state equilibrium, $g_s = g_N$, once again and the long run terms of trade now become:

$$\theta^* = \frac{sa(k_N)}{\sigma\pi'(k_s)} \tag{15}$$

This reveals that both savings rates now matter – σ in the South and s in the North – in dictating the equilibrium value for $\theta*$. Technologies in *both* regions also matter now. Similar to Findlay's prior result, demand elasticities are absent from the long-run story, although, in the short run, where the terms of trade equilibrate the balance of trade, they are very much present.

It also seems that it does not much matter that the North produces manufactures and the South primary products. What is different is the savings behaviour in the two regions – only profits are saved in the South, while some of both categories of income are saved in the North. As long as demand elasticities do not come into play it does not matter which region is producing which good, once persistent unemployment is present in both sites, in determining the long-run terms of trade.

Even the asymmetry in savings behaviour need not be maintained if we generalize each region's savings functions in Kaldor (1955) fashion. Suppose there are different propensities to save out of profits and wages in both North and South. Suppose also, again as Findlay does, that the rate of profit can be identified with the marginal product of capital.

The growth rate in the South now becomes:

$$g_s = (\sigma_p - \sigma_w)\theta\pi'(k_s) + \sigma_w\theta a(k_s) \tag{16}$$

In (16), σ_p is the savings rate out of profits, σ_w is the savings rate out of wages, θ still is the terms of trade, $\pi'(k_s)$ still is the marginal product of capital and $a(k_s)$ is the average product of capital in the South, and k_s, again, the capital–employment ratio in the South.

By parallel reasoning the growth rate in the North is:

$$g_N = (s_p - s_w)f'(k_N) + s_w a(k_N) \tag{17}$$

Under long-run/balanced growth the terms of trade will be:

$$\theta* = \frac{(s_p - s_w)f'(k_N) + s_w a(k_N)}{(\sigma_p - \sigma_w)\pi'(k_s) + \sigma_w a(k_s)} \tag{18}$$

Now the factors influencing the terms of trade in both regions are symmetrical – the invariant savings rates and production functions, or, some might say, tastes (for foregone consumption) and technology.[3]

If the extreme Kaleckian (1971) assumption is made, no savings in either region comes out of wages. Therefore, $s_w = \sigma_w = 0$, which means (18) simplifies to:

$$\theta* = \frac{s_p f'(k_N)}{\sigma\pi'(k_s)} \tag{19}$$

If the profit savings rate was higher in either region, or capital used less intensively, it would mean lower terms of trade over the long run for that region.

Thus far, the results examined have been derived under the assumption of neoclassical production functions and marginal product factor pricing. How might the long-run terms of trade be characterized under alternative assumptions about technology and distribution theory?

The Southern rate of profit, ρ_s, can be defined directly as a rate of return over capital, where capital is the manufactured good imported from the North.

$$\rho_s = \frac{P_s Y_s - w_s N_s}{P_N K_s} \tag{20}$$

P_s is the price of Southern output, Y_s is the quantity of Southern output, w_s is the nominal wage in the South, N_s is employment in the South, P_N is the price of the Northern good, and K_s is the Southern capital stock. Equation (20) is equivalent to:

$$\rho_s = \theta(C_s - \bar{w}_s/k_s) \tag{21}$$

In (21) C_s is the output–capital ratio in the South, and $\bar{w}_s$ is a fixed real wage measured in terms of Southern product.[4] If all savings is out of profits in the South, then we have:

$$g_s = \sigma\theta(C_s - \bar{w}_s/k_s) \tag{22}$$

In the North, with savings being drawn out of both categories of income at different rates, growth proceeds at the following rate:

$$g_N = (s_p - s_w)\rho_N + s_w C_N \tag{23}$$

In (23) ρ_N is the Northern profit rate, and C_N is the output–capital ratio in the North.

To push back towards the types of asymmetries that enliven North--South models, treat the North as following the dictates of a mark-up pricing rule in Kaldor–Kalecki–Weintraub fashion (see Reynolds, 1987, for a useful exposition). This also is closer to Prebisch (1959) and Singer's (1950) idea that the manufactured good producer exercises monopoly power in pricing. It also is similar to Taylor (1981), who confined mark-up pricing to the North.

With a mark-up over unit labour costs the North's manufacturing price will be:

$$P_N = (1+m)w_N l_N \tag{24}$$

P_N is once again the price of Northern manufactures, m is the mark-up, w_N is the North's nominal wage, and l_N is the employment–output ratio in the North.[5] Mark-up pricing implies that the Northern rate of profit can be defined as:

$$\rho_N = (\frac{m}{1+m})C_N \tag{25}$$

Substitution of (25) into (23) yields:

$$g_N = \{(s_p - s_w) \cdot (\frac{m}{1+m}) + s_w\} C_N \tag{26}$$

Setting $g_s = g_N$ means the long run terms of trade now will be:

$$\theta^* = \frac{\{(^*s_p - s_w)(\frac{m}{1+m}) + s_w\}C_N}{\sigma(C_s - \bar{w}_s/k_s)} \tag{27}$$

Of course, one can mix and match if desired. With a Kaldor–Kalecki–Weintraub North and a Lewis South (*à la* Findlay) the long-run terms of trade will be:

$$\theta^* = \frac{\{(s_p - s_w)(\frac{m}{1+m}) + s_w\}C_N}{\sigma\pi'(k_s)} \tag{28}$$

The K–K–W North in either case (27) or (28) yields an especially surprising result. The *higher* the North's mark-up the better the long-run terms of trade for the South. This is quite counter intuitive, and the exact opposite of results obtained elsewhere by Amitava Dutt (1988) and by Patrick Conway and myself (1988).

Recall the reluctance expressed above to treat θ as the variable adjusts to bring about steady-state growth. Rather, it is preferable to think of θ as having to take on a value consistent with steady-state growth if other forces get the world economy to grow in such a way. This result especially highlights the superiority of this interpretation. For when m enters into a model where the terms of trade bring about balance of trade equilibrium, a rise in the North's mark-up depresses the South's terms of trade (again see Dutt, 1986; and Conway and Darity, 1988). But when m enters into a model where the terms of trade must be consistent with steady-state growth, a higher mark-up in the North has adverse implications for the North's terms of trade.

There is another view of this result compatible with Lewis's cost-determined model of the terms of trade. In Lewis's scheme higher relative labour costs improve a nation's terms of trade. The same is true here as (27) demonstrates. If m falls (or labour's share rises in the North), the terms of trade will favour the North. If $\bar{w}_s/k_s$ rises in the South, the long-run terms of trade will favour the South more strongly. The Ricardian theory of values seems to return with a subtle vengeance.

4. TERMS OF TRADE IN THE LONG PERIOD

Findlay's long run is one of balanced, steady-state growth. But there is at least one alternative way to characterize equilibrium growth. This is the long-period concept where equilibrium prevails when rates of profit are uniform everywhere, a condition alluded to above with the Lewis model. This means that instead of having $g_N = g_s$ as the condition for dynamic equilibrium, we have $\rho_N = \rho_s$. And now, it makes more sense for the terms of trade to be viewed as a relative price that adjusts to help bring profit rates into equality as capital flows out of the low-return region towards the high-return region.

For example, suppose the South is a Lewis–Findlay economy; then its rate of profit is given by (9) above. If the North is a Kaldor–Kalecki–Weintraub economy then its rate of profit is given by (25) above. If rates of profit equalize, the *long-period* terms of trade will be:

$$\theta^* = (\frac{m}{1+m}) (\frac{C_N}{\pi'(k_s)}) \qquad (29)$$

Now even the regional savings propensities are irrelevant to the characterization of equilibrium terms of trade. Only the North's mark-up and the production conditions in each region determine θ^*. *Ceteris paribus* once more, paradoxically, a higher mark-up in the North implies improved terms of trade for the South. The relative cost of labour in the North would have to be higher to yield a higher long-period outcome for the terms of trade.

With mark-up pricing in both regions but with the North alone producing and exporting capital goods to the South, the long-period terms of trade will be:[6]

$$\theta^* = (\frac{m_N}{1+m_N}) (\frac{1+m_s}{m_s}) (\frac{a_{kN}}{1-a_{kN}}) \qquad (30)$$

The first two terms in brackets carry the effects of the fixed mark-ups on the terms of trade. The last term is the ratio of the share of the total capital stock utilized in the North to the share utilized in the South. Again, *ceteris paribus*, a higher mark-up in the home region implies lower terms of trade. Also, *ceteris paribus* a higher share in the capital stock reduces the terms of trade as well.

A higher m_N implies a higher P_N which implies a higher ρ_N. *Ceteris paribus*, θ^* must be higher to insure that ρ_s is in line with ρ_N. But would *ceteris paribus* necessarily obtain? No, because now we have a ready-made story to explain how ρ_s and ρ_N equalize. In Findlay's long-run analysis all savings are directed exclusively towards domestic accumulation. Capital once purchased and installed is immobile internationally. In contrast, in long-period analysis the customary mechanism for profit rate equalization is capital mobility. Any gap between ρ_N and ρ_s will be bridged by capital flows, and if ρ_N and ρ_s must equalize, the terms of trade must adapt to promote equalization, as the underlying regional capital stocks vary.

With capital mobility in the world economy, and long-period terms of trade given by expression (29), what happens to C_N will depend upon returns to scale. Consider a world economy growing in long-period equilibrium. Now the North experiences an exogenous rise in its mark-up. This implies that the Northern profit rate moves above the Southern rate, attracting capital flows northward, until increased Northern output depresses the Northern price sufficiently to restore equal profit rates. Under constant returns the capital–output ratio in the North will remain unchanged, so the higher mark-up must imply lower terms of trade for the North. Under increasing returns, the capital–output ratio will fall in the North, magnifying the adverse terms of trade effect of the increased mark-up. Only under conditions of decreasing returns could an increased mark-up lead to a favourable effect on Northern terms of trade. Only then could the higher mark-up be associated with higher costs of production.

In a world economy with long-period terms of trade given by (30), the inverse relationship between mark-ups and terms of trade holds, *regardless* of returns to scale. If an increased mark-up in either region pushes the world economy out of long-period equilibrium, capital will flow towards the region experiencing the higher mark-up due to the associated higher profit rate. Its share in global capital will necessarily rise until profit rates become uniform again. Hence its terms of trade will deteriorate.

Note also that equal profit rates need not mean equal growth rates. Hence the long period conceptualization provides an equilibrium framework for divergent development. For instance, the Southern growth rate persistently could be lower than the Northern growth rate, without any tendency for further relative price changes or net capital flows to take place, because profit rates are identical.

Although savings propensities are extinguished from the long-period characterization of the terms of trade, the functional distribution of income definitely matters. The mark-up, m, is by definition, the ratio of profits to wages in the North, and here it plays a direct role in setting the long-period terms of trade.

There are several lingering difficulties. Are centres of gravity for the terms of trade empirically as well as analytically of interest? Which sets of trading partners actually fit the various asymmetries assigned to North and South in this discussion? How does Lewis's observation about changing relative productivities and patterns of specialization influence the theoretical outcomes for the terms of trade? How do Marshall's (1920, p. 601) worrisome 'complex actions and reactions of credit' (and finance) impinge upon the conclusions reached here; is either the long run or long period truly independent of monetary considerations? These questions are not Solow's (1956, pp. 93–4) 'cobwebs' to be brushed lightly aside; these are serious issues to be pursued eagerly in extending the search for a serious and 'fundamental' explanation of the terms of trade between developed and developing countries.

NOTES

*   I am grateful to Andre Burgstaller, Patrick Conway, Amitava Dutt, Bobbie L. Horn, and participants at the Post-Keynesian International Workshop on Problems in Income Distribution held in Gatlinburg, Tennessee during 26 June – 3 July 1988 for useful comments and criticisms.
1. David Evans (1987) says that the empirical case does not unambiguously favour Lewis's claims of a sectoral bias in technical change in favour of temperate zone (Northern) agriculture. Evans also considers demand-side effects, asserting that a key role must be assigned to Engel curve effects in the determination of the terms of trade.
2. See Burgstaller's (1987) fifth and final stage of his classical model of trade and development.
3. There is a fundamental difference that lurks just below the surface. Northern output is a basic good while Southern output is a non-basic in a Sraffa (1960) sense. Consequently, the Northern profit rate depends only on the Northern wage ($\rho_n = f'[k_n(w_N)]$) and technology, while ρ_s depends on all the parameters in (18).
    I am grateful to Andre Burgstaller for pointing this out to me.
4. This assumption implies that Southern workers do not consume Northern output, an assumption that is made by Findlay (1981). If the more realistic assumption is made that Southern workers consume the output of both regions, then the fixed real wage must be calculated relative to a price index. If the price index, P, takes Cobb–Douglas form, for example, then $P = P_N^\lambda P_s^{1-\lambda}$. This would mean, in turn, that the Southern profit rate would be
    $$\rho_s = [\theta C_s - \theta^{(1-\lambda)} \bar{w}_s]/k_s \text{ instead of (21).}$$
5. Throughout what follows mark-ups are assumed fixed for institutional reasons described in Reynolds (1987).
6. In Burgstaller (1985), capital is treated as a wages fund rather than a produced means of production. The mobility of advances to labour across regions in response to profit rate differentials assures eventual equalization of returns. Under long-period conditions Burgstaller derives the following result for the terms of trade:

$$\theta^* = (w_s q_N)/(w_N q_s)$$

where each w_i is the wage rate in the corresponding region and each q_i is the output-labour ratio in each region. As w_i goes up or q_i goes down, production costs in each region rise. Burgstaller directly obtains a strictly classical result; the terms of trade improve as costs of production rise, and they deteriorate as costs of production decline. With capital as a produced means of production the classical result appears only indirectly, i.e. as the mark-up rises in particular region, labour's share in income falls, hence *relative* labour costs fall, and the terms of trade decline for that region. Also see the discussion in the main text at the close of section 3 above.

REFERENCES

Burgstaller, André, 'Industrialization, Deindustrialization, and North-South Trade, *American Economic Review*, Vol. 77. December 1987, pp. 1017–18.

Burgstaller, André, 'North–South Trade and Capital Flows in a Ricardian Model of Accumulation', *Journal of International Economics* Vol. 18, 1985, pp. 241–60.

Conway, Patrick and William Darity Jr, 'Growth and Trade With Asymmetric Returns to Scale: A Model for Nicholas Kaldor', mimeo, University of North Carolina at Chapel Hill, 1988.

Dutt, Amitava K., 'Monopoly Power and Uneven Development: Baran Revisited', *Journal of Development Studies* Vol. 24:2, January 1988, pp. 161–76.

Evans, David, 'The Long-Run Determinants of North–South Terms of Trade and Some Recent Empirical Evidence', *World Development,* Vol. 15:5, 1987, pp. 657–71.

Findlay, Ronald, 'The Fundamental Determinants of the Terms of Trade', in Sven Grassman and Erik Lundberg, (eds), *The World Economic Order: Past and Prospects*, London: Macmillan, 1981, pp. 425–57.

Kaldor, Nicholas, 'Alternative Theories of Distribution', *Review of Economic Studies*, Vol. 23, 1955, pp. 83–100.

Kalecki, Michal, *Selected Essays on the Dynamics of the Capitalist Economy*, Cambridge: Cambridge University Press, 1971.

Laursen, S. and L. A. Meltzer, 'Flexible Exchange Rates and the Theory of Employment', *Review of Economics and Statistics*, Vol. 32, November 1950, pp. 281–99.

Lewis, W. A., 'Economic Development With Unlimited Supplies of Labour', *The Manchester School*, Vol. 28, 1954, pp. 139–91.

Lewis, W. A., *Aspects of Tropical Trade* Stockholm: Almqvist Wicksell, 1969.

Marshall, Alfred, *Principles of Economics: An Introductory Volume*, London: Macmillan, 1920, 8th edition.

Prebisch, Raul, 'Commercial Policy in the Underdeveloped Countries', *American Economic Review*, Vol. 49, May 1959, pp. 251–73.

Reynolds, P. J. *Political Economy: A Synthesis of Kaleckian and Post Keynesian Economics*, New York: St Martin's Press, 1987.

Ricardo, David, *Principles of Political Economy and Taxation*, P. Sraffa and M. Dobb (eds), Cambridge: Cambridge University Press, 1951.

Singer, Hans, 'The Distribution of Gains Between Investing and Borrowing Countries', *American Economic Review*, Vol. 40, May 1950, pp. 473–85.

Solow, R. M., 'A Contribution to the Theory of Economic Growth', *Quarterly Journal of Economics*, Vol. 70, 1956, pp. 65–94.

Sraffa, Piero, *Production of Commodities By Means of Commodities*, Cambridge: Cambridge University Press, 1960.

Taylor, Lance, 'South–North Trade and Southern Growth: Bleak Prospects from A Structuralist Point of View', *Journal of International Economics* Vol. 11, 1981, pp. 589–601.

Weintraub, Sidney, 'Generalizing Kalecki and Simplifying Macroeconomics', *Journal of Post Keynesian Economics* Vol. I:3, Spring 1979, pp. 101–6.

10. The International Debt Trap: External and Internal Redistribution of Incomes

Sándor Nagy

The international debt crisis, one of the most pressing problems of the world economy today, is in fact an international, external distribution of incomes among sovereign countries participating in the international flow of trade and capital. The debt problem is an income distribution problem by origin and it remains one even when international money-lending has forced the debtor-countries into an international debt-trap which brings about a redistribution of incomes among the major classes within the individual countries, too.

For the international debt situation is far more than a simple net flow of resources first from the creditor-countries to the debtor-countries, and subsequently the other way around. The vast majority of the debtor-countries today are trapped in a situation where they are dependent not simply on a permanent inflow of external resources but on a constantly growing amount of foreign finance. On balance this situation means that they are highly dependent on the availability of external resources. Thus the servicing requirements of outstanding debt in these countries limits their sovereignty in economic policy and reduces their chances of growth.

EXTERNAL ASPECTS OF THE DEBT TRAP

It is generally believed that foreign credits contribute to the growth of a debtor-country if the external resources are invested so that the rate of return on investment exceeds the interest rate on foreign borrowing. Some earlier discussions of the problem (e.g. Domar, 1950; Avramovic, 1964); Solomon, 1977) have emphasized this aspect.

In the light of these contentions a country relying on external resources can avoid the permanent dependence on foreign credits by keeping domestic savings rates high and ensuring a high rate of return on

174

investment exceeding the international LIBOR-plus interest rate at the international money market.

Is it as simple as that?

Recent studies on international indebtedness (e.g. Bhaduri, A., 1981) have shown that the relationship between the interest rate on foreign borrowing and the rate of return on domestic investment is only a necessary but not a sufficient condition for avoiding permanent dependence on external resources.

On the basis of a suitably modified version of the Harrod–Domar growth model, Bhaduri has pointed out that the balance of foreign trade plays a crucial role in this relationship. Even if the first condition is fulfilled, i.e. the given country productively invests all its domestic saving and foreign borrowing and the productivity of these investments as measured by the incremental output–capital ratio is higher than the interest rate, the country must not touch foreign credits if imports permanently exceed exports.

Foreign credit is 'permissible' only if a second condition is fulfilled, i.e. the country runs a permanent export surplus the size of which is dependent on the productivity of investments, interest rates and the propensity to save, export and import. Some of these variables are effectively beyond the control of domestic policy-makers. Therefore, the fulfilment of the second requirement may prove to be impossible for the debtor-countries even if they successfully control some of the above variables.

It is clear that, within certain limits, economic policy is able to influence variables, such as the productivity of investment, and the propensity to save and import. However the propensity of a country to export depends largely on world economic conditions and, to a lesser extent, on the efforts of the given country. It hardly needs saying that fluctuations in the level of interest rates are beyond the reach of individual countries except for the major ones. These fluctuations are caused by the interplay of demand for and supply of foreign credits which have been heavily distorted by various factors over the last 15–20 years.

In the early 1970s the abundance of financial resources generated from the 'price explosion' of crude oil and other raw materials pushed down interest rates on foreign borrowing. Negative interest rates (in real terms) created favourable conditions for the developing countries and the Eastern bloc to incur large credits in the belief that this would facilitate their long-term growth.

However, in the late 1970s and the early 1980s the situation changed dramatically. The large budget deficit run up by the United States increased US demand for credits, and this pushed up interest rates. Rising interest rates coupled with sluggish world trade and falling world market prices wiped out all the debtor countries' efforts to exploit the resources they had borrowed from the creditor-countries because their financing requirements rose so dramatically that they could no longer meet them from the returns on effective domestic investments. Consequently the debtor-countries were forced to take up new credits to finance the old ones. This is a classic case of the international debt-trap.

Let me illustrate this with the case of Hungary. Computations carried out with Bhaduri's version of the Harrod–Domar growth model suggest that while in the early 1970s an export surplus of 8–10 per cent of GDP would have been enough to avoid the debt-trap, in the early 1980s 80–100 per cent of GDP would have been required as export surplus!

These are the external factors leading to the international debt-trap. However, there are internal processes which make it difficult for a debtor-country to fulfil the conditions necessary to avoid the debt trap. I shall next analyse those which are characteristic of the Eastern bloc.

INTERNAL ASPECTS OF THE DEBT TRAP

There are internal factors which move any given economy towards permanent dependence on foreign credits. However, they are not identical in the market economies and the Eastern bloc countries. One of the major differences is that the investment function in the socialist countries is a very simple one. In the developed market economies income saved is not necessarily invested (as Keynes and many others since have pointed out) therefore, external resources flowing in such economies are not necessarily invested; they may be used for many other purposes. In a socialist economy the investment behaviour of the managers of the (state-owned) enterprises face a permanent over-demand; a shortage situation of varying intensity on the market tends to be limitless and insatiable. Consequently, external resources flowing into such economies are necessarily invested and as a rule they never directly finance the consumption outlays of the household sector.

The second distinguishing feature is that due to the permanent shortage in the market in general and in the capital goods market in particular, there is strong pressure on imports that drives up the propensity of the country to import. This in turn threatens the realization of an export surplus. It is a general observation in these countries that whenever there is an upswing in general economic activity (i.e. measured in terms of growth rate) there is also an acceleration in the growth of imports. This has always occurred even on the surface in these countries whenever there was a general liberalization of import controls.

There is a distinguishing feature in respect to exports, too. The growth of exports is seriously retarded by internal shortages. However, it is difficult to increase exports because of world market conditions. According to the above-mentioned version of the Harrod–Domar growth model in relation to borrowing foreign resources, it is not enough to invest them productively and realize an export surplus in the field of foreign trade but the increment in production received from the investment of external resources should appear in those commodities accepted by the world market without serious deterioration in the terms of trade of the country. The world market never favours small countries with medium-level development.

Once a country is in the debt-trap it is forced to export at almost any cost in order to earn hard currency to pay interest on the outstanding debt and to try to reduce its level of indebtedness. However, the forced growth of exports and the 'pressure' of the world market in general leads to losses which are unevenly distributed in the economy. As a matter of course the bulk of these losses is concentrated on enterprises which sell their products in the world market and these happen to be, by Hungarian standards, the big enterprises which account for some two-thirds of Hungarian exports to the world market. Small (private and state) business very rarely takes part in the export activity of such countries.

This seems to be a major reason why many large Hungarian enterprises appear to be inefficient. In total, the fact that the country is in the debt-trap leads to a redistribution of income among the enterprises, in favour of the non-exporting ones. All this has contributed greatly to the emergence and the popularity of the belief in Hungary that only small businesses can be really effective.

As a consequence a redistribution of income has taken place among households. The income level of workers in the big enterprises started to lag behind that of workers in other enterprises, especially of those with (legal and semi-legal) access to other sources of income. Moreover policy measures taken to improve this situation (e.g. breaking up big enterprises into smaller ones) has adversely affected the workers in these big enterprises. (A great part of the unemployed belong to this group.)

The above redistribution of income among households and the various groups of workers have political implications in Hungary. The big enterprises were created in the early 1950s and they have become traditional centres of the working class, the political basis of the regime. Consequently, the adverse effects of the debt-trap and the policy measures following from it squeezes the working class and thus threatens the political and economic stability of the regime. Therefore, the handling of the present debt-trap in countries like Hungary needs considerable political tact, care and patience not only on the part of the domestic policy-makers but also on the part of the creditor banks and countries.

11. Taxation and Income Distribution: A Kaleckian Approach*

Andrea Szegö

Kalecki distinguished between two types of economies: demand-constrained and resource-constrained. The first type he identified with the advanced capitalist, the latter with the socialist countries.

Taxation has been applied as one of the more or less successful instruments of economic policy in the advanced capitalist countries suffering from a lack of effective demand. In the socialist countries suffering from excess demand, i.e. permanent shortages, the most recent rounds of economic reforms have focused attention on the application of various tax systems as possible means to curb excess demand. In fact, in Hungary, a value added and a personal income tax system were introduced on 1 January 1988.

There is a fairly wide-scale belief that these tax systems tend to operate in the socialist countries more or less in the same way as in the advanced capitalist countries. In the present chapter we shall challenge this contention.

It is a well-known fact that taxation is the income of the state. However, Hungarian economists seem to be less aware of the question of how income distribution is influenced by taxation and spending of tax receipts by the state.

By income distribution the distribution of both nominal and real incomes are understood, since for economic and social policy the latter is of fundamental importance because only in view of changes in the distribution of real incomes can one answer the question 'who carries the tax burden?'

The present chapter is concerned with the short-run effects of taxation on income distribution, i.e. it does not analyse how the secondary price and wage modifications influence the positions of the individual income owners in the long run. The reason for this is that the influence of taxation on price formation is very difficult to separate from other components. It is, however, an elementary fact that in the short run under conditions of permanent excess demand prevailing in a socialist economy the turnover tax raises the price level by its total amount. It is also a realistic assumption that the total amount of profit tax can also be charged to the consumer.

MACRO-PROFIT THEORY AND TAX INCIDENCE

According to popular reasoning in economics indirect taxes (turnover taxes) are paid in the final analysis by the consumer, whereas direct taxes can partly be further charged. Thus, it is assumed that capitalists can charge a part of their profit taxes to the consumers and its exact proportion is determined by the specific demand supply conditions.

A conclusion is usually drawn from this in welfare policy, according to which indirect taxes are of the most anti-social character and income and especially profit taxes are suitable tools to meet the requirements of social justice to bring about a certain degree of levelling of income differences. These conclusions relate exclusively to the positions of individual income owners and thus do not examine changes taking place at the aggregate level of the main sectors of the economy (the corporate sector, households, the state). However, tax policy cannot approach these questions with the logic of microeconomics since in this field it is the macro economic changes (i.e. shifts in the income positions of the individual classes, social sectors) that are the issues to be examined.

In fact, even the microeconomic analysis of the effects of taxation tries to explain macroeconomic phenomena since the question is always how modifications in tax incidence and tax rates influence the distribution of income among the corporate sector, households and state budget. However, this approach presupposes the application of an adequate macroeconomic income theory. Therefore, in the present chapter the income effects of taxation are discussed in the light of Kalecki's macro-profit theory.

In this theory Kalecki lays main emphasis on the fact that the state not only collects taxes but also spends them. From this he draws the conclusion that in the case of a balanced budget profit taxes raise by their total amount the level of profit compared to the situation without taxation. Consequently, taxation does not reduce the level of profit.

On the surface this theory is not concerned with tax incidence since it places emphasis on the balance of the budget in the generation of profit. Following from this the advocates of the Kaleckian political economy arrive at the conclusion that – provided that the budget is balanced – profit tax does not place a burden on capitalists as a class since as a consequence of state intervention there is a rise in the level of national income and this increment finances the additional expenditures of the state and the state employees. However, this result holds only if capacities are not fully utilized in the economy.

ELEMENTS OF MACRO-PROFIT AND THEIR RELATIONSHIP

The individual components of macro-profit are usually examined separately. However, these components are closely interrelated: these relationships rest on direct mechanisms in some cases and on deeper economic laws working themselves through in a rather complicated and indirect manner in others.

The direct automatism appears in the first place in the field of inventory accumulation since, except for certain specific budget implications, changes in any profit component influence the level of inventory accumulation in the enterprises. The basic theoretical reason for this is that in the course of the production process, commodities constituting national income or GDP are held by the capitalist class – or by the corporate sector in the socialist economies – consequently every individual act of exchange modifies the volume of commodities held by them.

In cases of corporate investment in fixed capital or in inventories, the total volume of these commodities remains unchanged; their value, however, increases since for the sellers these commodities were accounted in factor costs only. This implies that investment in fixed capital is necessarily a disinvestment in inventories and the amount of profit generated is, in fact, equal to the amount of inventory disinvestment. The same applies to consumption by capitalists.

In the case of purchases made by other income owners, it is obvious that the volume of commodities held by the capitalist class – the corporate sector in the socialist economies – decreases and is replaced by the amount of money received. It follows from this that the purchases made by the state budget, the households or the rest of the world increase the amount of macro-profit realized not by their total sum but only by the difference between the total amount of money received and of the inventory disinvestment.

Similar complications may arise in understanding the influence of the state budget on corporate profits. Here the most important thing is that purchases made from the state budget, i.e. the flow of commodities from the corporate sector to the state, have a different impact on the generation of profit from transfers from the state budget, i.e. the flow of money without the counter-flow of commodities. State purchases modify the amount of commodities held by the corporate sector. Thus these purchases constitute a part of the inventory adjustments as against the purely financial transfers (subsidies) from the state budget.

Inventory adjustment is absent in the case of taxation and transfers from the state budget since inventory adjustment does not function if there are only money flows without counter-flows of commodities between the main income owners. It is quite probable that this phenomenon explains why in everyday life, tax appears as a tool for centralizing incomes in the state budget and state transfers and subsidies appear as increases in corporate profits. In publications on socialist economies this is not only accepted but, under the heading state redistribution and paternalism, it is raised to the status of a general theory.

Indirect relationships operate primarily through decisions of other income owners (state, households, rest of the world). One of Kalecki's well-known statements is that, in the so-called pure model, by determining the level of investment and consumption, capitalists decide for themselves the level of their income, i.e. their profit. However, the relationship described above indicate that the profit level of the capitalist class is also influenced by the behaviour of the other income owners. Saving and investment by capitalists may be equal (i.e. the duplication of savings into commodities, real assets and money ceases to exist) only if the savings of other income owners are equal to zero.

In this relationship the state, the wage earners and the rest of the world play a direct role, although they do not determine the direction of their activity completely independently of the corporate sector. In the case of the state and the rest of the world, we can speak of deliberate economic policy actions coordinated at the macro-level (e.g. deficit financing economic policy or the so-called export-led economic growth path). However, when elaborating the theory of political cycles, Kalecki cautioned that although a budget deficit increases the current profits of the capitalist class, they may still exert political pressure on the state to follow an orthodox (balanced) budget policy.

In view of the internal relationships of the profit components one can draw the conclusion, a lesson for the regulation of the socialist economy, that the control of the inventory automatism seems to be decisive nowadays for both economic theory and practical economic policy. For in view of the investment over-demand, the socialist state cannot do without the regulation of accumulation within the corporate sector and this is possible if not only investment in fixed capital but also investment in inventories is under the direct control of the state.

Unsuccessful attempts made to date in Hungary to bring cycles of fixed capital investment and inventory accumulation under control indicate that the regulation of the process of inventory accumulation presupposes knowledge of the whole system of inventory automatism. This would put economic policy organs in a situation where a not fully developed investment cycle has to be curbed, and consequently the less direct instruments of control can be used. Thus our research work in this field (in contrast to the current reform concept based on the idea of the self-regulating market) indicates we should renew economic planning, i.e. lay the foundations of an alternative theory for the reform of the socialist economy.

Non-automatic relationships among profit components are at least of similar importance for the macroeconomic analysis. We should focus our attention on the relationship between state budget and the balance of foreign trade, the level of consumption and of investment and the export surplus. However we shall not analyse the latter here.

TAX INCIDENCE AND INVENTORY AUTOMATISM

Due to the interrelatedness of the profit components discussed above, tax incidence does have an influence on the level of macro-profit. If profit tax pushes prices up, enterprises replenish their inventories at higher prices and thus *ceteris paribus* the real value of their net inventory accumulation decreases. Such an effect would not appear in the case of traditional taxes on sales (turnover taxes) since, as it is commonly known, they only increase consumer prices. Wage taxes also leave the level of macro-profit unchanged in the short run as long as they do not have an effect on prices.

Taxation on profit in fact reduces the level of real profits through changes in inventories, in contrast to taxes on wages and sales which modify the distribution of real incomes only in the long run as a result of successful wage rounds. Thus, for the capitalist class it is still advantageous to have a tax structure in which taxes on wages and sales account for the larger part.

An analysis of the influence of the tax structure on real incomes permits us to answer the question: 'Who carries the tax burden?' In the case of wage and turnover taxes (as we shall see in the model computations) wage and salary earners are adversely affected since turnover taxes do nor reduce the consumption outlays of the capitalists. In the case of profit tax, the burden is shared (in the short run) between those receiving income from capital and those income from employment.

In the case of nominal incomes a different situation arises. *Ceteris paribus,* neither wage nor turnover taxes influence the level of nominal profit since they do not modify the price level of any profit component. However, profit tax raises the level of nominal profit if the rate of inflation is higher than the rate of cost increases taking place due to taxation.

To the many paradoxes of the Kaleckian theory, we think, a new one can be added: an increase in nominal macro-profit can be accompanied by a decline in real profit, (provided the balance of the state budget remains unchanged). If, however, price increases only counter-balance the tax burden or lag behind them nominal profit declines despite increasing prices on capital goods and inventories, because – if the level of GDP remains unchanged – the volume of use values (commodities held by the corporate sector) will decrease.

In view of the analysis of how income distribution is influenced by taxation, we have to modify the contention according to which profit tax increases by its own amount the level of macro-profit compared to the situation without taxation.

As an immediate response, the spending of taxes results in a reduction in the level of net inventory accumulation which means that the level of after-tax profit will be smaller by the above reduction in the value of inventories (which is equal to the $c + v$ value element of the commodities sold) than the level of profit without taxation.

This relationship is usually presented not as a necessary connection among the profit components, as the rule of the inventory automatism but as the mutual transition between cost and income elements. (The real content of this transition is that income accrual is a decline in inventories.)

It follows from this that profit tax raises the level of profit compared to the situation without taxation by its own amount only if the spending of taxes is accompanied by such secondary multiplier effects which through increases in the level of production and prices counter-balance the decrease in the value of inventories. A presentation of the precise functioning of the multipliers in this context is still missing from the (Hungarian) professional literature.

Profit before tax presents almost the whole spending from the state budget as deficit financing which, due to inventory automatism, also increases the level of macro-profit by an amount equal to total spending less the decline in inventories. Consequently, it is obvious that (*ceteris paribus*) the level of profit before tax is much higher than that of profit without taxation, however, the difference cannot be the same as the sum of taxes.

Therefore, in the case of a balanced budget the profit-decreasing effect of taxation can in fact be counter-balanced only by a multiplier mechanism and it is exclusively a coincidence if a tax produces an increment in profits compared to the level which would be produced without taxation which happened to be equal to its own amount.

Kalecki's macro-profit theory proves that although Lassalle and his advocates did not follow up their statements concerning taxation to the end, and they only examined microeconomic implications, they nevertheless arrived at correct conclusions in relation to welfare policy, i.e. they gave the right answer to the question: 'Who pays the taxes?'

As a matter of fact even Marx did not analyse the influence of taxation on the distribution of incomes. In his message on the occasion of the foundation of the First International (like Lassalle) he took the stand that the working class had to struggle to replace indirect taxes by direct taxes, although the clarification of this question is missing from his economic theory.

In the appendix we illustrate this argument with the help of the Marxian schemes of reproduction. In these calculations it is assumed that the individual taxes are newly introduced and their effect is examined in comparison to the situation prevailing before the introduction of the given tax. Consequently, the cross-impacts of various taxes are not analysed. Another constraint of the model is that the level of GDP remains constant, which means that our investigation is confined to the effects of western-type taxes introduced into a socialist (i.e. resource-constrained) economy.

APPENDIX
AN ANALYSIS OF THE INFLUENCE OF TAXATION ON INCOME DISTRIBUTION BASED ON THE MARXIAN SCHEMES OF REPRODUCTION

In the following analysis the calculations are carried out with the following version of the Marxian schemes of reproduction:

The economy consists of four enterprises and the rate of profit tax is 10 per cent for each enterprise. In order to simplify calculations amortization is ignored.

Enterprise A: $100c + 50v + 50m = 200T$
Enterprise B: $100c + 50v + 50m = 200T$
Enterprise C: $100c + 50v + 50m = 200T$
Enterprise D: $100c + 50v + 50m = 200T$

where T stands for commodity.

I. The Influence of Profit Tax on Income Distribution

In response to the 10 per cent profit tax each enterprise raises prices by 5 units, i.e. charges the total amount of profit tax to the consumers. The value of the output of the individual enterprises increases correspondingly from 200 to 205.

Step 1

Wages are paid. 0 profit = 200 units of net inventory accumulation – 200 units wage saved.

Step 2

Workers purchase for 200v .200T from enterprise D where the equation is: 97.56c + 48.78v + 53.66m = 200T, i.e. 53,66P units of profit was realized. (P stands for profit.)
    53.66P = (200 – 146.34 = 53.66) inventory accumulation.
    Enterprise D holds an inventory valued in factor costs: 2.44c + 1.22v = 3.66. (When calculated in selling prices its value is 2.44c + 1.22v + 1.22m = 5T.)
    After the wages are spent the distribution of national income in current prices:

Enterprise A: 50   units
Enterprise B: 50   units
Enterprise C: 50   units
Enterprise D: – 96.34 units (1.22 – 97.56 = – 96.34)
Workers: 200 units

Enterprise sector total: 53.66 units
Workers total: 200   units

National income total: 253.66 units

After wages are spent the distribution of national income in constant prices:

Enterprise A: 50   units
Enterprise B: 50   units
Enterprise C: 50   units
Enterprise D: – 96.34 units (1.22 – 97.56 = – 96.34)
Workers: 195.12 units

Enterprise sector total: 53.66 units
Workers total: 195.12 units

National income total: 248.78 units

Step 3

Enterprise A buys 200T units of commodities from enterprise B to hold them as inventory. The equation for enterprise B: 97.56c + 48.78v + 53.66m = 200T: Profit realized 53.66P units. 107.33P = 107.33 inventory accumulation. Enterprise B holds output inventory valued in factor cost according to the following equation: 2.44c + 1.22v = 3.66.
    The distribution of national income in current prices:

Enterprise A: 250   units
Enterprise B: – 94.34 units (1.22 – 97.56 = – 96.34)
Enterprise C: 50   units
Enterprise D: – 96.34 units (1.22 – 97.56 = – 96.34)
Workers: 200 units

Enterprise sector total: 107.32 units
Workers total: 200   units

National income total: 307.32 units

The distribution of national income in constant prices:

Enterprise A: 245.12 units (50 + 195.12 = 245.12)
Enterprise B: −96.34 units (1.22 − 97.56 = −96.34)
Enterprise C: 50   units
Enterprise D: −96.34 units (1.22 − 97.56 = −96.34)
Workers: 195.12 units

Enterprise sector total: 102.44 units
Workers total: 195.12 units

National income total: 297.56 units

Step 4

Enterprises B and D pay the state the profit tax. Its total amount is 10.73a units. (Where a stands for tax.) Their profit after tax is 107.33 − 10.733 = 96.597P.
   96.597P = 107.33 units of net inventory accumulation − 10.733 budget surplus.

Step 5

From the 10a units of tax receipts the state purchases 5T units of commodity from enterprises B and D each.
   The corresponding equations are:

Enterprise B: 2.44c + 1.22v + 1.22m + 0.12a = 5T
Enterprise D: 2.44c + 1.22v + 1.22m + 0.12a = 5T

The amount of profit realized at enterprises B and D is 1.34P respectively, 2.68 in total.
   99.277P = 100.01 units of net inventory accumulation − 0.733 budget surplus.
   The distribution of national income in current prices:

Enterprise A: 250   units
Enterprise B: −100   units
Enterprise C: 50   units
Enterprise D: −100   units
Workers: 200   units
State budget: 10   units

Enterprise sector total: 100   units
Workers total: 200   units
State budget total: 10   units

National income total: 310   units

The distribution of national income in constant prices:

Enterprise A: 245.12 units
Enterprise B: −100   units

Enterprise C: 50   units
Enterprise D: − 100   units
Workers: 195.12 units
State budget: 9.76 units

Enterprise sector total: 95.12 units
Workers total: 195.12 units
State budget total: 9.76 units

National income total: 300   units

This means that the 9.76 unit real consumption of the state was financed in 50 to 50 per cent by the enterprise and household sector. (4.88 unit decline in consumption in real terms in each sector.)

After step 5. enterprises B and D have sold their total output. Enterprises A and C have sold nothing. The distribution of purchases made:

200T (195.12T in real terms) units by enterprise A;
10T (9.76T in real terms) units by the state budget;
200T (195.12T in real terms) units by the workers.

There was a decline in inventories at enterprise D y 100T in both nominal and real terms, by OT in nominal and by − 4.88T in real terms at the enterprise A.

Step 6

Enterprise D purchases 200T units of commodity from enterprise A to replenish inventories. The equation for enterprise A: $97.56c + 48.78v + 53.66m = 200T$, i.e. profit realized is 53.66P units.

152.937P = 153.67 units of net inventory accumulation − 0.733 budget surplus. The distribution of national income in current prices:

Enterprise A: 103.66 units (200 + 1.22 − 97.56 = 103.66)
Enterprise B: − 100   units
Enterprise C: 50   units
Enterprise D: 100   units
Workers: 200   units
State budget: 10   units

Enterprise sector total: 153.66 units
Workers total: 200   units
State budget total: 10   units

National income total: 363.66 units

The distribution of national income in constant prices:

Enterprise A: 98.78 units (195.12 + 1.22 − 97.56 = 98.78)
Enterprise B: − 100   units
Enterprise C: 50   units
Enterprise D: 95.12 units

Workers: 195.12 units
State budget: 9.76 units

Enterprise sector total: 143.90 units
Workers total: 195.12 units
State budget total: 9.76 units

National income total: 348.78 units

Step 7

Enterprise B purchases 200T units of commodity to accumulate as inventory. The equation for enterprise C: $97.56c + 48.78v + 53.66m = 200T$ i.e. profit realised is 53.66P.

$206.597P = 207.33$ units of net inventory accumulation − 0.733 budget surplus.

The distribution of national income in current prices:

Enterprise A: 103.66 units
Enterprise B: 100   units
Enterprise C: − 96.34 units $(1.22 − 97.56 = 96.34)$
Enterprise D: 100   units
Workers: 200   units
State budget: 10   units

Enterprise sector total: 207.32 units
Workers total: 200   units
State budget total: 10   units

National income total: 417.32 units

The distribution of national income in constant prices:

Enterprise A: 98.78 units
Enterprise B: 95.12 units
Enterprise C: − 96.34 units
Enterprise D: 95.12 units
Workers: 195.12 units
State budget: 9.76 units

Enterprise sector total: 192.68 units
Workers total: 195.12 units
State budget total: 9.76 units

National income total: 397.56 units

Step 8

Enterprises A and C pay the profit tax into the state budget. Its amount being 10.733a. The total amount of profit after tax is 195.864P $(206.957P − 10.733a)$.

195.846P = 207.33 units of net inventory accumulation − 11.466 budget surplus.

Step 9

From the 10a units of tax receipts the state budget purchases from enterprises A and C 5 − 5 units of commodity each. The corresponding equations are:

Enterprise A: 2.44c + 1.22v + 1.22m + 0.12a = 5T
Enterprise C: 2.44c + 1.22v + 1.22m + 0.12a = 5T

The total amount of profit realised is 2.68P units (1.34P + 1.34P).
198.544P = 200 units of net inventory accumulation − 1.466 budget surplus.
The distribution of national income in current prices:

Enterprise A: 100   units (103.66 − 3.66 = 100)
Enterprise B: 100   units
Enterprise C: − 100   units
Enterprise D: 100   units
Workers: 200   units
State budget: 20   units

Enterprise sector total: 200   units
Workers total: 200   units
State budget total: 20   units

National income total: 420   units

The distribution of national income in constant prices:

Enterprise A: 95.12 units
Enterprise B: 95.12 units
Enterprise C: − 100   units
Enterprise D: 95.12 units
Workers: 195.12 units
State budget: 19.52 units

Enterprise sector total: 185.36 units
Workers total: 195.12 units
State budget total: 19.52 units

National income total: 400   units

In real terms of the 19.52 unit purchases made by the state budget 14.64, i.e. $\frac{3}{4}$, was charged to the enterprise sector and 4.88, i.e. $\frac{1}{3}$, to the household sector, i.e. to the wage and salary earners, despite the fact that in the situation without taxation, state budget the distribution of national income between the above two sectors was 50 − 50 per cent. The explanation for this is that inventory accumulation which in current prices seemed to be an inventory replenishment was an inventory disinvestment in constant prices.

The distribution of the tax burden is proportional to purchases made: the total purchase of the enterprises was 615T in current prices and that of the population 205T (with the value of social product being 4 times 205 = 820T). This means that $\frac{3}{4}$ of social product was held by the enterprises and 50 per cent of this was inventory replenishment and 25 per cent net inventory accumulation. The consumption of the population accounted for $\frac{1}{4}$ of the social product.

As a result of state purchase the distribution of the social product – in constant prices – was the following:

Enterprises	73.13%	((185.36 + 400)/800)
Workers	24.39%	(195.12/800)
State	2.44%	(19.52/800)

The corresponding figures in current prices:

Enterprises	73.17%	(600/820)
Workers	24.33%	(200/820)
State	2.44%	(20/820)

Incomes realized by the enterprise sector constitute, in real terms, inventory disinvestment – 9.76 units, consequently real income of the enterprise sector corrected for inventory desinvestment is 185.36 units.

In the present model an increase in the prices of inventories did not lead to an increase in the level of nominal profit because simultaneously with this there was a decline in inventories and the two factors counter balanced one another.

Unit price of inventory before tax was 200/200 = 1, after tax 205/200 = 1.025. Without state taxation the inventory accumulation of enterprises amounts to 200 × 1 = 200. In the case of purchases made from the state budget it is 1.025 × 195.12 = 199.999, i.e. the nominal value of inventory accumulation is identical in both cases, since in the second case there was a minor budget surplus the level of nominal profit was somewhat lower.

A conclusion can be drawn from all this that budget surplus leads to an increase in the level of macro-profit only if the level of national income or GDP increases, too.

II. The Influence of Wage and Turnover Taxes on the Distribution of Real Incomes

A. The influence of wage tax

Our basic assumption is that a 10 per cent wage tax is levied and 50 per cent of the tax receipts are spent by the state on purchase of commodities and services and the other 50 per cent is paid as salary to the state employees. (In SNA this latter item is also regarded as a purchase of services.)

If the state and the state employees spend their incomes and save nothing nominal demand remains unchanged. Let us assume that due to unchanged demand prices remain stable, too.

The model used here consists also of 4 equations:

Enterprise A: 100c + 50c + 50m = 200T
Enterprise B: 100c + 50v + 50m = 200T
Enterprise C: 100c + 50v + 50m = 200T
Enterprise D: 100c + 50v + 50m = 200T

Step 1

Wages are paid.
0 Profit = 200 units of net inventory accumulation − 200 units saved by the population.

Step 2

Wage taxes are collected by the state.
0 Profit = 200 units of net inventory accumulation − 180 units saved by the population − 20 units budget surplus.

Step 3

State employees receive 10v2 units of salary.
0 Profit = 200 units of net inventory accumulation − 190 units saved by the population − 10 units budget surplus.

Step 4

Workers buy 180v units of consumer goods from enterprise D. The corresponding equation for enterprise D: 90c + 45v + 45m = 180T i.e. 45P units of profit are realised.
45P units Profit = 65 units of net inventory accumulation − 10 units saved by the employees − 10 units budget surplus.

Step 5

The employees buy 10T units of commodity for 10v2 from enterprise D. The corresponding equation for enterprise D: 5c + 2.5v + 2.5m = 10T, i.e. 2.5P units of profit are realised.
47.5P units Profit = 57.5 units of net inventory accumulation − − 10 units budget surplus.

Step 6

The state buys for 10 units of tax 10T units of commodity from enterprise D. The corresponding equation for enterprise D: 5c + 2.5v + 2.5m = 10T i.e. 2.5P units of profit are realised again.
50P = 50 units of net inventory accumulation.

Step 7

After this enterprises make purchases among themselves. Since enterprise D sold total output total turnover amounts to 600T of which 400T inventory replenishment, 100T inventory accumulation and 100T investment. (This distribution is not necessarily so!)

200P = 100 units of net inventory accumulation + 100 investment.

After all the purchases were made the distribution of national income is the following among the main income owners: enterprise sector: 200T; workers: 180T; state employees: 10T; state budget: 10T.

As a consequence of the wage tax both nominal and real profits remained unchanged in the short run and the expenditures of the state budget and state employees were charged exclusively to the workers.

Decrease in the real wages of the workers = expenditures of the stable budget and state employees.

B.   The influence of the turnover tax

The total amount of turnover tax collected by the state is identical with the 20 unit wage tax if the tax rate is 10 per cent and it is levied on state purchases, too. Due to this tax the total value of the output of enterprise D increases to 220T.

Step 1

Wages are paid.

0 Profit = 200 units of net inventory accumulation – 200 units saved by the population.

Step 2

For 200v units of wage the workers buy consumer goods 200T units in current prices and 181.8T units in real terms from enterprise D.

The corresponding equation for enterprise D: 90.90c + 45.45v + 45.45m + 18.2a = 200T i.e. 45.45P units of profit were realised after 18.2 units of tax were paid.

45.45P = 63.65 units of net inventory accumulation – 18.2 units budget surplus.

Step 3

The state pays 10v2 units of salary to the state employees.

45.45P = 63.65 units of net inventory accumulation – 10 units saved by the state employees – 8.2 budget surplus.

Step 4

State employees purchase for their 10v2 units of salary 10T units of commodity, 8.9 units in real terms from enterprise D.

The corresponding equation for enterprise D: $4.545c + 2.2725v + 2.2725m + 0.905a = 10T$ i.e. $2.2725P$ units of profit were realised after 0.905 units of tax were paid.

$47.7225P = 56.8325$ units of net inventory accumulation $- 9.10518.2$ units budget surplus.

Step 5

For the 9.105 units of turnover tax and .895 units of short term credit the state buys 10T units of commodity (8.9 units in real terms) from enterprise D which sold by this its total output.

The corresponding equation for enterprise D: $4.545c + 2.2725c + 2.2725m + 0.905a = 10T$ i.e. $2.2725P$ units of profit were realised again after 0.905 units of tax were paid.

$49.995P = 50.015$ units of net inventory accumulation $- 0.10\ 18.2$ units budget surplus.

The final sum of turnover tax paid is 2.01 units which is in fact 20 units. If the 0.01 unit of budget (tax) surplus is ignored the distribution of nominal incomes is: Workers 200v; state employees 10v2; state 10a; enterprise sector 200P.

The distribution of real national income:

Real accumulation of the enterprise sector	200T
Real consumption of the workers	181.8T
Real consumption of state employees	9.09T
Real consumption of the state	9.09T
Total	399.99T

It is clear again that the consumption of the state and the state employees is a deduction from the consumption of the workers. Since turnover tax was levied also on commodities purchased by the state and state employees the real consumption of the workers was only slightly higher here than in the case of 10 per cent wage tax. Therefore, the influence of wage and turnover taxes can be taken as practically identical.

NOTE

* Based on a joint paper with G. Weiner.

12. Some Short- and Long-Term Barriers to Income Redistribution in a Monetary Production Economy: An Illustration from the Recent Brazilian Experience*

Fernando J. Cardim de Carvalho

1. INCOME DISTRIBUTION IN A MONETARY ECONOMY

In 1933 Keynes published a paper where he stated that he was working towards the construction of a new notion in economics. He was looking for a meaningful concept of monetary economy (or a monetary production economy), where money was not neutral either in the long or in the short period. Keynes's paper was only the announcement of a revolution, with few details of how it would come about. By the time the paper was being published, however, Keynes was working on a series of drafts of the *General Theory* where the concept of monetary economy was taking definite form. Classical economics focused either on 'cooperative' economies, where transactions were made in kind, or on 'neutral' economies, where

> the factors [of production] are hired by entrepreneurs for money but where there is a mechanism of some kind to ensure that the exchange value of the money incomes of the factors is always equal in the aggregate to the proportion of current output which would have been the factor's share in a cooperative economy. . . (Keynes, 1979, p. 78)

In contrast, in a monetary (or entrepreneur) economy, 'entrepreneurs hire the factors for money but without such a mechanism as the above' characteristic of neutral economies (ibid.). According to Keynes, 'it is obvious . . . that it is in an entrepreneur economy that we actually live today' (ibid.). In such an economy, 'the volume of output which yields the maximum value of product in excess of real cost may be "unprofitable" ' (ibid., p. 67). This may happen because in monetary economies effective

195

demand may be deficient (ibid., pp. 80–1, 86).

The implications of these principles for the theory of employment are well known. But even a quick glance at the way Keynes presented his notion of a monetary economy is sufficient also to identify the lines along which the discussion of the determinants of the profile of income distribution should proceed.

Two main features defined the way a monetary economy works. On the one hand, purchases and sales are contracted in terms of money instead of goods. Sellers and buyers enter into forward money contracts on the basis of their expectations of the evolution of purchasing power of money in terms of their relevant baskets of goods. When the time comes, agents receive money, not goods, which they can spend whenever they want to in whatever goods they may desire. On the other hand, these economies lack mechanisms of pre-coordination of decisions. There are no means by which would-be spenders can (or have to) specify the nature and the timing of their demands to orient sellers with certainty.

From these features, two main implications may be derived. First, as Davidson (1982, p. 68) has put it in his criticism of Clower's Say's Principle, it is liquidity, not real income, that constrains purchases. In a monetary economy money buys goods; but money can be earned as income or be obtained by issuing debt. Secondly, the level of income (and of employment) to be generated depends on the expectations of firms as to how much they will be able to gain when the period of production is over and sales are completed.

A model of income distribution for a monetary economy has to be compatible with these features. It has to deal with money forward contracts, liquidity, financial transactions, expectations of money profits and changes in money prices and wages. However, none of the available models of income distribution, which in some sense are connected to Keynes, complies fully with these requirements.

2.   KEYNESIAN AND RELATED MODELS

Keynesian models of income distribution draw their foundations from two main sources: 1. Kalecki's papers on the determination of profits [1] relating the *structure* of aggregate demand to income distribution; and 2. Harrod's extension of the *General Theory* to long-period analysis, in which the equilibrium growth path of the economy was related to its propensity to save.

Kaldor was the pioneer among the authors of post- (or neo-) Keynesian models combining these features. To put it very succinctly, the central proposition of these models is that an economy can adjust to an (externally given) equilibrium growth path through changes in income distribution. If a given growth rate requires an amount of investment that exceeds full-employment savings, inflation redistributes income in favour of profits. The propensity to save out of profits is supposed to be higher than that out of wages, so that redistribution ensures that the growth path can then be sustained.[2]

The solution to Harrod's 'knife-edge' problem was thus proposed to reside in changes in distribution. Investment expenditures had a priority claim on income. As Kaldor assumed full employment, this meant that consumption was determined as a residual. Given the assumption that most (or all) of investment was financed out of profits, while most (or all) the consumption was financed out of wages, the distribution of full-employment income between profits and wages was then determined.[3]

Compared to Kaldor's neo-Keynesian model of distribution, Kalecki's approach is less definite in its results. Kalecki proposes a theory of profits in which only capitalists' expenditures may be independent of current income. Workers neither save nor dis-save, having their expenditures constrained by wage-income. As capitalists' expenditures are not constrained by earned profits, the necessary equality, under conditions specified by Kalecki, between aggregate profits and aggregate value of investment and capitalist consumption led him to propose that causality runs from the latter to the former.[4]

Kalecki's theory is much less definite about the profit share, that is the relation between profits and wages. The model is generally closed by assuming a definite relationship between profits and wages based on microeconomic relations, such as the degree of monopoly. Kalecki, however, never offered a satisfactory theory of the degree of monopoly. In his *Theory of Economic Dynamics* he presented a measure of it and some brief remarks about what may influence its size. A measure, however, is not a theory.

In some of his works Kalecki introduced an instrument borrowed from Rosa Luxemburg and, more distantly, from Marx (Kalecki, 1971, ch. 14). He assumed that all productive sectors could be aggregated in three 'departments': department I producing investment goods; department II producing luxuries for capitalists' consumption; and department III producing wage goods. According to Kalecki, the departments should be taken to include the production of their inputs, being completely vertically integrated.[5] In this model, if the difference between wage goods and luxuries is well marked so that workers cannot consume goods from department II, once capitalists decide how much to invest and to consume, the amount of employment in sectors I and II is determined. The amount of employment in department III then has to be sufficient to supply wage goods to workers in departments I and II as well as to its own workers. Thus, for a given wage, the aggregate shares are determined. Possibilities of income redistribution in such an economy are limited by the size (or growth rate) of department III.

The central difficulty of the model resides in its necessity of sharply differentiating wage goods from goods consumed by capitalists. More general versions of this kind of model, such as Marx's own (Marx, 1978) rely only on the difference between consumption and investment goods. In modern capitalist economies, mass production probably falsifies Kalecki's hypothesis in determining the results again.[6]

If Kalecki's premises are insufficient to close a model of income distribution, one should recognize that Kaldor's model does it only at the cost of having to introduce some heroic assumptions. First, the model is built for full employment conditions, making it possible to treat income as given. Changes in aggregate profits then become changes in profit shares. The second assumption is that investment is externally given. Again, in a steady-state model with an accelerator-type of investment function at full employment, one is prevented from investigating other possible feedbacks on investment or investigating the possibility of changing demand patterns. Technology is introduced in the model through a technical progress function that gives the equilibrium rate of investment to which income distribution has to be adjusted.

Both Kaldor's and Kalecki's models are insufficient as explanations of income distribution in a monetary economy. They are basically 'real' models in which demands in real terms determine income shares. Kaldor does introduce price variations but as an *ad hoc* mechanism of adjustment requiring a full employment assumption. Kalecki does not deal with money prices and his treatment of financial variables is rather perfunctory. He assumes that the supply of finance is infinitely elastic to capitalists but completely inelastic to workers. As a consequence, once an expenditure plan is adopted by capitalists nothing can prevent it from being implemented and, therefore, the profits from materializing.[7] The whole discussion is actually conducted in real terms, so there is no space for monetary or financial variables in the model.[8] Both models actually try to determine the behaviour of profits, introducing strong arbitrary assumptions to obtain also the behaviour of income shares.

The perplexities of the question are not eased by appealing to other non-orthodox models, such as the neo-Ricardian production prices model. Nor does this approach deal with money prices or remunerations, but with the distribution of surpluses of goods an economy may generate, given technology, above its physical reproduction. In reality, neo-Ricardian models are concerned with the effects of distribution on relative prices rather than distribution itself. The model is open with respect to shares as long as some minimum requirements are respected, such as the real wages being sufficient to ensure the survival of workers, etc.

In conclusion, the principles that define the workings of a monetary economy, although obviously related to the question of income distribution, are not yet adequately integrated into even Keynesian models. These models can be used to describe, under certain assumptions, a given distribution profile but they do not allow us to understand how it was actually achieved nor how it could be modified. This is so because they do not show how real-world variables, such as money wages and prices, are set or finance is obtained. One still largely relies on treatments that may even be incompatible with the fundamentals of a monetary economy.

3. DETERMINANTS OF INCOME DISTRIBUTION IN A MONETARY ECONOMY

The core of Keynes's *General Theory* could be seen as consisting in the rejection of the orthodox view that a decentralized market economy had a unique equilibrium position determined by objective factors such as technology and availability of materials and/or labour force. A monetary economy, in contrast, may find itself in any number of 'unemployment equilibrium' positions, depending on the state of expectations and the policy of the authorities. As Keynes noted in a fragment dated November 1932, the point was not just a difference between the variety of possibilities open in the short period against the uniqueness of long-period results. He stated that 'there is no unique long-period position of equilibrium equally valid regardless of the character of the policy of the monetary authority' (Keynes, 1979, p. 55).

That Keynes did not think this 'indeterminacy' to be restricted to the level of income but also to attach to income distribution is witnessed by the opening pages of chapter 24 of *The General Theory* (Keynes, 1964, pp. 372–4). The profile of income distribution is not solely the result of the operation of purely economic mechanisms. It is the result of a conflict that is ultimately decided by power. These power relations are reflected in the institutions and rules that limit and organize the distributive conflict. Being part of a larger social process, there is no *a priori* reason to suppose a unique distribution profile to be compatible with the operation of a given economy.

Joan Robinson has noted that '[t]he capitalist rules of the game are favourable to establishing property in debts' (Robinson, 1969, p. 7). More generally, however, one could say that the rules of the game in a monetary economy are favourable to profits against labour incomes. This has been known at least since Adam Smith pointed out the greater ease with which capitalists can organize themselves when contrasted to the association of workers (Smith, 1974). Smith's argument, however, and all of its modern variants, refer to a power balance that can change and has changed. The rise of large and powerful unions in the twentieth century has shown that big numbers need not be an impediment to organization. There is a deeper sense, however, in which we may say that the rules favour profits and it has to do with the way prices are set.

Atemporal neoclassical theory tends to make us forget the sequential nature of capitalist production. In contrast to general equilibrium models, exchanges in real capitalist economies are not all simultaneous. Goods and factor services are not traded directly for each other, with all prices being determined at the same instant. In the real world, production (and investment) takes time and has to be organized before the sale of final goods can take place. Pricing of factors of production and of final goods face different constraints.

Firms operating in a monetary production economy have to develop strategies to cope with an uncertain future. They do not limit themselves to react to the environment but they try to shape it in their favour. Controlling financial resources and physical means of production, their expectations and decisions largely determine important elements of the environment in which they operate, such as the income of buyers (Keynes, 1964, ch.3). Nevertheless, no isolated firm or even a group of firms can guarantee individual success. As Keynes has proposed, in a monetary economy every enterprise is speculative (Keynes, 1981, p. 114), and firms have to deal with uncertainty.

Firms, like workers, make their calculations and set their income expectations in terms of money.[9] Firms invest money to obtain more money: 'It has no object in the world except to end up with more money than it started with. This is the essential characteristic of an entrepreneur economy' (Keynes, 1979, p. 89). In this context, the existence of forward contracts in terms of money becomes essential to organize productive activity in a complex interrelated system.[10] This is the foundation of the liquidity premium of money (Keynes, 1964, ch. 17).

Hence, the concentration upon money does not result from any kind of money illusion. It relies on the assumption that money is a good 'liquidity time-machine', transporting purchasing power through time, in the wings of forward money contracts (Davidson, 1978). Agents, then, make their bids to income shares in terms of money, based on their expectations of what it will mean in terms of real incomes when the process is over.

The process of price formation, for labour and goods, is the arena where the bids are made. It is here that the rules favour profits. In an uncertain world, to be able to wait is a bonus. In a Walrasian world of simultaneous transactions in all markets, including those of factors, this makes no difference. In a Keynesian monetary economy, the price of labour is a cost that must be known to the firm in order to fix the prices of goods. Labour is sold, then, through forward contracts, predetermining money wages for the period covered by the contract. No such need to sign forward contracts exists for the final goods. As a matter of fact, a system of complete future markets for final goods is incompatible with a monetary economy. Therefore, prices of final goods do not have to be set in advance as the price of labour does. This means that when firms set their prices, making their bids to income-to-be-generated, money wages are already determined. Workers have to make decisions based on expectations of prices of goods. Firms make decisions on the knowledge of wages. If firms have target rates of return, they can scale up money-wage costs when the latter are established to defend their goals.

Under uncertainty mark-up pricing is the most rational strategy open to firms (Davidson, 1978; Sylos-Labini, 1984). Firms can adjust their mark-up and prices in order to maintain the financial feasibility of their plans when there is a change in the environment there (Eichner, 1980) including changes in money wages.

These principles underlie Keynes's statement that workers can fix their money wage but not their real wage, which does not, thus, depend on any special assumption such as money illusion by workers. It is just a result of the way prices are formed in a monetary economy, that allows firms to set their own strategy *after* the workers have made their bid. In this sense, even the introduction of escalator clauses does not change the situation because all it does is to set a rule to change money wages. In any case, firms can and will change their prices after workers have set theirs. Escalators then probably become no more than sources of price instability, being unable to change the situation of workers. In a monetary production economy, the rules will favour firms against workers.

The above discussion does not mean that any action by workers is useless, but that redistribution strategies that do not interfere with this mechanism in some way are destined to fail.

This discussion, so far, has concentrated mainly on microeconomic mechanisms, since we could say that it is in this level that the bids to *expected* income are made. Furthermore, income expectations by firms determine the point of effective demand and therefore the amount of income to be distributed.

In the *General Theory* Keynes assumed that entrepreneurs always entertained 'correct' short-term expectations (Keynes, 1973b, p. 182).

This assumption allowed him to concentrate on more important subjects than 'deficient foresight' and was supported by Keynes's views on probability (Carvalho, 1988). Be it as it may, it is assumed that entrepreneurs are able to estimate incoming demand for consumption goods, which is induced by income changes, but also demand for investment goods, which is not.

The existence of credit makes demand at least partially independent of income. At this point, again, the rules are favourable to capitalists. Credit is supplied by financial institutions on the basis of security margins, that is, depending on the possession of some kind of asset that can be used to liquidate the debt in case of insolvency (Minsky, 1982). Both the amount of credit to be supplied, and its terms, are related to the size of the margin.

Workers may have access to external finance but in a more limited scale because the more uncertain nature of its main 'asset': human capital. A labour asset is illiquid and cannot be taken over by a bank to cover a debt. Moreover, its returns are also uncertain, given the possibility of unemployment. Capitalists have tangible assets. Besides, they may and do use credit to buy assets rather than consumption goods, which means that at least part of the debt issued by capitalists is self-liquidating.

Easier access to credit allows capitalists to exercise demand over goods beyond or in advance of their income to an extent that is not permitted to workers. As Kalecki argued, this is what gives capitalists the power to 'determine' their profits.

In sum, the rules of the game are favourable to profits, because of the way prices are formed in a monetary economy and external finance is supplied. All this means that redistribution of income in favour of wages can only be achieved through some kind of intervention in the pricing mechanism.

As Pasinetti (1961/2) has noted, if workers were allowed to save, and supposing these savings to be borrowed by capitalists to finance investment, the distribution of real income would no longer correspond to the distribution of claims on income. Capitalists would be exercising a real demand with workers' resources. Financial relations would have then to be introduced to allow us to understand the sequence of events leading to the final profile. On the other hand, if workers could borrow from capitalists or from some other external source the demand for wage goods would increase, and the share of profit-earners in the appropriation of real income would fall. This would be equivalent to a reduction in the average profit/wage ratio in terms of real income even if not in terms of earned income.

If workers can actually reduce the average profit/wage ratio of the economy, the same amount of expenditure on investment goods will induce a higher aggregate expenditure in consumption goods. The aggregate profit share falls but not the aggregate amount of profits.

In conclusion, a monetary theory of income distribution cannot evade the issue of how money wages and prices are formed and how purchases are financed. In both issues the rules are biased in favour of profits. As the historical record shows, however, the rules tend to conserve rather than to determine a profile. Profit shares are found to be widely different in a comparison between countries although its stability through time seems to be common to a large number of experiences. The differences may be due to practices or institutions that are particular to each country and show that income may be redistributed if those circumstances are changed. It is worth while to examine some of them.

4. INFLUENCES ON THE PROFIT SHARE

The profit share may be different from one context to another depending on the limitations and the environment in which the wage/price mechanism is affected and demand is determined. If the relevant features of the context can be identified, redistribution policies attempting to change the distribution profile may be designed. These features, however, may be different in the short and long period.

The Wage/Price Mechanism

According to Kalecki, the ratio between prices and wages (the latter being the main element of prime costs) is a measure of the degree of monopoly of an industry and can thus be used as a distributive parameter to obtain income shares. The degree of monopoly, however, in most models is completely indeterminate, except in its limits.

Degrees of monopoly are reflected in the mark-ups firms can impose over production costs. Sylos-Labini (1966) related them to barriers to entry. Steindl (1976) used a kind of Ricardian approach, based on differentials of productivity among firms. The mark-up of the marginal firm, however, as the rent of the marginal land, is left unexplained, expecially when all firms are large. Kalecki himself offered a measure rather than a theory.

Part of the revenues earned with the mark-up have the character of expenses (overheads, fixed capital depreciation, etc.) that have to be recovered by firms. The remaining part of it shares the character of a monopoly rent and reflects 'exploitation'. To limit the degree of monopoly and to reduce exploitation, it is necessary to control the power to mark up costs. In the short period, there are two main ways of affecting the degree of monopoly. First, it is possible to increase competition in the short period by increasing imports. As Sylos-Labini (1984, ch. 1) has shown, this had an important effect in reducing mark ups in Italy in the 1960s and 1970s. A second possibility is the imposition of extensive price controls simultaneously with increases in money wages, as Brazil did in 1986.

Both means may be effective in the very short period but are not necessarily sustainable in the longer term. Continually increasing imports may create balance-of-payments problems. Price controls when aggregate demand is growing may create queues and stimulate black markets. Besides, measures like these, if they are deep enough to promote a change in income distribution, may depress investments and ultimately stagnate the economy.

Redistribution changes aggregate demand patterns. In capitalist economies it has to be profitable to satisfy the new demands. Thus sustainable changes require longer-term measures, such as industrial policies designed to increase competitiveness both internally and externally at the same time in which production is adapted to the new demands. Price controls may be useful to promote short-term changes in distribution but they cannot bear the burden of permanent redistribution.[11]

Finance

Availability of finance influences the ability to demand goods and services. For this reason, changes in access to goods caused by reorientations in the supply of credit are more efficacious in the short term. Especially in situations of income concentration when a large segment of the public has a repressed demand for more expensive goods, demand is very elastic with respect to the availability of credit. To democratize access to credit is then a way of facilitating these segments to become part of those markets. Again, if increases in demand supported by a larger credit supply is not to be dissipated by price increases, the structure of production has to be prepared to satisfy these demands.

In conclusion, changes in the degree of monopoly or in the supply of finance make it possible to change the profit share in aggregate private income. There are, of course, other means of redistribution that may be, to a certain extent, more efficient. Taxation of excess profits to finance indirect wages and other public goods has been an effective way of redistribution in the more advanced countries. Nevertheless, in some cases it may also be important to promote some change in *private* income distribution. The government provides public goods, but larger markets for privately produced goods may be healthy for the economy. In developing countries, where redistribution is an important subject, it is necessary to integrate larger fractions of society into private markets. Fiscal redistribution, then, is not an alternative but a complement.

5.   REDISTRIBUTION IN A MONETARY ECONOMY: THE BRAZILIAN EXPERIENCE IN 1986

On 28 February 1986, the President of Brazil announced a series of decrees directed at stabilizing prices which had been growing at two-digit monthly rates over the previous year. The new policy included a general freeze of prices and wages and the creation of a new currency. The indexation system was to be dismantled and forward contracts denominated in money (which generally contained some generous allowances for expected inflation) should be deflated according to rules defined by the government. The package of measures was to be followed by a fiscal reform, as well as a reform in government institutions in order to adapt them to the requirements of a modern economy with stable prices. The financial systems would also be changed, to spur competitiveness and efficiency, leading to a reduction in interest rates. The price freeze included exchange rates.

The plan was inspired by European experiences in combating hyperinflation. In the last stages of hyperinflation, as Kaldor has suggested, most or all price increases are synchronized to such an extent that at any given moment relative prices and remuneration are roughly in equilibrium. That result was obtained by indexing all prices and wages to the exchange rate and having practically instantaneous adjustments to its variations. Under these conditions, the process could be stopped without leaving traces in the form of 'wrong' relative prices. Inflation in Brazil was high and there was a risk of its accelerating into hyperinflation. Nevertheless, the situation was *not* one of hyperinflation in the sense that prices and wages adjustments to inflation took place only after relatively long intervals. That meant that a price freeze would most probably find 'wrong' relative prices and wages. For those firms or workers that had just had their prices and wages corrected for past inflation the relative position would be improved by a freeze. The opposite would be the case for those next in line for adjustments.

To avoid this situation (and the pressures that would spring from it) the government tried to correct relative imbalances beforehand. It was done for wages (but not for prices) by calculating the average real income of workers grouped according to the dates of their collective contract bargaining, then calculating the money value of that average income at 28 February prices and then freezing them at that level. The government assumed workers would accept the relative position into which they were frozen once it was shown to them that their past efforts to improve it were nullified by inflation.

As a result, at 28 February, money wages were increased for those workers that had 'lagged' real incomes. In addition, Brazilian policy-makers feared that the stabilization policy could abort the recovery initiated in 1984 that had ended the deepest recession the Brazilian economy has known since World War II. The Brazilian economy and society are ill-prepared to deal with stagnation. Population growth is still high, poverty is intense and there is no real support for the unemployed. Self-employment and disguised unemployment are not always easy to distinguish, and the demand for their services depends heavily on private income. Urbanization and industrialization, on the other hand, have raised the expected or desired standards of living of a large number of people, including unionized workers in the manufacturing and service sectors. Under these conditions, periods of stagnation or, which is much worse, recession create not only economic discomfort but also political instability. To avoid recessionary impulses that could threaten newly-achieved price stability (in the sense that only a growing economy could accommodate increasing demands on the social product avoiding inflationary conflicts) it was seen as necessary to prevent reductions in aggregate demand. This was intended to preserve fiscal deficits, achieve low interest rates and stimulate consumption. Partly for this reason and partly because of political motives (such as placating unions that received the new wages policy with deep suspicion) the government decided to concede a general 8 per cent increase in money wages simultaneously with the price freeze.

In sum, however unintentional this result may have been, the anti-inflationary policy adopted on 28 February consisted in large part of a powerful combination of redistribution measures. Employment was reviving both for 'natural' reasons (the end of the 1982/83 recession; the recovery of exports) and because of expansionary fiscal and monetary policies. Money wages were generally raised at the same time that prices were frozen, leading to steep increases in real wages.

Table 12.1 shows data on growth rates of urban wages in 1986 in the metropolitan area of Sao Paulo. The State of Sao Paulo was responsible for 37 per cent of Brazil's GDP in 1980. Most of the industrial and tertiary activities are concentrated in or around its capital. The second column shows real wage increases of workers with a formal labour contract. These workers, in general, because their contracts cover longer periods, benefited practically only from the increases conceded by the government. Informal (those without formal contracts) and self-employed workers benefited, on the other hand, from the growth of aggregate demand (that increased the opportunities for these kinds of activities) and from the price

Table 12.1   *Growth rate of workers' real earnings – Sao Paulo (%)*
             (base: same period of 1985)

Period	Total	Formally Employed	Informally Employed	Self-Employed	Average Manufacturing Wage	Total Payroll*
Jan/Feb	15.7	9.7	21.2	30.2	10.1	20.3
Mar/Aug	27.9	16.2	32.2	57.4	6.8	17.6
Sep/Dec	30.2	14.6	38.1	70.2	3.9	14.3
Jan/Dec	26.9	14.6	32.6	58.1	6.3	16.9

*Manufacturing sector

Sources:
FIBGE, FIESP.

freeze. The gains of the latter groups were significantly higher than those of formally employed people. In terms of manufacturing industry (last two columns), one can see that real wage increases were relatively more modest but the expansion of employment, however, was very effective in increasing workers' real income.

The policy-makers (and most of the academic community) were taken by surprise by the vigour of the post-February increase in demand. It was in sharp contrast to what was expected, having the end of hyperinflation as the only indication as to what could happen in a shock treatment of inflation.

Brazilian economists also seemed unprepared to deal with the composition of aggregate demand that was revealed after the stabilization plan. Generally, one expected that poorer people would use their newly increased income to meet their basic needs. The modern sector of the economy, the manufacturing industry installed after the 1950s, producing capital goods and durable consumption goods, would be penalized by redistribution because its market was constituted by higher income classes.

Actually, there was a double error in the reasoning. First, the increase in real income was very steep (supported by the general feeling that inflationary erosion was a problem of the past). As shown in Table 12.1, between March and August *real* earnings in Sao Paulo increased by an average of 27 per cent compared to the same period in 1985. With hindsight, under these conditions a smooth adjustment to new levels of income cannot be expected. Long-repressed demand for those goods that define a modern standard of living was suddenly liberated. Income elasticities of demand for most goods were unknown. In any case, knowledge from the past was not likely to prove particularly useful in a situation of almost revolutionary change like that experienced in 1986 (government, firms and the

Table 12.2   Industrial production – annual rates of growth (%)

Demand Classes	1984	June 85	Dec 85	June 86	Dec 86
Total	7.1	7.2	8.5	11.3	10.9
Capital goods	14.8	13.1	12.8	21.1	21.6
Intermediate goods	10.2	7.5	7.2	8.3	8.4
Durable consumer goods	− 7.5	1.2	15.4	33.5	20.3
Non-durable consumer goods	2.1	5.2	7.9	9.9	8.9

Source:
FIBGE.

Table 12.3   Growth rates of sales – durable goods for domestic use (physical units – %)

Jan./Sept. (Base: same period of preceding year)				
Item	1986	1985	1984	1983
Portable electric goods	14.6	10.2	− 5.2	3.2
Domestic electronics	40.1	20.1	− 9.8	− 17.4
Air conditioners	50.1	1.6	14.1	10.1
Refrigerators	27.1	− 0.6	− 9.4	6.8
Total	34.6	14.6	− 8.1	− 7.9

Source:
Abinee/FGV.

general public felt that way). Tables 12.2 and 12.3 show that demand for manufactured goods was concentrated on consumption durables. Refrigerators and domestic electric goods were in heavy demand, to the point of exhausting available stocks and creating waiting lists in department stores that lasted sometimes more than two months.

A second point to be noted is price elasticity of demand. Controls were much more effective when imposed on firms producing modern manufactured goods. Domestic appliances had their relative prices reduced when compared to goods that were more difficult to control. Table 12.4 shows that domestic appliance prices increased in line with the average change in the consumer price index, much below clothing (which is a highly differentiated good, almost impossible to control) and transportation (with price increases mainly concentrated in the last two months of 1986). In addition, food prices listed in Table 12.4 are completely illusory. By the second semester of 1986 items like beef, eggs, cheese and milk had all but disappeared from the 'official' (controlled) market. Nobody could buy any of those items at official prices. Beef, however, was readily available on the black market and anyone choosing to ignore controls could

Table 12.4 *Monthly rates of change – consumer price index, 1986*

Month	Total	Food	Housing	Domestic appliances	Clothing	Transport	Health	Personal Services
Jan.	17.2	17.8	14.9	13.4	11.7	32.8	9.5	16.9
Feb.	14.8	18.1	12.3	10.8	8.3	9.5	11.1	16.4
Mar.	—	—	—	—	—	—	—	—
Apr.	.43	-.74	.82	2.08	4.13	1.23	1.17	.55
May	1.08	.11	1.04	2.16	6.21	1.48	.39	.89
June	.97	.42	.49	1.65	4.04	1.64	.35	.83
Jul.	.91	.28	.94	1.65	2.26	2.97	.13	.94
Aug.	1.43	.35	1.92	1.57	2.63	5.87	.18	.94
Sept.	1.19	.33	.44	1.22	2.63	5.87	.18	1.75
Oct.	1.43	.62	.52	1.71	5.32	2.94	.41	.89
Nov.	3.29	3.13	4.07	1.54	5.84	5.45	.43	1.51
Dec.	7.27	4.93	9.02	3.59	4.96	25.71	.61	1.32
Mar./Dec.	19.29	9.69	19.53	18.52	48.74	60.32	1.99	7.37
							5.78	17.06

Source:
Banco Central do Brasil.

Table 12.5   Average rates of capacity utilization (%)

Sector	Jan. 86	Apr. 86	Jul. 86	Oct. 86	Jan. 87
Consumption goods	81	79	82	83	81
Capital goods	70	75	76	81	75
Construction materials	76	73	79	81	82
Intermediate goods	85	84	84	91	90

purchase it. The government made confrontation with cattle-ranchers a point of honour. It even sent the federal police to farms to confiscate animals, but the attempt ended in an embarrassing failure, signalling forcefully to the general public that the system of controls could not last for long without some (possibly great) changes. In sum, actual food prices, especially high income elasticity goods like beef or cheese, rose so fast that price indices could not keep up. As a result, actual relative prices of appliances were probably reduced with respect to food prices.

The Brazilian consumption durable sector was not geared to meet such a widespread demand, especially if it occurs so suddenly. Previously, lower income classes had access mainly to second-hand items, allowing middle income classes to renew their stocks of durable goods. Low income families were mostly excluded from the new products. When their demand was liberated, it represented an overwhelming pressure on the productive capacity of industry. The industrial sector was in the first stages of a recovery process, after a long and deep crisis. Data on investment being incomplete and unreliable do not allow any reliable conclusion as to growth in productive capacity in 1985 and 1986. The pressure of demand on available capacity is not shown in the survey of capacity utilization (Table 12.5) but it does appear clearly in Table 12.6, where entrepreneurs were asked about limits to expansion of production at the end of the period under analysis. Producers of consumption goods did not seem to worry about demand. In contrast, entrepreneurs representing 66 per cent of the value of production of that sector pointed out lack of inputs and an additional 9 per cent the unavailability of packaging materials as the operative limit on the expansion of their production. Capacity utilization 'at the end of the line' was low because of supply restrictions, not of demand.

A short-term means of alleviating demand pressures and allowing income redistribution is by liberalizing imports. The Brazilian economy is still basically closed (see Table 12.7). In 1986, imports were allowed to increase (and exports to be reduced). The frozen exchange rate was, in addition, favourable to this move. This allowed some reduction of internal tensions, but in an economy with external problems such as

Table 12.6 *Limits to expansion of production*
(% of answers weighted by value of production)

Sector	Deficient demand	Lack of inputs	Lack of labour	Lack of short-term finance	Lack of packaging	Other
Consumption goods	5	66	1	4	9	1
Capital goods	20	58	3	8	0	1
Construction materials	35	42	1	0	5	1
Intermediate goods	8	23	1	1	3	1
Total	12	51	2	3	5	1

Source:
For Tables 12.5 and 12.6: Entrepreneurs' Survey – FGV.

Table 12.7   Degree of openness of Brazilian Economy (%)

Year	Exports/GDP	Imports/GDP
1975	7.9	11.1
1976	6.6	8.1
1977	6.9	6.8
1978	6.3	6.8
1979	6.8	8.1
1980	8.4	9.6
1981	8.9	8.3
1982	7.5	7.2
1983	10.7	7.5
1984	12.8	6.6
1985	11.6	6.1

Source:
FGV.

Table 12.8   Foreign transactions, 1986 (US$ million)

Month	Reserves	Trade balance
Jan.	7,279	701
Feb.	7,093	628
Mar.	7,425	1,136
Apr.	7,665	1,292
May	7,792	1,340
June	7,274	1,072
July	6,982	1,009
Aug.	6,668	1,029
Sept.	6,777	823
Oct.	5,566	210
Nov.	4,901	131
Dec.	4,585	156

Source:
IEI/UFRJ.

Brazil's it is not an effective instrument for the longer term. The external position of the economy deteriorated rapidly (see Table 12.8), leading to potential insolvency and to a moratorium in 1987.

In sum, a large measure of redistribution was achieved in 1986. Real wages were effectively increased through central controls that conceded rises in money wages and prevented firms from shifting it to prices. In contrast to wage indexation, that by itself does not allow workers to set their real wage, direct intervention in the pricing mechanism achieved redistribution. Workers were given access to modern consumption patterns by the increase of their real incomes.

The difficulty of a redistribution process is to sustain it. The structure of supply is more or less rigid in the short term and it may not be feasible to rely on imports to cover a transition period to a new distribution profile. Kalecki's intuitions about the relations between supply patterns and income distribution become relevant in this context.

It seems that the historical experience is not favourable to attempts to change the distribution of private income. Fiscal instruments seem to be more effective. Nevertheless, private income concentration in Brazil is still extreme. Recent data supplied by the United Nations Industrial Development Organization show that the wage share in the income of the Brazilian industrial sector was the lowest of all countries being studied – 17 per cent as compared to 34 per cent in Bolivia, 37 per cent in Mexico, 38 per cent in Italy, 39 per cent in Greece, 42 per cent in Portugal and 46 per cent in Spain.

Fiscal means of redistribution tend to concentrate on supplying public goods such as health and education. There is no doubt that these are deeply-felt needs and should be continued to be provided by the state. This is so especially when one considers than when these goods are supplied by the state they are not replacing previous private expenditures but really covering an absolute lack. But there is also an argument for redistribution of private income in order to bring to modern consumption larger sections of the population. It may serve to give strength to the economy and stability to politics. To show how it may be done in a monetary production economy is a strength of Keynes's theory.

NOTES

*   The author wishes to thank Ademar Santos Mineiro, Ary Silva Jr and Fernanda Carvalho for discussions of the ideas presented in this chapter. Comments and suggestions by Jan Kregel much improved the final version. The responsibility for the final product is, however, entirely the author's. Financial support from the National Council of Scientific and Technological Development of Brazil (CNPq) is gratefully acknowledged.

1.   Kalecki's famous aphorism that 'capitalists earn what they spend' had also been proposed by Keynes in *A Treatise on Money*, with the image of the widow's cruse. Kalecki, however, has had in this particular point much more influence than Keynes. The widow's cruse metaphor seemed to have left a bad impression even on Keynes's closest collaborators. See Keynes (1973a, pp. 339–42).
2.   See Asimakopulos (1980/81) and Kregel (1971) for a more detailed discussion of Kaldor's growth model.
3.   Although not the distribution between workers and capitalists. Pasinetti offered a model where this distinction is developed. See Pasinetti (1961/62) and Kregel (1971).
4.   For a closed economy without government.
5.   Marx's departments were not vertically integrated. The premises underlying Kalecki's treatment were criticized by Keynes (1983).
6.   On the other hand, in developing countries, where markets are smaller, and income is

highly concentrated for historical reasons, demand patterns are sharply discontinuous, and Kalecki's model may fit better.

7. Again, see Keynes (1983) for a discussion of the point with Kalecki.
8. In the first versions of his model of business cycle the rate of interest was present but Kalecki eliminated it on the grounds that 'the rate of interest is an increasing function of gross profitability', variable already included in the model (Kalecki, 1971, p. 7).
9. As Joan Robinson put it:

> The reason why the plain man concentrates upon money is that he can hope (according to his personal circumstances) by working, saving, speculating, employing labour, demanding a rise in pay, to increase his command over money, whereas the purchasing power over goods and services that a unit of money represents is something arising out of the total operation of the economy, which he can do nothing about. (1969, p. 25)

10. See Davidson (1978a pp. 57 and 60).
11. Short-term possibilities to attend new demands are increased by appealing to imports. The extent to which this may be efficacious depends on balance of payments restrictions.

REFERENCES

Asimakopulos, A., 'Themes in a Post Keynesian Theory of Income Distribution', *Journal of Post-Keynesian Economics* (III)2, Winter 1980/81.

Carvalho, F., 'Keynes on Probability, Uncertainty and Decision-Making', *Journal of Post-Keynesian Economics* (XI)1, Fall 1988.

Davidson, P. *Money and the Real World*, 2nd edition, London: Macmillan, 1978.

Davidson, P., 'Why Money Matters', *Journal of Post-Keynesian Economics* (I) 1, Fall 1978a.

Davidson, P., *International Money and the Real World*, New York: John Wiley and Sons, 1982.

Eichner, A., *The Megacorp and Oligopoly*, White Plains: M. E. Sharpe, 1980.

Kalecki, M., *Selected Essays in the Dynamics of Capitalist Economies*, Cambridge: Cambridge University Press, 1971.

Keynes, J. M., *The General Theory of Employment, Interest and Money*, New York: Harcourt, Brace, Jovanovich, 1964.

Keynes, J. M., *The General Theory and After. Preparation. The Collected Writings of John Maynard Keynes*, vol. XIII, London: Macmillan, 1973a.

Keynes, J. M., *The General Theory and After: Defence and Development. The Collected Writings of John Maynard Keynes*, vol. XIV, London: Macmillan 1973b.

Keynes, J. M. *The General Theory and After. A Supplement. The Collected Writings of John Maynard Keynes*, vol. XXIX. London: Macmillan 1979.

Keynes, J. M., *Activities 1922-1929. The Return to Gold and Industrial Policy. The Collected Writings of John Maynard Keynes*, vol. XIX. London: Macmillan, 1981.

Keynes, J. M., *Economic Articles and Correspondence. Investment and Editorial. The Collected Writings of John Maynard Keynes*, vol. XII. London: Macmillan, 1983.

Kregel, J., *Rate of Profit, Distribution and Growth: Two Views*. London: Macmillan, 1971.

Marx, K., *Capital.*, vol. II. Harmondsworth: Penguin, 1978.

Minsky, H P., *Can 'IT' Happen Again?*, Armonk: M. E. Sharpe, 1982.

Pasinetti, L., 'Rate of Profit and Income Distribution in Relation to the Rate of Economic Growth', *Review of Economic Studies*, vol. 29, 1961/62.

Robinson, J., *The Accumulation of Capital*, London: Macmillan, 1969.

Smith, A., *The Wealth of Nations*, A. Skinner (ed.), Harmondsworth: Penguin, 1974.

Steindl, J., *Maturity and Stagnation in American Capitalism*, New York: Monthly Review Press, 1976.

Sylos-Labini, P., *Oligopolio y Progreso Tecnico*. Madrid: Oikos-Tau, 1966.

Sylos-Labini, P., *Ensaios sobre Desenvolvimento e Precos*, Rio de Janeiro: Forense-Universitaria, 1984.

13. Income and Citizens' Rights Distribution*

Eduardo Matarazzo Suplicy

---

1. INTRODUCTION

Lucimar Maria da Silva, black, 38 years old, with five children, is the head of the family and, until May 1988 was living in the Favela JK slum (named after former President Juscelino Kubischeck), in Itaim, an upper/middle-class district of Sao Paulo, the largest city in Brazil. She is a typical black woman. According to the Brazilian Demographic Census of 1980, prepared by the IBGE Foundation, 21.7 per cent of black women in the Female Active Economic Population are heads of families (the ratio for white women by contrast is 15.2 per cent). The percentage of women who act as main providers for the family in poor communities is even higher: 30.5 per cent of black women and 28.5 per cent of women in the Female Economic Active Population who earn up to three times the minimum wages.[1]

The father of Lucimar's first three children has not given them any allowance since their separation and the father of the younger two, although living in the same slum, has not either. He now has another family and is barely able to support them. The older girls, aged 15 and 12, take turns in their school time to help look after their 8 and 6-year-old brothers and the 2-year-old sister, so that their mother can work.

Lucimar was working as a janitor, from 6.30 a.m. to 3.30 p.m., in the same district, where she was earning 9000 cruzados a month (around US $60, equivalent to the minimum wage). She was struggling to support her five children in their simple rent-free house. She had lived there 26 years. Born in Joao Pessoa, Pareiba, in the north-east, she first moved with her parents to Rio de Janeiro when she was two years old, and later to Sao Paulo, when she was 12. Her father, now dead, had been a night-watchman. Her mother, Isaura Maria da Silva, aged 57, was one of the first to form the Favela JK. Today, she still works as a caretaker.

Last May, just as the Brazilian government was celebrating the 100th year of the Abolition of Slavery, Lucimar was going through great

216

upheavals in her life. By request of the Municipality of Sao Paulo, supported by a court order, 'Favela JK', located on Juscelino Kubischeck Avenue, was demolished. The great majority of residents, some 300 families, including Lucimar Maria da Silva's, were forceably removed to the Sao Nicolau Housing Complex, built by the Municipal Housing Company, in Vila Prudente, a working-class district located 28 km away. Other families went to Sitio Conceicao, in Guaianazes District located some 75 km away, or to other areas in the city; still others returned to their state of origin, such as Alagoas, Bahia or Paraiba, in the north-east. It is registered in the records of the legal proceedings that the residents of Favela JK will be given the right of preference to be transferred to the Jardim Arpoador Housing Complex, located in the area of the Raposo Tavares Highway, which is much closer to Itaim, but was not due to be completed until the end of 1988.

This case is typical of the precarious state of Brazil's poorest citizens, particularly of the blacks, who normally can be found in greater number in the slums, in the prison system, and in institutions that look after abandoned or deviant adolescents. Today, one can still feel strongly the effects of three centuries of slavery and 100 years of no effective measures that would allow a sudden change in the living conditions that result from the lack of proper educational opportunities, decent housing and a healthy life for the blacks and their descendants. They represent practically half of the Brazilian population (44.34% in 1980, according to the Census of the Brazilian Institute of Geography and Statistics Foundation, a ratio that keeps increasing from 35.85%, in 1940; to 41.0% in 1950; and 38.2% in 1970).[2]

The 1980 Census is the most recent picture of the situation to which the blacks in Brazil have been relegated in terms of opportunities. Of all Brazilians aged 5 years or over, in that year, 35 per cent had not had access to at least one year of schooling. In the case of blacks (including blacks and browns according to the IBGE classification) this percentage is 38 per cent. On the other hand, while 3.6 per cent of the same group had enjoyed tertiary education, only 0.9 per cent of browns and 0.5 per cent of blacks had 12 or more years of schooling.

In 1980, the Economic Active Population (EAP) indicated that 2.6 per cent of the population as a whole were employers. But browns and blacks were only 1 and 0.4 per cent employers, respectively. In the same year, 33 per cent of the EAP earned only up to the minimum wage. But this ratio increased to 44.7 per cent of browns and 46.9 per cent blacks. At the other end of the spectrum, the percentage of people with incomes more than 10 times the minimum wage was 3.72 per cent, of whom 1 per cent were browns and a mere 0.4 per cent blacks.

Taking into account the whole Brazilian population aged 10 years or more, in 1980, the percentage of those without any income is much larger for the 44.7 million women – at 67.1 per cent – than for the 43.5 million men – 24.7 per cent. Of all men aged 10 years or more, those not earning any income together with those receiving the minimum wage only amount to 48.9 per cent, whereas among women this ratio is 84.4 per cent reaching 90.4 and 87.4 per cent, respectively, in the case of *brown* and black women. At the other extreme, 4.1 per cent of men and 0.5 per cent of women earn more than 10 times the minimum wage; of brown and black men, 1.1 and 0.4 per cent respectively, and of brown and black women, 0.09 and 0.03 per cent, respectively.

Lucimar Maria da Silva, earning more or less the minimum wage, is one of the 33 per cent of the population with low incomes. She is also among the 50 per cent poorest people in the EAP who, in 1986, according to the National Survey of Housing Sampling (carried out by the IBGE Foundation) received only 13.5 per cent of Domestic Income, compared with the 47.5 per cent received by the 10 per cent richest, or the 15.2 per cent received by the 1 per cent richest.[3] This picture of income distribution, in the 1970s, continues to rank Brazil as one of the leaders in inequality compared to the rest of the world. If we consider the share of the 10 per cent richest, among all the 50 countries listed in the *1987 World Development Report*, of the World Bank, for which there are available data, Brazil was the country with the largest share. 39.6 per cent in 1960, 46.7 per cent in 1970, peaking at 52.6 per cent in 1972, before falling back to 47.7 per cent in 1980 and 1985, and 47.5 per cent in 1986.

In developing countries like Bangladesh and India, the share of the 10 per cent richest was 29.5 per cent (1981–82) and 33.6 per cent (1975–76) respectively. In Argentina and Mexico which have approximately the same per capita income as Brazil, the percentage is 40.6 per cent (1977) and 35.2 per cent (1970), respectively. In socialist economies, such as Yugoslavia and Hungary, we find 22.9 per cent (1978) and 20.5 per cent (in 1982), respectively. In industrial market economies, such as Japan and the United States, the 10 per cent richest had, 22.4 per cent (1979) and 23.3 per cent (1980) respectively of Domestic Income.[4]

In Brazil the share of the 1 per cent richest, rose from 11.9 per cent in 1960, 14.7 per cent in 1970, 14.9 per cent in 1980, 14.3 per cent in 1985, and 15.2 per cent in 1986. By contrast the 50 per cent poorest saw their share fall, in the corresponding years from 17.4 per cent, to 14.9, 14.2, 13.1 and 13.5 per cent.

These figures indicate that, in terms of market signals, to which the manufacturing sector responds by marketing goods and services, the 1 per cent richest, since 1970, has more 'voting' power than the 50 per cent poorest of the population.

When we bear in mind that one of the objectives proclaimed by those in government is the building of democracy, for this to make sense from both the political and the economic perspective, we can see that the purchasing power of the different sectors of the population is extremely different. The average income of the 1 per cent richest, in 1986, was 150 times higher than the average income of the 10 per cent poorest.[5] If, as far as market decision-making is concerned, the situation has very little to do with democracy, in terms of equality of rights, it is important to question the power of the poorest segments of the population, particularly the blacks, to influence the decision-making at the muncipal, state and federal levels, in comparison to that of the richest segments.

Income disparity is one of the reasons why socioeconomic indicators in Brazil are below what one should expect for a country with an annual per capita income of about 2000 dollars (reached in 1987). Thus, life expectancy according to the IBGE Foundation, increased from 42.74 years in 1940, to 45.90 in 1950, 52.37 in 1960, 52.67 in 1970, 60.08 in 1980 and 64.5 years in 1985. Infant mortality (0–12 months) for each 1000 born alive, declined from 118.13, in the 1950s, to 116.94 in the 1960s, 87.86 in the 1970s, 82.4 in 1975/80 and 67 in 1985. The illiteracy rate among those aged 15 years and over fell from 51 per cent in 1950, to 39 per cent in 1960, 33 per cent in 1970, 23 per cent in 1980, and 20.7 per cent in 1985, which represented 17,284,056 people in 1985, slightly below the figure of 18,146,977 who could not read and write in 1970.

The slow progress of those indicators are in stark contrast to the case of Cuba, which also has an annual per capita income of 2000 dollars. According to the 1987 Cuban Statistics Year-Book, life expectancy at birth in 1960 was 62 years, increasing to 67 in 1965, 70 in 1970 and 75 in 1985. Infant mortality rate per 1,000 live-born fell from aproximately 60–70, according to imperfect estimates in the late 1950s, to 38.7 in 1970, 19.6 in 1980, 16.5 in 1985, and 13.3 in 1987. The illiteracy rate among those aged ten years and over was 23.6 per cent in 1953, dropped to 3.9 per cent in 1961, and is practically zero today. The three indicators are near those reached by the industrialized developed countries with annual per capita income over 10,000 dollars, such as the United States and the Federal Republic of Germany, where life expectancy at birth is 75.5 years, infant mortality, respectively, 11 and 10, in 1985, and illiteracy rate also near zero.

Here we return to what happened in Favela JK to Lucimar Maria da Silva and 300 other families, each with a serious problem, that is likely to be experienced by each of the 1594 slums registered in Sao Paulo in 1987. Between 1973 to 1987, whereas the population of Sao Paulo as a whole grew by 59.89 per cent, from 6,600,693 to 10,554,107, the number of slum residents increased 1039.86 per cent, from 71,840 to 818,872. In 1987, 7.76 per cent of the people of Sao Paulo were living in slums 'conglomerates of housing units, built out of wood, zinc, tin, fiberboard, or even brick, generally distributed in an unorganized form in areas where the individual property is not legalized by those who occupy it'.[6]

If they could choose to remain in the shanty, Lucimar and the rest of the residents would certainly prefer to do so, thinking of the possibility of upgrading their roughly built homes, the majority of which have two floors, built in one area of 2.873 m^2, into respectable brick houses, with full facilities with the help of architects and urban planners appointed by the municipal administration.

In fact, although they did not have any legal documentation in relation to their property, this was about to become a legal right guaranteed by the new Constitution, now being voted by the National Constituent Assembly. In its Article 188, Chapter 20, Title VII, of the Financial and Economic Order, it anticipates the right of *usucapiao*: 'the one that possesses, as his own, an urban area up to 250 square metres, for five years, uninterruptedly and uncontested, utilizing it for his or his family's residence, it will acquire its domain, under the condition that he has no other urban or rural real property.' This right will not be valid for public areas. The new Constitution, however was only promulgated in October 1988.

The area where Lucimar lives was originally privately owned but was disappropriated in two stages in 1971 and 1974. The municipality must allocate it within a five year period, or risk losing its rights, to do so but it has not done anything to date. On the contrary, it has allowed the families to remain there and, in response to their demands, has made improvements in the area. In 1979/80 it installed running water, then electricity and, in 1984/5, sewerage. In the neighbourhood, it provided schools, nurseries and, just in front of the favela, a public telephone. Favela JK has several bars and grocery stores. The majority of residents work in the vicinity, in an area where job opportunities are reasonably good. This offers the advantage for the residents of being able to walk to work – a 10–20-minute walk. Typical occupations are attendants, nightwatchmen, bricklayers, painters, carpenters, factory hands, office-boys, domestic servants, who earn 1–3 times the minimum wage.

Originally, the municipal administration intended to use the area to extend Faria Lima Avenue, one of the main arteries in the vicinity. On this pretext, and quoting that the area 'would be utilized in an improvement named the "Iguatemi Project" approved by the Municipal Law no. 7107 of 1/3/68', on 6 August 1987 the Municipality sued in Court for the right of 'domain reintegration'. Judge Nivaldo Balzano, of the 4th Jurisdiction of the Acts of the Municipal Treasury, determined, in April 1988, a 90-day maximum term for the clearance of the slum, instructing the justice official however that the process could start immediately, and that the police could be brought in in case of resistance.

The decision is part of a policy of clearing slums from areas which are considered inappropriate for housing, e.g. areas subject to flooding, or high-value urban areas. This latter is the case of the Favela JK, since it was built in one of the most expensive areas of the city, in an avenue where one of the major public investments of the present administration is taking place: the linking of Morumbi, a district with the highest concentration of mansions, to 23 de Maio Avenue, by building two tunnels, one under the river Pinheiros and the other under Ibirapuera Park. Juscelino Kubis-check Avenue, which is being rebuilt, will be the link between the two.

The residents of Favela JK have tried to organize themselves. They formed an association, held weekly meetings, engaged lawyers and political parties to help them, and entered a measure into the Justice Court, to halt or postpone the slum clearance, at least until they received a guarantee that the families would be rehoused in decent units. In the Court, however, the pressure exerted by the municipal administration was much more effective, so that the 4th Jurisdiction Judge showed no sympathy for the argument that the Housing Complex of Jardim Sao Nicolau, to which the majority of residents were to be moved, was without any facilities. He was not concerned about the long distance to the city centre or to the original shanty, or about the fact that fares in Sao Paulo are high for low-paid workers. He told this author that he had to transfer the families promptly because he could not trust the Municipality to keep the housing units, which were on the point of being appropriated by other poor families. It is odd that the judge had requested that the police should monitor the removal (both state and the metropolitan police were brought in) that lasted almost one month, but had not considered that they could have been used to protect the housing units in Jardim Sao Nicolau until the energy, water and sewerage were installed.

Even though the federal, state and municipal authorities have pro-grammes for the construction of cheap housing, the resources necessary to do so were insufficient to solve the demand for new houses – the available money was repeatedly diverted to other prestige projects – in a country where the population has been growing in the 1980s, at a rate of 2.3 per cent a year. In Sao Paulo alone, the number of people waiting for cheap housing according to figures provided by COHAB (the Municipal Hous-ing Company) is close to 600,000.

Here we shall consider the question concerning the priority given to public works. What is the cost-benefit ratio to different sectors of the urban population, of an investment such as the two-tunnel complex with an estimated cost of 300–500 million dollars, when compared with other types of investment, e.g. the expansion of the present housing programme to meet the urgent need for cheap housing to give to more than one million slum-dwellers, and more than 2 million people living in inadequate housing, in the so-called 'cortico', a decent home? Wouldn't it be better, if possible, if the money were used to build 200,000 cheap housing units?

Who, in fact, influences the decisions involving public spending? Can't we contest the decisions made by the present Mayor, Janio Quadros, who was elected in 1985 with only 37 per cent of the vote? To what extent do they fulfil the objectives of building a democracy, and a just society that provides equal rights to all?

In fact, there are highly organized economic interests, such as the large construction companies, that are able to coordinate the raising of funds at international financial institutions. These in turn are able to influence the decision-making concerning the destination of public resources.

The construction of tunnels to serve the upper classes, those who own cars, is given priority over the construction of basic housing units, education, health, and improved and cheap transport for the poor and more numerous population.[7] This coordination of interests usually takes place during expensive electoral campaigns and is generously financed by those who later become active participants in public projects. It is worth mentioning that the tunnel will be designed for private automobiles only. It is foreseen in the project that it will *not* serve buses or other public means of transportation. The construction companies have much more interest in building tunnels, viaducts, roads, etc., than cheap housing, since this type of construction is more profitable.

City-level decision influencing also occurs at the state level, and in even higher intensity at federal level, not least because, since 1961, Brazil has not been governed by a directly elected president. The indirect electoral system by an electoral college has only aggravated the situation, facilitating the access of powerful private economic groups to the decision-making process. The José Sarney administration, in order to guarantee a five-year term, instead of four-year, as most of the population expected, used multiple mechanisms to distribute favours, appointing people to new positions in state-owned companies and administration agencies, granting radio and television broadcasting stations, in addition to providing economic assistance to groups selected by those constituents who voted favourably to the President's wishes.

A notable example of funds allocation carried out according to the best interests of the large construction companies was the announcement by

President José Sarney, in 1987, that he would build during his administration (1985–89) the North–South Railroad, that will link Brasilia, the federal capital, the mid-west, to Acailandia, in the state of Maranhao, in the north, a distance of 1570 km. In his award-winning article, of 13 May 1987, the journalist Janio de Feitas, of *Folha de S. Paulo*, was able to show that even before the public tender had been published, the eighteen construction companies knew beforehand which part of the work, estimated at 2.5 billion dollars, would be given to each company.[9] This revelation forced the government to postpone the beginning of the work and they had to convince the public that the work could be justified on cost-benefit terms compared to the alternatives.

In large public projects such as this, the interests of the large construction and industrial companies coincide with the interests of international credit institutions. This may not be obvious, but it works to avoid the control of the National Congress, Legislative Assemblies and the City House of Representatives. The author was a Federal Representative for the Workers' Party, from March 1983 to January 1987, during which time, and in spite of obstacles, he had the opportunity to see this at work.

Thus, for instance, in 1984/85 the Swiss Bank Corporation offered to loan $150 million to Electricidade de Sao Paulo S.A.–Eletropaulo, a state-owned company responsible for providing electricity to the State of Sao Paulo, for the expansion of transmission lines of electric power in the State of Sao Paulo. The terms of the loan demanded that at least $85 million should be spent in the purchase of equipment from a consortium of seven companies led by Brown-Bowery S.A.,[10] a Swiss company that manufactures transformers and other equipment in Osasco, Sao Paulo. There had been an attempt to overcharge significantly for the operation, with no public tender. The system consisted of simply checking to see if the prices were higher in real terms than those charged in the market in the last two years. For speeding up the operation, at least one company received a 1.5 per cent commission of the total amount of purchases carried out with the consortium. By making this public at the time, the author, according to the President of Eletropaulo, Professor Jose Goldenberg, brought about a sudden price cut in the cost of equipment.

In January 1987, the author noted that the Department of Water and Sewerage (DAEE) of the State of Sao Paulo was carrying out a public tender, budgeted at $150 million dollars, for the enlargement of the Tiete river chute that runs through the middle of the city, in order to avoid constant flooding in the rainy season. The work would be financed by an international institution, the World Bank, as part of a larger contract of $350 million signed by Companhia de Saneamento Basico do Estado de Sao Paulo-SABESP (The Public Sanitation Company for the State of Sao

Paulo). Julio Cerqueira Neto, Director of Planning for DAEE, who resigned shortly after this, told the author that two months before the bid was announced, the work had already been assigned to four major construction companies: sections 203–378 were assigned to Andrade Gutierrez SA; 378–628 to Companhia Brasileira de Projetos e Obras-CBPO; 628–1033 to Construcoes e Comercio Camargo Correa; and 1490–1650 to Constran SA Construcoes e Comercio. Even though the author has alerted the press, and the case has been examined by the Court of Public Accounts, the public tender was published in two months, with the same results as those predicted by former Director, Julio Cerqueira Cesar Neto. Today, the work is being carried out by these four construction companies.

The spending ratio of the Federal Government in relation to GNP, in 1985, was 21.1 per cent. However, if we consider expenditures incurred by the state and municipal governments, as well as operations of state-owned companies at these three government levels, we can reach the conclusion that government influence whether on the side of taxes collected or expenditures, plays a very important role in the Brazilian economy. Another fact to be considered is the way official financial institutions allocate subsidized credit. This is one of the main mechanisms responsible for the concentration of wealth in the hands of those who influence the power centres.

In order to evaluate the limitations of influence of the low income population with regard to public decision-making, the author carried out some detailed interviews with the community leaders of some of slum-dwellers in the city of Sao Paulo.[11]

Maria Margarida Diniz, aged 40, 'cabocla' from Esperanca, State of Paraiba, came to Sao Paulo with her parents when she was 13 years old. She is president of the Association of Dwellers of Favela JK where she has lived since 1975, because she could not afford to pay rent and found no other alternative that would allow her to educate and feed her three daughters, one of whom is adopted – a common occurrence in the favelas. Like Lucimar Maria da Silva, she is separated from her husband and is now the only provider in the family. Her father used to work in the street market but had to stop working when he went blind. Her mother is a maid. Maria Margarida has worked since she was 14, first in the market, then in factories and in pharmacies or stores as a clerk or package wrapper.

Maria Margarida Diniz has not had an easy life and she now fights for decent and respectful treatment for the people of Favela JK. She told the author that from the beginning of the Janio Quadros administration, the mayor would go past the favela every day, stopping to impose fines on vehicles illegally parked on the pavement, and, without ever entering the favela, would tell the residents that they had to clean the pavements and paint the front of the houses that faced the street.

One day in 1986, just after the clearance of Favela Cidade Jardim which was located in an expensive area of the city and after hearing rumours that the next in line would the JK, one of the residents boasted in an interview with *O Estado de S. Paulo* that if this did happen he might even kill the mayor (he was probably a bit drunk at the time). The story was published in the newspaper the following day, and the mayor was there at 5.30 in the morning demanding to know who was responsible. He also demanded the presence, in his chambers, of the president of the Association of the Dwellers of Favela JK. He informed her that, not that year, but very soon, he would clear the favela. He ordered that the residents should hose down the pavement in front of the favela every day. This was frequently done by Margarida herself who now began to hear daily threats of JK's clearance. To the press the mayor said that he would remove, 'whether they like it or not', the 'pigs', the 'thieves' and the 'drunks'.

According to the mayor, the favela is an 'ignominy, a collective shame that reaches every one of us', an observation one cannot disagree with. He continues: 'if in one hand it assists the unassisted, it is full of drug addicts, prostitutes and professional bums who distort the character of minors and of large sectors of the population', which is a biased conclusion. A detailed examination of the favelas shows that the people living at the margins hardly differ from those found in the richest areas of the city, though they are disguised under sophisticated schemes. It also shows that the great majority of the favela dwellers are workers who could not find alternative accommodation. To compensate for their standard of living, there is a high sense of solidarity and mutual help between members of the favelas, the multiple ways families find to help each other in difficult times is something talked of but not easily found in wealthy districts.

The judicial order finally came in April and was inforced in May 1988. On 9 June 1988, the last shanty was demolished and the last family removed. Neither the mayor nor the judge cared whether there was electricity, water or sewerage in the Jardim Sao Nicolau Housing Complex located in Vila Prudente, 28 km from JK, or in the housing complexes located in Guainases, 75 km away. They were not interested to know that there were only 20 more days to go for the children to finish their school term.

In fact, there was no urgent need to remove the families from Favela JK as revealed by the mayor to the judge. He claimed the area was needed for the construction of the extension of Faria Lima Avenue, however, no other building was demolished in the surrounding area. The only work done was a street linking Juscelino Kubischeck Avenue with a back street and a park. On 13 June 1988, in a press release, Mayor Janio Quadros finally showed that he had indeed other things in mind for the area, rather the extension of the avenue. To reassure other residents in the area, who were worried about the possible compulsory appropriation and demolition of buildings that would certainly occur with the construction of the 'Iguatemi Project', the mayor stated: 'I solemnly state, for public knowledge, that I do not intend to carry out any expropriation in this district or in any adjacent area for the construction of a boulevard'. This satisfied those who were willing to see poverty at a distance. However, poverty still exists. And where once there was favela, there is now a park.

Certainly, life in the favela was precarious. Inadequate construction materials were used, the place was infested by rats, which they tried to eradicate with a large number of cats. At times there would be disputes between residents who had had a bit too much to drink. There were also young men who smoked marijuana and would sell it to occasional visitors, people with a higher income, and this was a cause for concern for the authorities. It was said that the favela served as a refuge for criminals. People in the adjacent districts complained to City Hall officials, demanding the clearance of the favela because, according to them, most of the robberies that occurred in the area were committed by residents or frequent visitors to Favela JK. This was not the opinion, however, of the residents of the favela, who led normal working lives. (A fact attested by City Hall officials during the registration process of all the families involved.)

Today, a lot further from their place of work, former JK residents still face many hardships. Those who moved back to their states of origin, with only a pittance received for transportation costs of personal belongings, will soon find themselves in the same desperate situation that drove them to migrate to Sao Paulo in the first place. Maybe after basic utilities are installed in Jardim Sao Nicolau, things will improve, because it is a vast area and there is enough space for each family to expand a little on their $28m^2$ house. It will be a while before this happens. First, the population will have to claim their right to citizenship that has been denied them since slavery times until today.

A similar situation was experienced by Joaquim Satiro da Silva, President of the Association of Residents of former Favela Cidade Jardim, a slum located in a prime area in the city of Sao Paulo. Without consulting the 103 families who had lived there for over ten years, the mayor removed them to Jardim Adventista Housing Complex, some 15 km away, in the District of Campo Limpo. Where the favela had once stood, an area inappropriate for housing, due to heavy traffic in the surrounding area, a park has been built for the pleasure of the upper-class

Figure 13.1   % of income of the economic active population 1986

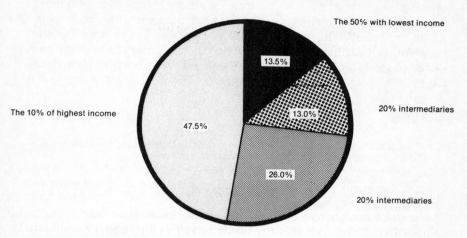

families who live in the area.

Residents of Favelas Paraisopolis and Jardim Panorama are alert to the fact that they may be next since their homes are located in privileged areas like Morumbi, according to information collected from Maria Betania Ferreira Mendonca and Luis Gomes da Silva, both presidents of the favela residents association. According to an official source, the Sao Paulo City Hall has a provisional plan to redevelop the entire region where Favela Paraisopolis, one of the largest in the city, is located with 5500 houses and aproximately 25,000 residents who are organizing themselves to assert their rights to have access to any information concerning the Municipality's plan and also to participate in decisions over their future.

Table 13.1   Distribution of income of the economic active population with income

Classes of Percentage	% of income				
	1960	1970	1980	1985	1986
The 50% with lowest income	17.4	14.9	14.2	13.1	13.5
20% intermediaries	16.5	13.3	12.7	12.3	13.0
20% intermediaries	26.5	25.1	25.4	26.9	26.0
The 10% of highest income	39.6	46.7	47.7	47.7	47.5
The 5% of highest income	28.3	34.1	34.9	34.2	34.3
The 1% of highest income	11.9	14.7	14.9	14.3	15.2

Sources:
IBGE – Censos de 1960, 1970, 1980;
PNAD 1985, 1986.

In the city and in the countryside, throughout Brazil, one can clearly see growing trend towards better organization among the lower classes, those who struggle for their right to a piece of land, a decent home, education, health, and above all, their right to life. Democracy cannot be realistic hope for all Brazilians while the country is still going through serious socio-economic and power influence inequalities which has characterized Brazil in the past and still exists today.

NOTES

*   I am grateful to the Instituto Latino Americano de Desenvolvimento Economico e Social, Ildes, that advanced funds that made this work possible.
      I would like to thank Liliane Jeanne Baldacci, my research assistant, for her collaboration in this paper.

1.   IBGE, *Relatorio de Indicadores Sociais*, 1988, the chapter on 'A Familia Negra em Questao' (The Black Family in Spot).
2.   Suplicy, Eduardo Matarzzo, 'Desigualdades Socias e Raciais no Brasil,' *Revista de Economia Politica* no. 8, Oct.-Dec. 1982, Editora Brasiliense, Tables 1–6.
3.   IBGE, *Anuario Estatistico do Brasil*, 1987.
4.   World Bank, World Development Report, 1987, Table 26, on distribution of income.
5.   IBGE, *Pesquisa Nacional por Amonstra de Domicilios, 1985–86*.
6.   Sao Paulo City Hall, Housing Secretariat, 1988, *Censo das Favelas, 1987*, published by *O Diario Oficial do Municipio*, 28 April 1988, pp. 3–7.
7.   The companies actually involved in the construction of the tunnel under the Ibirapuera Park are Constran S/A–Construcoes e Comercio and CBPO–Companhia Brasileira de Projetos e Obras. The tunnel under the Pinheiros river is the responsibility of Construtora Camargo Correa; and the reconstruction of Juscelino Kubischeck Avenue, linking both tunnels, is in the hands of Servent-Civilsan and Badra.
8.   The newspapers *O Estado de S. Paulo, Folha de S. Paulo, Jornal do Brasil, O Globo* published many articles highlighting the event in the months of May and June of 1988. Journalist Gilberto Dimenstein, of *Folha de S. Paulo*, reveals the way the Jose Sarney Administration has distributed favours with public resources in exchange for a favourable political position on its projects. The book is titled *A Republica dos Padrinhos, Chamtagem e Corrupcao em Brasilia* (Republic of Godfathers – Blackmail and Corruption in Brasilia), Editora Brasiliense, 1988.
9.   Journalist Janio de Freitas was given the Esso Journalism Award for the publication in code of an ad in the classified section of Folha de Sao Paulo, dated 13 May 1987, before the final announcement of the results of the public tender. The ad consisted of a code containing the exact information of the stretches of road to be built by each company, as follows: Lot 1A – Norberto Odebrecht; Lot 2A – Queiroz Galvao, Lot 3A – Nendes Juniro, Lot 5A – CR Almeida, Lot 6A – Serveng, Lot 7A – EIT, Lot 8A – COWAN, Lot 9A – CESA, Lot 1B – CBPO, Lot 2B – Camargo Correa, Lot 3B – Andrade Gutierrez, Lot 5B – Constran, Lot 6B – Sultepa, Lot 7B – Construtora Brasil, Lot 8B – Alcindo Vieira, Lot 9B – Tratex, Lot 10B – Paranapanema, Lot 11B – Ferreira Guedes.
10.   The seven companies forming the consortium were: Industria Eletrica Brown Boweri S/A; Camargo Correa Brown Boveri S.A.; SACE S/A–Equipamentos Eletrodomesticos – these three are part of the industrial group Brown Boveri–Siemens S.A. Insat–Industria de Sistemas de Alta Tensa S.A. and Transformadores Uniao Ltda. The alert was given by the author of the paper on 8 May 1985, when he also published, in *Folha de Sao Paulo*, the article titled *Risco de Cobranca de Sobre-Preco em Compra de Equipamentos pela ELETROPAULO* (Risk of Charging Over-prices for Equipment Purchased by ELECTROPAULO).

It is indeed an interesting coincidence that among the several cases of public construction works mentioned above, the construction of the tunnel by the Municipality, the expansion of the botton of the Tiete river by the State Government and the expansion of the retransmission lines of electric power, by Eletropaulo, also a state-owned company, and the North–South Railroad, a Federal Government project, the only company to appear in all of these projects is Camargo Correa Construtora e Comercio, the largest construction company operating in Brazil and working on more than 1000 public works in the country. The company's main shareholder, Seabastiao Camargo, was considered by Forbes and Fortune the richest man in Brazil in 1987, with one of the 50 largest fortunes in the world, with a total wealth estimated in US dollars at 1.2 billion.

11. Interviews with Maria Margarida Diniz, Maria Beatania Ferreira Mendonca, Joaquim Satiro da Silva and Luia Gomes da Silva, presidents of the Association of Residents of Favelas JK, Cidade Jardim and Jardim Panorama, respectively.

14. Inflation and Market as Alternative Systems of Regulation*

Paul Singer

INTRODUCTION

This is a very exploratory paper, inspired by the idea that – in contemporary capitalist democracies – inflation may be more than an economic aberration. From the angle of political economy, it is clear that inflation often performs functions, particularly in relation to distributional conflicts. The power to distribute value 'created from nothing' enables the governmental arbiter to solve conflicts, without having to deny grievances or inflict losses. But here I venture further along this path, asking if high inflation rates that persist over decades do not become systems of macro-regulation for the economy as a whole.

The hypothesis seems well grounded, at least for countries like Brazil, which has experienced continuous inflation since the 1940s at least, and has been suffering from 3-digit inflation since 1980. During the 1960s, Brazil was part of what seemed to be the 'Latin American inflationary syndrome', but since then the number of countries with permanent high inflation is growing fast. The syndrome is spreading preferentially to countries undergoing sharp economic and social change.

The rate and persistence of inflation in these cases is evidence of its major impact on social life. But, since social life is 'reproduced' under such circumstances, its 'regularity' is conditioned not only by inflation but also by the endless attempts to get rid of it. And, of course, by the regular failure of these attempts.

In section 1 of this chapter we consider why endemic inflation remains at high rates without evolving into hyperinflation. From this, the working of an economy regulated by inflation is examined, taking into account economic as well as political factors. In section 2, the question is how economies without inflation are regulated. Here, the historical experience of developed capitalist countries becomes relevant, particularly from 1973 on, when economic losses had to be allocated and this question occasioned an inflationary wave that persisted for several years. Successful stabiliza-

230

tion restored the marketplace as a regulator in these economies. But this required a political explanation, which leads to speculation about the future of the labour movements in these countries. Finally, in section 3, some more abstract conclusions about economic stagnation, distributional conflicts and inflation are reached.

As usual in exploratory papers, none of the leads is pursued in depth. An assessment seems necessary, in order to verify if it is worthwhile going along such lines.

1.   INFLATION AS A REGULATORY SYSTEM

Inflation is too often regarded as an anomaly, as an episodic evil that should and could be 'cured' by adequate 'adjustment' policies. But there are countries in which inflation is chronic, being a permanent feature of economic, social and political life. In Latin America there are many such countries and in the 1980s these have been joined by others (e.g. Mexico, Colombia, Venezuela). It is conceivable that chronic inflation is also becoming the plight of countries in transition from centrally planned to market economies (e.g. Yugoslavia, Hungary, Poland, China), not to mention the NICs of Asia and Europe, in which inflation is also high and chronic.

Considering only the capitalist countries, these can be classified in two types, from the point of view of their regulatory systems: 1. countries in which the adjustment of global demand to global supply is achieved through fiscal and monetary policies, having as targets the level of activity and employment and the balance of payments; 2. countries in which fiscal and monetary policies are conditioned by past inflation, so that the adjustment of global demand to global supply has to be made by the rise of prices, that is, by present inflation.

In order to examine the workings of inflation as a regulatory system let us consider an economy that has experienced high inflation over so many years that: (a) the original causes of inflation are forgotten; the only factors that are relevant are those that made inflation reach its present level and are still at work, possibly tending to lead it to higher plateaux; (b) inflation is expected to continue, so that most nominal prices, taxes, rents, interest and foreign exchange rates are 'indexed', i.e. readjusted at different time intervals, according to the variation of different indexes of price levels.

In such a setting, fiscal policy has one overreaching aim: to hold in check the public deficit. The deficit is there because inflation increases public expenses *before* it augments tax revenue. Since taxes have to be collected on *past* transactions or incomes, governments are always paying prices (or wages, etc.) of today with tax revenues which correspond to prices of several months earlier. The inflation between these points in time occasions an unavoidable loss of revenue in real terms. To combat the public deficit, expenditure may be curtailed and/or taxes may be raised. Both are difficult to achieve. Expenditure cuts hurt political interests, particularly in rapidly changing societies, like the NICs or of New Market Economies (NMEs). Social change requires massive public expenditure in economic infrastructure, in social services and social infrastructure. The logical thing would be not to reduce expenditure but to increase tax rates. But this is doubly difficult because increased taxation is incorporated in all inflation indexes and results in readjusted incomes 'after taxes' that literally 'crowd out' the tax increase through higher inflation. Suppose that a value-added tax of 10 per cent is collected in a time interval during which a 30 per cent inflation deprives it of 23 per cent of its real value.[1] In order to combat the deficit, the tax is raised to 15 per cent. A higher tax stimulates a larger tax evasion. Let us assume that the elasticity of tax evasion to tax increase is 1, so that a 50 per cent tax rise induces a 50 per cent marginal tax evasion. So nominal tax revenue grows from 100 to 125 (instead of the 150 that would have come about if tax evasion would have remained constant). If inflation during the time interval goes up, mainly due to the tax increase, from 30 to 62.3 per cent, the real value of the tax revenue remains the same as before.[2] This example shows how improbable it is that, under high chronic inflation, a nominal tax increase may render significant changes in the real tax revenue.

Monetary policy is to a large extent conditioned by the outcome of fiscal policy. As is often the case, persistent public deficits over a long period pile up into very large public debts, the service of which being one of the main causes of the current public deficit. This narrows the alternatives for monetary policy. If a more restrictive policy is adopted, in order to finance the public deficit or most of it, the issue of securities will drive the interest rate upwards. Not much new money will be put into circulation, so that the scarcity of means of payment[3] ratifies the increase of the rate of interest. This should reduce effective demand and help to damp down inflation. But, in the meanwhile, most price-makers will increase their mark-ups in order to achieve a rate of return on their capital which will be commensurate with the higher interest rate. So initially inflation will go up instead of down, the public deficit will be even larger, due to bigger interest payments on the public debt and due to higher inflation, which increases public expenditure much more than tax revenue. This in turn will force the monetary authorities to restrict even more credit and the money supply and so on, until the recession, brought about by the decline of effective demand, is exerting sufficient downward pressure on prices to counteract the reactions that accelerate inflation.

A restrictive monetary policy eventually brings about a decline of inflation by shifting the burden of adjustment mainly on price-takers – small and medium entrepreneurs in competitive markets – and wage earners. Price-takers cannot shift the burden of higher interest payments to their clients and so are forced to narrow their profit margins, even more so when facing a declining demand. In the process, many of them are ruined. Wage earners also have to cope with a strong reduction in the labour force. The growth of unemployment undermines the indexation of wages, which normally is anyway somewhat below current inflation. Under the pressure of the unemployed, a black labour market develops – real wages decline, reinforcing powerfully the decrease of effective demand.

Although economically feasible, a restrictive monetary policy unavoidably provokes growing social resistance, that eventually develops into overwhelming political opposition. Since this policy hurts the interests of the majority of the electorate and brings positive results (i.e. the decline of inflation) only later, it becomes very likely that political opposition will kill the policy before it has any chance to show its stabilizing virtues. In order to make the restrictive monetary policy politically feasible, government is force to compensate its most painful effects by means of subsidies and transfers. Hard-pressed farmers receive 'special' credits with lower interest, owners of mortgaged homes get subsidies, the unemployed workers get benefits. All this impinges on the public deficit, making the monetary policy even more restrictive, accelerating inflation and *delaying* its stabilizing effects. The delay is caused by the fact that all compensating measures alleviate the recession, holding back the decline of effective demand. In the end, an uneasy mix of restrictive and permissive policies is put into practice, which most probably *stabilizes* the inflation at a high level instead of bringing it down.

The story of economics under permanent high inflation is full of such episodes. Nowhere is high inflation passively endured, without repeated attempts to get rid of it. The fight against inflation in such countries becomes a real obsession, and is taken up by each new government and each new Finance Minister. Although inflation is seen as a universal evil – often as *the* evil – the losses derived from the fight against inflation, by means of reducing effective demand, become unbearable after a time and the revolt so provoked, which often gains expression at the polls, defeats the alliance in power and imposes a more permissive fiscal and monetary policy. The succeeding battles against inflation, ending in more or less complete defeat, make up the routine dynamics of these economies. It is probable that high – let us say, 3-digit – inflation, if not subject to persisting attempts to hold it down, would rapidly explode into hyperinflation. From this point of view, the failures in eliminating inflation are certainly not without effect. The penalties imposed by succeeding recessions are, after all, not wholly in vain. They are 'rewarded' by the relative stabilization of the pace of price increases, an increase which, thanks to indexation, eventually becomes 'neutral' from the point of view of income distribution.

That is the way in which inflation becomes permanent. But how does an economy work under the pressure of continuously rising nominal values? Obviously, prices can only grow because buyers are prepared to pay them. This defines a situation in which global demand is in chronic excess of global supply. But global demand is held in check by restrictive fiscal and monetary policies, so that prices may go up *now* at much the same speed they did in the *past*. At least, that would be the logical outcome of indexation: if all 'leading' prices (prices of the most 'basic' goods, in the sense of Sraffa's system) grow at the same pace as the average level of prices, the inflation rate, required to adjust global demand and supply, should be constant, unless elements of the 'real' economy – consumers' preferences, costs of production, foreign competition etc. – change. But, in reality, such an equilibrium model of inflationary adjustment ignores one essential trait: under high, permanent inflation, a complex, interlocking set of *distributional conflicts* is always changing relative prices, wages, rents, etc., and thereby modifying the overall distribution of income. All *real* values and incomes are always moving upwards or downwards, due to the basic fact that, although at each moment *some* values are rising, *most* of them are *not*. That is the decisive difference between heavy inflation and hyperinflation. Under hyperinflation, it is most likely that *all* prices move up daily. But under common inflation, particularly an inflation that is heavy but is not 'running away' each nominal value changes at certain intervals, but only some financial values rise *every* day. Most contractual values – like wages and rents – are readjusted each month, couple of months, quarter, etc. Prices of many goods in wholesale trade are also fixed for the length of contractually-defined supply periods. In such a situation, *at each moment*, income is redistributed to the few groupings the prices (or wages, rents, etc.) of which are *now* rising; income is being lost by other agents, who are paying those higher prices. At the *next moment, another* set of groupings will be favoured by nominal price readjustments, and so on.

Each grouping (essentially composed of sellers of the same commodity: a good, a service, labour force under the same collective contract, etc.) is losing *real* income most of the time, as its purchases become continuously more expensive, while its nominal income is not changing; then comes the moment in which *its* price is readjusted, so that it can recover its past losses and face its future losses. For each grouping, the amount of readjustment of its nominal income is very important, since it provides a larger or smaller safety margin against the future increases of its costs, which are expected to occur until its turn of readjustment arrives again.

So, all groupings strive to maximize their price readjustments, and that is the gist of most distributional conflicts. A number of important prices are subject to legal indexation, so their readjustment depends on legal norms. Important political struggles are fought around such norms, particularly around readjustments of wages, rents and tariffs of public services, like bus fares; less open, but none the less heavy are the struggles around the readjustment of different taxes, foreign exchange rates, interest rates and prices of fuels, electricity, basic raw materials and support prices of agricultural products. Other prices are not subject to legal norms but are freely bargained in the marketplace. But not all markets are equally competitive. In many, sellers and/or buyers have a considerable degree of monopoly. Under high inflation, the distinction between price-makers and price-takers is crucial, much more so that under light inflation or average price stability. Price-makers may fully shift increased costs to their prices, keeping their real incomes intact *as an average* in each period. Price-takers cannot do that, unless the demand for their products has low price elasticity. Which indeed becomes more frequent when heavy inflation numbs the buyers' sensibility to price differentials.

Normally anyone who goes shopping for items of small value (current consumption goods) has a pretty good idea of the prices she (he) expects to pay. But, when prices are rising rapidly and the rate of increase becomes unpredictably large, price expectations get muddled and one pays almost anything, without bothering to verify if the competition is charging the same. This means that each grocer, butcher, drugstore or supermarket gets a much larger degree of monopoly. In practical terms, each retailer may increase her (his) prices more than the competition without having to fear a significant loss of sales.

As a result of this set of heightened distributional conflicts, inflation is under steady upward pressure. If leading prices get out of hand, due to the behaviour of groupings endowed with a higher degree of monopoly or increased leverage on the state, indexation spreads the increase to most other prices, so that the groupings which took the lead quickly lose their relative gains. They may, of course, react by increasing their prices even more, so that inflation accelerates continuously until it turns into hyperinflation. To avoid this danger, governments try to keep distributional conflicts under strict control, by means of specific value regulations *and* by undermining effective demand through succeeding stabilization policies.

That is how inflation, high and enduring enough to warrant generalized indexation, functions as a regulatory system of market economies undergoing rapid economic and social change. It regulates economic behaviour by replacing market and liquidity constraints, which seem to originate from the unbridled interaction of economic agents by explicit legal and contractual 'pricing' norms. The contrast between these two 'modes' or 'systems' of regulation can help to understand changes that present-day capitalism is undergoing.

2. MARKET REGULATION OF DEMOCRATIC CAPITALIST SOCIETIES

We have described and to some extent analysed a bizarre mode of regulation, in which the all-pervading scarcity of use values (consumption goods and services) is translated into permanent high inflation. Scarcity in this case is most 'social', the demand for commodities being produced by social competition. Inflation is the result of overdemand and its permanence is made possible by the steady reproduction of overdemand. In this way, the constraint of a limited effective demand is overcome but its place is taken by a different constraint, that of a continuous degradation of all real values.

Scarcity as such leads naturally to an enhancement of values: the price rise due to a failure of crops or a lost war may not reproduce itself, that means, it does not have to be the start of an inflationary process. If it is not, if after the rise prices are stabilized, most people become poorer but the wealthy become even richer than before, because the relative distance between incomes matters (when unemployment increases sharply, menial services become cheaper and easier to get, making the lives of the rich that much better). In the mode of regulation by which the general price level is *not* allowed to rise continuously, scarcity is translated into poverty and poverty is allocated more or less permanently by market mechanisms. The losers in the economic game may get welfare transfers from the state but only to the limit defined by tax revenue less other expenditure. This limit is often the object of hard social struggles, but at each moment it is given and is not violated.

The political implication of market regulation is that the state may only redistribute marginal income, a share of incremental income, as long as global income is growing. This is so because, with a stable general price level, nominal global income grows only to the extent that real income is growing; if the state would redistribute *more* than the increment of income, some of the higher income groups would have to *lose* real income. This is not impossible, but highly unlikely. Higher income groups hold most of the financial wealth in all capitalist countries. If a government dares to deprive these groups of some of their income, even in a most modest degree, they react by transferring part of their assets out of the country,[5] occasioning the devaluation of the national currency and losses in foreign accounts. Capital flight is soon followed by an investment strike and both bring about economic crisis, a state of affairs no government can endure for long. There are a number of historical examples of such a sequence of events, which show that under democratic capitalism the extent to which income can be redistributed is limited, although far from negligible in the longer run.

When the economy is growing steadily, as it did in all capitalist developed countries, from 1945 to 1973, even without much income redistribution, absolute poverty can be – and in several countries *has* been – almost entirely eliminated. The market allocation of poverty was increasingly attenuated by growing real wages for unskilled labour and social expenditure for the benefit of most underprivileged groups. Price stability was politically feasible because it was coupled with permanently growing incomes – monetary and non-monetary.

The reversal came after 1973, when most developed capitalist countries suffered severe losses from the first and second oil shocks. The market regulation failed then, because income losses could not be definitely allocated by the interaction of supply and demand. The price rise of fuels spread to many other prices and unions were able to get corresponding adjustments of wages. The regularities, described in section 1, followed. During the rest of the 1970s, most developed countries lived under low but persistent inflation. What prevented this inflation from becoming high and permanent? The answer cannot be in the technique of stabilization policies, which are also perfectly well known in all countries under inflationary regulation. It has to be in the *political sphere*, in the acceptance by workers of crushing rates of unemployment and by inhabitants of old industrial strongholds of rapid economy decay.

Such acceptance was never peaceful; bitter strikes and protests had to be crushed before the straightforward translation of increased scarcity into impoverishment, allocated by the market, could be successfully imposed in one country after another. One noteworthy aspect of this process was that the victories over working-class resistance could be achieved everywhere without violating the rules of political democracy. After the second oil shock and the worst wave of inflation, conservative parties won elections in almost all capitalist developed countries and mustered enough strength ruthlessly to impose stabilization policies, which reverted the system of regulation from inflation to market allocation. The answer seems to be that, in these countries, the higher income groups are in a majority or are able to gather a majority behind them.

At the beginning of the 1980s the choice facing many developed capitalist countries was between regulation by the market and regulation by inflation. Of course, no party endorsed 'inflation *cum* indexation' as its platform. Everybody repudiated inflation but not everybody was prepared to pay the social price required by the achievement of stability. In fact, almost everywhere the majority chose stability, and even so, after the worst post-war recession (1980–82), inflation was reduced to the 3–5 per cent level, which is low but significantly more than zero. The option for the market regulation was clearly in the interest of wealth owners. Decades of steadily growing earnings also made many workers owners of property and financial assets. The 'adjustment' by means of recession and the closing down of whole industries hurt a large number of people, but certainly *not* the majority. At last, a large share of working-class voters joined the neo-conservative majority and denied solidarity to those whom the market chose to impoverish.

In the process, union membership began to shrink and the belief that economic policy could and should keep the economy near to full employment was abandoned even by labour parties. The change, of course, was much wider than merely about how the economy should be regulated. But this was the central issue and everywhere pre-Keynesian concepts, which seemed to have been buried during the 1930s, were successfully revived. Ideological reversals such as these must be related to deep social change. Now, what really changed in most developed capitalist countries was the relative number of the poor, which fell to negligible levels. This seems to be the big historical achievement of the labour movement, guided by socialist ideologies, in the broadest sense. The *raison de'être* of the labour movement, at least in this form, seems to near exhaustion. The labour movement conquered universal suffrage during the first half of the twentieth century, and used it during the second half to raise the standard of living of most workers much above the subsistence level; besides that, many workers accumulated savings and became, in spirit at least, 'petty capitalists'. Others lost their livelihood, their property, being forced to join the ranks of the unemployed or underemployed. Their conspicuous presence in the labour market forces unions to accept wage-cuts in the hope of keeping members in jobs. And labour governments practise adjustment policies that expand unemployment, besides making the startling discovery that profits finance investment and investment creates jobs – so profits must be protected against the greedy inroads of ignorant trade unions.

The conversion of most labour parties to the market regulation of capitalist economies – a process still underway – seems to remove the last resistance against this mode of regulation. But, now the market regulation is not quite the same as that which prevailed before 1930, when the gold standard and some free trade guaranteed the absence of government from the economic scene. The size of the public sector is too big and the degree of monopoly too high to leave the macro-regulation of the economy entirely to the vagaries of markets (among which, financial markets play the leading role). Nowadays the market regulation is, so to say, 'produced' by deliberate economic policies, which aim mainly to keep in bounds the rise of prices. Even countries which have near-zero inflation cannot be sure that price stability will prevail in the future. So, monetary policy is not tied automatically to the state of the balance of payments but is part of a set of economic policies through which government tries to manage effective demand in order to keep stable the domestic price level and external accounts. One may wonder if market regulation, as it is practised today, is not a case of repressed inflation, which succeeds due to the weakening of distributional conflicts in most developed capitalist countries.

3.   CONCLUSIONS

Distributional conflicts seem, for the time being, to have weakened in the developed countries, but that is certainly *not* the case in countries that are undergoing sharp social transformations, as the result of industrialization and/or transition from centrally planned to market economies. In such countries, structural changes, brought about by the applications of advanced technology, by the creation of new branches of industry or by the opening of whole sectors of the economy to private enterprises, disrupt the hitherto distribution of income in such a way that the market allocation of gains and losses in never peacefully accepted. Distributional conflicts arise and have to be arbitrated by government. Permanent and heavy inflation is the most likely outcome, mainly because, as was seen, 'stabilization' is socially and politically unfeasible.

It seems that, once under way, inflation itself provokes so many distributional conflicts that the permanence of inflation does not depend on new conflicts, originated by structural changes. That may be so, but in the absence of structural change, the repetition of the same conflicts, pitting against each other always the same social actors, would possibly stabilize inflation and increase the chances of success of the 'heterodox' stabilization strategy. That may be the main reason why stabilization, be it orthodox or heterodox, seems to require economic stagnation to succeed. If so, then recession has the double role of repressing in the short run the rise of prices by means of lack of demand and, in the longer run, to prevent distributional conflicts by maintaining income distribution relatively unchanged.

The correlation between income changes and distributional conflicts is likely to be high. Distributional conflicts don't spring up from a sudden perception of distributive injustice. They result from changes: the opening of collective bargaining, the increase of needs due to the appearance of new goods or services on the market, the loss of real income due to inflation, the recognition of profitable investment opportunities etc. In a stagnating economy with stable prices, such changes are infrequent, so that the likelihood of distributional conflicts is small. In an economy under permanent high inflation, however, real incomes change virtually all the time and distributional conflicts become a central feature of social life. The mode of regulation, therefore, has profound consequences not only in the economic but also in the political sphere.

NOTES

*   Paper presented at the Seminar on 'Democratizing Economics: discourse and praxis', at the university of São Paulo, São Paulo, 25–29 July, 1988.
1.   Nominal tax revenue = 100; price index = 130; $100/130 = 0.77$.
2.   Nominal tax revenue = 125; price index = 162.3; $125.5/162.3 = 0.77$.
3.   If inflation is high but stable, the demand for money should expand at the same pace as prices rise. If inflation accelerates, the cost of holding cash increases and as a consequence the demand for money should expand less than the new current inflation rate, and vice versa.
4.   Low inflation implies an annual price rise of less than 20 per cent and high inflation prices rise more than 50 per cent a year. Such figures are indicative only. The 'weight' of the same quantitative inflation may be very different in different institutional settings.
5.   This overreaction should be ascribed not only to the economic loss but also to the political climate which usually prevails when drastic income redistribution is implemented.

15. Medium-Run Keynesianism: Hysteresis and Capital Scrapping*

David Soskice and Wendy Carlin

1. INTRODUCTION

This chapter was stimulated by the puzzle posed by two sets of empirical observations for the UK economy. On the one hand, as Chart 15.1 illustrates, in the upswing of 1985 capacity utilization has returned to a level very close to that of 1973 while the rate of unemployment has continued to rise.[1] The second observation is that estimates of the NAIRU or non-accelerating inflation rate of unemployment have risen with the actual rate of unemployment over the period from the mid-1970s to the mid-1980s resulting in the pattern depicted in Chart 15.2. A possible explanation would be that of a continuous upward shift in the NAIRU. But the standard exogenous variables accounting for such a shift (such as continued worsening of the terms of trade or increasing strength of unions) are of doubtful power from the perspective of the 1980s. Alternative explanations of the phenomenon of the upward shift of the NAIRU with the rise in actual unemployment have centred on the phenomenon of hysteresis. The most frequently cited microeconomic foundation for hysteresis is the so-called insider–outsider model (e.g. Lindbeck and Snower, 1984; Blanchard and Summers, 1986). In these models, the monopoly power of insiders associated with the turnover cost of hiring and firing means that it is the change in unemployment rather than its level which is important for bargaining.

This Chapter suggests an alternative route to hysteresis focusing on the effect of changes in capacity utilization on pricing decisions. We develop a simple model which, in the context of a specific policy rule pursued by the government, would produce results consistent with the observations in Charts 15.1 and 15.2. The model is in the NAIRU tradition in the short run, but changes in the NAIRU over a longer period are seen as the consequence of the effect of deflationary policies on the capital stock. This is the sense in which the model displays medium-run Keynesianism.

241

Chart 15.1   UK unemployment and capacity utilization, 1973–87

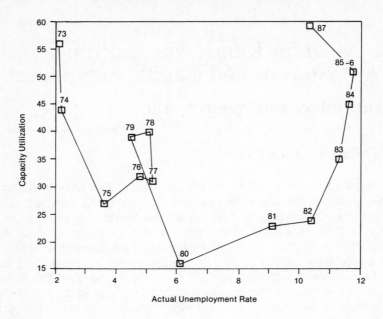

Note:
Capacity utilization is derived from the CBI *Industrial Trends Survey* and shows 100 minus the percentage of respondents stating that they are working below full capacity.

Sources:
Capacity utilization from CBI *Industrial Trends Survey* results for October each year, reported in *National Institute Economic Review*, 3. 1988, Table 5, p. 95. Years before 1978 from earlier *NIER*s. Unemployment rate from OECD *Economic Outlook*, 1. 1988, Table R18.

2.   A STANDARD NAIRU MODEL

A very simple macroeconomic model is derived which, for ease of exposition, is characterized in equilibrium by a stationary state, i.e. in equilibrium, the growth rate of the capital stock and of output is zero. There are four component equations: first, the equation which determines the rate of net investment and thus the growth rate of the capital stock as a function of the difference between actual and desired capacity utilization. The second is a short-run utilization or production function that determincs the rate of unemployment associated with any given level of capacity utilization for a fixed level of the capital stock. Third, is the

Chart 15.2   UK actual unemployment rate and NAIRU, 1966–85

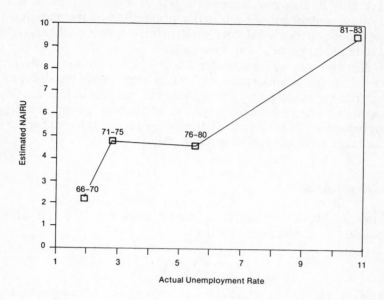

Source:
O. Blanchard, R. Dornbusch and R. Layard, *Restoring Europe's Prosperity*, 1986, Table 18, p. 80.

aggregate demand function that determines the actual level of capacity utilization through a simple multiplier relation. Finally, the model is completed by an equation that specifies the combinations of capacity utilization and unemployment at which inflation is constant. This 'competing claims equilibrium' reflects the fact that if a higher rate of capacity utilization permits businesses to raise their profit margins and a lower rate of unemployment permits unions to negotiate a higher expected real wage through money wage negotiations, then any increase in capacity utilization will require an increase in unemployment if inflation is to remain constant.

In the short run, the level of capacity utilization and unemployment is fixed by the level of aggregate demand, given the capital stock. Only if this short-run equilibrium pair (capacity utilization, unemployment) lies on the competing claims equilibrium schedule will the rate of inflation be constant. Full long-run equilibrium in the model is defined by constant inflation and a constant capital stock (which requires that capacity utilization is at its target level). However, in the medium run, as the capital stock rises or falls, the rate of unemployment at which inflation is constant will generally be changing. Hence, the rate of unemployment at which inflation is constant will depend in the medium run on the pattern over time of changes in the capital stock which in turn depends on the aggregate demand implications of government policy.[2]

It is also demonstrated that, with particular patterns of the relationship between the mark-up and capacity utilization, problems of instability may characterize the model over a specific range of capacity utilization. Over such a range, a fixed government policy rule expressed in terms of a target rate of reduction of the rate of inflation can result in a destabilizing fall in capacity utilization and rise in unemployment.

Net Investment

The rate of growth of the fixed capital stock (i.e. the rate of net investment), $\dot{K}$, is determined by:

$$\dot{K} = \mu (v - v^*) \tag{1}$$

where $\dot{K} = dK/dt$, v is actual capacity utilization, v^* is target capacity utilization, and μ is the accelerator-type coefficient. v^* is assumed exogenously determined by considerations of oligopolistic strategy in the product market (e.g. Dixit, 1980). Hence, firms will undertake investment to remove any discrepancy between actual and target utilization.

Short-run Production Function

The simplest possible structure is assumed with fixed coefficients in the short-run production or utilization function. Unit labour requirements are a_L and unit capital requirements are a_K. Thus,

$E = a_L y$ where E is the total number employed and y, real output;
$K \geq a_K y$; and
$v = \dfrac{a_K y}{K} \leq 1$.

On the assumption that the labour force, L, is constant, there is a short-run production function relation between the degree of capacity utilization and the rate of unemployment, given the capital stock.

Figure 15.1   Short-run production function

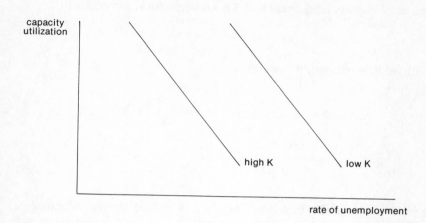

$$v = \frac{a_K}{a_L} \cdot \frac{E}{L} \cdot \frac{L}{K} = \frac{a_K}{a_L} \cdot (1 - u) \cdot \frac{L}{K} \tag{2}$$

where u, the rate of unemployment is defined as $1 - E/L$.

For any given capital stock, equation (2) defines a downward-sloping relationship between the rate of capacity utilization and the rate of unemployment (Figure 15.1). From equation (3), defined below, the level of aggregate demand fixes the rate of capacity utilization which, via equation (2), determines the rate of unemployment. A decline in capacity utilization with fixed coefficients implies a fall in employment, which with a constant labour force implies a rise in the rate of unemployment. A lower level of the capital stock shifts this short-run production function to the right since with a given rate of capacity utilization, a lower capital stock implies lower employment (Figure 15.1).

Aggregate Demand: The Actual Level of Capacity Utilization

Once again, an extremely simple structure is used. Product market equilibrium is defined by:

$$I + NG = S$$

where NG is net government expenditure in real terms (the public sector deficit). I is gross investment and S is savings with s, a constant

$$S = sy$$

With no depreciation, we can write

$$NG + \mu (v - v^*) = sy = \frac{s}{a_K} \cdot v \cdot K$$

$$\therefore \quad v = \frac{NG - \mu v^*}{\frac{s}{aK} K \mu} \tag{3}$$

Equation (3) is the multiplier relation, with the degree of capacity utilization demand-determined, as long as $sK/a_K > \mu$. For simplicity, net government expenditure is the only element of autonomous demand. Other elements could be introduced without altering the structure of the model.

Competing Claims Equilibrium Schedule

Common to a number of competing claims NAIRU type models[3] is the assumption that the expected real wage is determined through collective bargaining and is a function of the rate of unemployment. Money wage negotiations are conducted on the basis of a particular expected rate of inflation.

Thus $w^N = w^N (u)$ where w^N is the expected negotiated real wage and $w^N{}'(u) \leq 0$.

The actual real wage, on the assumption that prices are set immediately after wage negotiations is determined by mark-up pricing:

$$w = a_L^{-1} \cdot (1 - m (v))$$

where w is the actual real wage, and m(v) is the real profit margin. Various possibilities can arise – the profit margin may be positively, negatively or unrelated to the rate of capacity utilization, and the function need not be monotonic.

Figure 15.2   Competing claims equilibrium schedules

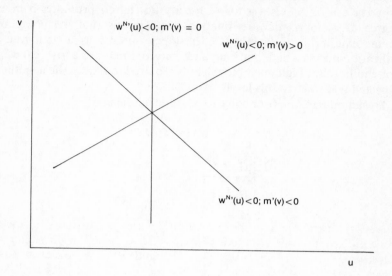

The competing claims equilibrium schedule is defined by equality between the negotiated expected real wage, w^N and the actual real wage, w, i.e. by:

$$w^N(u) = a_L^{-1}(1 - m(v))$$

(4)

The slope of the competing claims equilibrium schedule (CCE) is:

$$\frac{dv}{du} = -\frac{w^{N\,\prime}(u)}{m'(v)}.$$

Depending on the responsiveness of the profit margin to capacity utilization and of the negotiated expected real wage to the rate of unemployment, a number of possible shapes for the competing claims equilibrium exist and are shown in Figure 15.2.

3.   THE EXTENDED MODEL: THE MARKUP RISES WITH CAPACITY UTILIZATION ($w^{N\,\prime}(u) < 0$; $m'(v) > 0$)

Let us take as the standard case the situation in which the negotiated expected real wage varies negatively with the rate of unemployment and the mark-up varies positively with the degree of capacity utilization. Thus it is assumed that businesses are able to raise their profit margins when capacity utilization rises – high-capacity utilization promotes a higher degree of oligopolistic coordination. This means that the competing claims equilibrium schedule (CCE) slopes upward as a high rate of utilization means a high mark-up and therefore requires a low real wage. For equilibrium, high unemployment is required to reduce the negotiated expected real wage to this level.

To summarize, the four equations of the model are:

$$\dot{K} = \mu \, (v - v^*) \tag{1}$$

$$v = \frac{NG - \mu \, v^*}{\frac{s}{aK} K - \mu} \tag{3}$$

$$u = 1 - v.\frac{K}{L} \frac{a_L}{a_K} \tag{2}$$

$$w^N(u) = a_L^{-1} \, (1 - m(v)) \tag{4'}$$

Since for any level of the capital stock equation (3) determines the level of capacity utilization and equation (2), the rate of unemployment, equation (4) will not in general hold. Out of equilibrium, the wage and price-setting behaviour represented in equation (4) will produce increasing or decreasing inflation according to equation (4):

$$\ddot{P} = \tau \, [\, w^N(u) - a_L^{-1} \, (1 - m(v))] \tag{4'}$$

where $\ddot{P}$ is the rate of change of the rate of inflation, $\tau > 0$.

Figure 15.3 depicts the system of equations. Equation (3) simply identifies the actual rate of capacity utilization along the downward sloping line representing the short-run production function (eq. 2).

To examine the dynamic behaviour of the model, it is necessary to specify a government policy rule. Suppose that the government embarks on a medium run programme (five to ten years) to reduce the rate of inflation by a fixed amount of $x\%$ each year. In the context of the model, this will require that net government spending takes a path over time to ensure that

$$w^N(u) + \alpha = a_L \, (1 - m(v)).$$

In other words, for inflation to fall at $x\%$ per year, the rate of capacity utilization and unemployment must be such that from equation 4',

Figure 15.3   The model – mark-up varies positively with capacity utilization

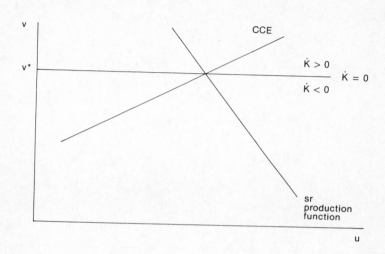

$$-x = \tau [w^N - a_L^{-1} (1 - m(v))].$$

This implies that

$$a_L^{-1} (1 - m(v)) - x/\tau = w^N$$

i.e.

$$\alpha = x/\tau,$$

where, for simplicity τ is assumed to be a constant.

Hence, to ensure that the rate of inflation falls by $x\%$ per year, the government must set the public sector deficit such that actual capacity utilization is at the intersection of the CCE + α schedule and the short run production function $u(v; K_t)$ where K_t is the current capital stock. Thus from an initial long-run equilibrium at A_1 in Figure 15.4 where actual unemployment is equal to the NAIRU, (u_1^*),[4] the government cuts net government expenditure to reduce the rate of capacity utilization to v_2. Unemployment rises from $u_1 (= u_1^*)$ to u_2. Unemployment is now above the NAIRU (u_1^*) and the rate of inflation is falling both because the fall in

*Figure 15.4   Dynamic adjustment in response to policy rule of reducing
inflation each year*

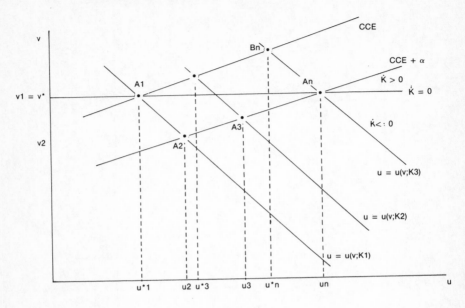

capacity utilization has reduced the mark-up and because higher unemployment reduces the negotiable expected real wage.

However, at A_1 with capacity utilization below the target level, businesses will be scrapping part of the capital stock so as to restore the desired level of utilization. The capital stock is falling over time and the economy moves up the CCE + α line. For example, when the capital stock has fallen to K_2, the economy is at A_3 with unemployment equal to u_3. At this point, the NAIRU has risen from u_1^* to u_3^*, since with the lower capital stock K_2, capacity utilization is higher and thus the unemployment rate must be higher than in the initial situation for inflation to be constant (the NAIRU) and higher still for inflation to be falling at $x\%$ (u_3).

This process will continue until the point A_n is reached as long as the government maintains its policy stance unchanged. At A_n, with capacity utilization back to the target level, there will be no further change in the level of the capital stock. The economy can remain indefinitely at A_n with unemployment of u_n and with inflation falling at a constant $x\%$ per year. The NAIRU has risen to u_n^*. The path of capacity utilization and unemployment are shown in Figure 15.5 and of actual unemployment and the NAIRU in Figure 15.6.

Figure 15.5   The path of unemployment and the NAIRU

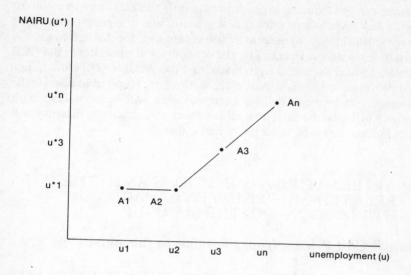

Figure 15.6   The path of capacity utilization and unemployment

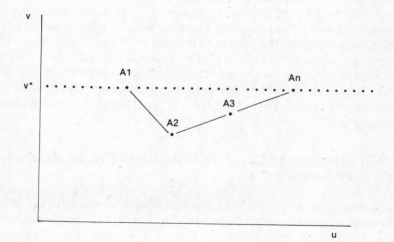

Should the government decide to allow inflation to stabilize (for example, when the inflation rate has fallen close to zero), then it will increase net government expenditure to shift the economy to point B_n (Figure 15.4). With the economy now in a situation of greater than desired capacity utilization, investment will increase and the capital stock will begin to grow again. Eventually, the economy will move down the CCE schedule toward the initial equilibrium and the initial NAIRU, u_1^*. Actual unemployment will be falling as more workers are required to operate the growing capital stock. Falling unemployment will be consistent with constant inflation because the falling level of capacity utilization will mean falling mark-ups and a rising real wage.

4.   ALTERNATIVE ASSUMPTIONS AS TO THE RELATIONSHIP BETWEEN CAPACITY UTILIZATION AND THE MARK-UP

Normal Cost Pricing from the 1950s to the mid-1970s

It was assumed in section 3 as a standard case that the mark-up varies positively with capacity utilization. However, evidence on pricing behaviour in the period from the 1950s to the mid-1970s supports the hypothesis of normal cost pricing – i.e. that the mark-up does not vary with capacity utilization (e.g. Godley and Nordhaus, 1972). With $m'(v) = 0$ and $w^N{}'(u) < 0$, the competing claims equilibrium schedule would be vertical. A change in capacity utilization produces no change in profit margins and therefore in the real wage: there is a unique rate of unemployment at which inflation is constant irrespective of the rate of capacity utilization. This would be consistent with the finding that the NAIRU was relatively constant over the period of the 1950s and 1960s. As can be seen in Figure 15.7, the pursuit of a policy similar to that pursued in section 3 would see the economy shifting from A_1 to A_2 to A_n but the NAIRU would remain constant at u_1^*.

Profit Margins and Capacity Utilization: Pricing Behaviour in a Deep Recession

Little empirical work has been done on business pricing behaviour in response to the much larger fluctuations in capacity utilization which have been experienced from the mid-1970s. We illustrate how changes in pricing behaviour in response to the reduction in capacity utilization

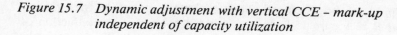

*Figure 15.7   Dynamic adjustment with vertical CCE – mark-up
independent of capacity utilization*

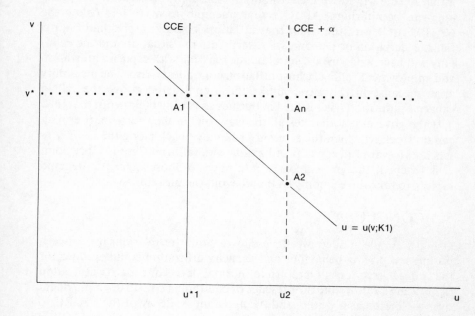

below the 'normal range' can create instability in the context of a
government pursuing a policy rule to reduce inflation. Two different
pricing responses are examined:

(i)   raising margins as utilization falls. Firms feel able to raise their profit
      margins as the result of a reduction in the likelihood of new entry
      into an oligopolistic industry; an extreme form of this tendency is
      cartelization.

(ii) Competitive price-cutting, i.e. profit margins fall as oligopolistic
      coordination collapses in the face of shrinking markets.[5]

These different pricing responses can be represented in the capacity
utilization/unemployment diagram in Figure 15.8. To illustrate the instability case, it is assumed that as capacity utilization falls below the normal
range, there is first a zone of cartelization and then as capacity utilization
falls further, price wars begin. The possibility that there is a region in
which the mark-up rises with a fall in capacity utilization means that the
pursuit of a policy of reducing inflation by x% per year may be unstable.

For example, if the government deflates sharply and pushes the economy to point B in Figure 15.8, then continued pursuit of the reduction of inflation rule will move the economy further and further away from the long-run equilibrium. At B, actual unemployment (u_2) is *below* the NAIRU (u^*_2) with the result that inflation is rising rather than falling. Further deflation of demand will exacerbate the situation and the economy will be in a downward spiral on the real side with capacity utilization and employment falling, whilst inflation continues to rise. The instability arises because in this case, unlike those considered above the fall in capacity utilization has resulted in businesses raising their profit margins.

If the government deflates all the way to C in the short run (i.e. with capital stock K_1), then the economy will move back along the CCE $+ \alpha$ schedule toward full capacity utilization with falling inflation. Once point D is reached, the government would have to boost aggregate demand rapidly to take the economy to E and avoid the unstable region.

5.   CONCLUSION

Using a simple model, we have shown how the relationship between businesses' pricing behaviour and capacity utilization could account for the twin observations of a return to 'normal' levels of capacity utilization in 1979 and 1985 despite the presence of continuing rises in unemployment over the period as a whole, and the apparent tendency of the NAIRU to move upward with the actual rate of unemployment over this period. The implications for the capital stock and for unemployment of following a policy rule of reducing inflation each year over an extended period in an economy which is characterized by wage and price setting for the type assumed here have been illustrated.

These results highlight the importance of research into the relationship between mark-ups and capacity utilization in the recent period. It would also be useful to know whether v* the desired level of capacity utilization responds to the expected growth of output or to the variance in the growth rate. In the face of the adoption of a deflationary government strategy, v* might be expected to rise (i.e. the desired margin of spare capacity would fall) as the likelihood of entry declines. If as is reasonable to assume, investment is a function of the expected growth rate of demand as well as the difference between actual and desired capacity utilization, then this would presumably make the likelihood of instability greater.

Finally, from the labour market side, a process very similar to the one described in this paper may also occur as a result of the decline in the stock of marketable skills in the economy as a result of a prolonged period of deflation.

Figure 15.8   Possible instability as pricing behaviour changes with falling capacity utilization

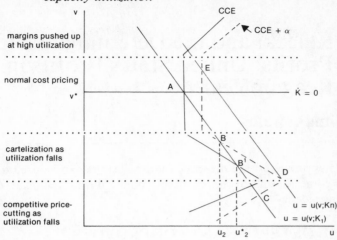

NOTES

*   We wish to thank V. Bhaskar and Andrew Glyn for constructive suggestions.
1.   The estimates in Chart 15.1 come from the CBI's regular survey of businesses. A similar picture is presented in the OECD's *Economic Survey of the United Kingdom*, 1985, diagram 7, p. 27, where capacity utilization was estimated using the phase-average-trend method of calculating potential GDP.
2.   Rowthorn (1977) hints at these effects in the note on p. 222.
3.   For example Rowthorn (1977) and Layard and Nickell (1985).
4.   Note that u* refers to a NAIRU; u refers to the actual unemployment rate.
5.   Blair (1959) identifies and discusses these two responses.

REFERENCES

Blair, J. M., 'Administered Prices: a phenomenon in search of a theory', *American Economic Review*, Vol. 49, 1959, pp. 431–50.

Blanchard, O. and L. Summers, 'Hysteresis and the European Unemployment Problem', in S. Fisher (ed.), *NBER Macroeconomics Annual*, vol. 1, MIT Press, 1986.

Blanchard, O., R. Dornbusch, and R. Layard (eds), *Restoring Europe's Prosperity*, MIT Press, 1986.

Dixit, A., 'The Role of Investment in Entry-deterrence', *Economic Journal*, 90, 1980, pp. 95–106.

Layard, R. and S. Nickell, 'Causes of British Unemployment', *National Institute Economic Review*, February 1985.

Lindbeck, A. and D. J. Snower, 'Involuntary Unemployment as an Insider-Outsider Dilemma', Seminar Paper No. 282, Institute for International Economics, Stockholm, 1984.

Rowthorn, R. E., 'Conflict, Inflation and Money', *Cambridge Journal of Economics*, No. 1, 1971, pp. 215–39.

16. Kalecki and the Determinants of Profits: United States Profits in the Reagan Years*

A. Asimakopulos

Kalecki's approach to the determination of profits can be used to shed light on some aspects of US economic policy during the years of the Reagan presidency.

1. THE DETERMINANTS OF PROFITS – THE SIMPLE CASE

Kalecki's theory of profits, which was first presented in his 1933 article on the business cycle (Kalecki 1971, ch. 1), was restated in a short article (Kalecki 1942)[1] that paid particular attention to the direction of causation. A closed economy with no saving by workers, and a balanced government budget, was assumed.[2] The profits equation was derived from the definitional equality between gross national product and gross national expenditure. Kalecki attributed causal significance to the resulting equation between gross profits and the sum of gross investment and capitalists' consumption (given the assumption of no workers' saving) after considering the following question: 'Does it mean that profits in a given period determine capitalists' consumption and investment, or the other way round?' (Kalecki, 1942, p. 259). He argued that capitalists' expenditures are subject to their decisions, while their earnings are not: 'It is therefore their investment and consumption decisions which determine profits, and not the other way round' (ibid.). But this observation on the variables subject to capitalists' decisions is not sufficient to establish Kalecki's conclusion that capitalists' expenditures determine current profits. Also required is that capitalists' expenditures in the period be *independent* of profits in the same period (cf. Asimakopulos, 1987). If they are not independent, then the profits equation simply shows that profits are either consumed or invested (saved), with no presumption of one-way causality from expenditures to profits. The length of the unit time-period, and the time-lags in the relation of capitalist expenditures to profits, are thus necessary elements in the attribution of causal significance to equality between profits and capitalists' expenditures.

Kalecki did go on to observe that if the period considered is 'short', 'we may say that capitalists' investment and consumption are determined by decisions formed in the *past*' (Kalecki, 1942, p. 259). A time-lag between capitalists' consumption expenditures and profits is thus recognized in addition to the time-lags between investment decisions and expenditures that were always present in Kalecki's analysis. 'For the execution of investment orders takes a certain time, and as to the capitalists' consumption, it is only with a certain delay that the capitalists' standard of living reacts to the change of factors which influence it' (ibid.). But he did not state that it is only for a time-period in which capitalists' expenditures can be taken as pre-determined, that the equality between profits and these expenditures provides a causal explanation for the level of profits.

There was recognition that certain qualifications may have to be added to the statement that current profits are determined by capitalists' expenditure decisions made in the past, because these decisions may not be fully executed. In particular, investment in the period might be affected by unexpected changes in inventories. Kalecki sees capitalists' expenditure decisions as being made in real terms, while the value of current expenditures is also dependent on current prices, and he expresses his profits equation in real terms by deflating both sides of the equation by suitable price indices. 'We may now conclude that the real gross profits in a given short period are determined by decisions of capitalists as to their consumption and investment formed in the past, subject to the correction for the unexpected changes in the volume of stocks' (ibid., p. 260).

To complete the analysis of the determination of profits in his basic model, Kalecki considered the effects of changes in the factors determining income shares. With the level of current profits dependent only on predetermined values for capitalists' expenditures, an increase in the degree of monopoly that is reflected in a higher mark-up cannot affect the level of profits in real terms, but must result in lower output and real wages. The higher price of wage goods, given money-wage rates, results in a fall in workers' consumption and thus in total output. With the level of real profits constant, given the assumption of unchanged capitalists' expenditures, the profit share has increased. Kalecki concludes that '[H]owever great the margin of profit on a unit of output, the capitalists cannot make more in total profits than they consume and invest (inclusive of accumulation of unsold goods)' (ibid.).

This independence of the level of profits from the degree of monopoly is a feature found only in Kalecki's simplest model of a closed economy, in which workers do not save and the government budget is balanced. As soon as any one of these special assumptions is relaxed, then the level of profits, as well as the profits share, can be affected by changes in mark-ups (Asimakopulos, 1975, p. 333). Kalecki never drew attention to the very special circumstances that are required in order to make the level of profits independent of the factors affecting distribution. Even Joan Robinson, a close student of Kalecki's work, was misled into pointing to this 'independence' as a central feature of his theory of distribution.

> There are two elements in Kalecki's analysis of profits: the share of gross profit in the product of industry is determined by the level of gross margin, while the total flow of profits per annum depends upon the total flow of capitalists' expenditure on investment and consumption.
> Combining these two theories, we find the very striking proposition that firms, considered as a whole, cannot increase their profits merely by raising prices. Raising profit margins reduces real wages and consequently employment in wage-good industries. The *share* of profit is increased but the total profits remain equal to the flow to capitalists' expenditure. (Robinson, 1979, p. 192; italics in original)

In Kalecki's general model, to which we now turn, a change in the degree of monopoly can affect the level of profits, even if capitalists' expenditures are unchanged.

2.   THE DETERMINANTS OF PROFITS – THE GENERAL CASE

Kalecki returned once again to the consideration of the determinants of profits in his *Theory of Economic Dynamics (1954)*. He began with the simplified model discussed above and, as in Kalecki (1942), the national income identity was used to derive the profits equation. A slightly different variant of the simplified model was examined. Government expenditure and taxation are assumed to be negligible, and there are thus no taxes to be deducted from the profits in the profits equation. Kalecki reproduces the 1942 statement that attributes causal significance to this equation, and his only reference to the role of the degree of monopoly occurs before he examines the more general case. No indication is given that the degree of monopoly could also affect the level of profits in this general case.

> The above clarifies the role of the 'distribution factors', i.e. factors determining the distribution of income (such as degree of monopoly) in the theory of profits. Given that profits are determined by capitalists' consumption and investment, it is the workers' income (equal here to workers' consumption) which is determined by the 'distribution factors'. In this way capitalists' consumption and investment conjointly with the 'distribution factors' determine the workers'

consumption and consequently the national output and employment. The national output will be pushed up to the point where profits carved out of it in accordance with the 'distribution factors' are equal to the sum of capitalists' consumption and investment. (Kalecki 1954, p. 47)

The message is the same as it was when only the simplified model was being examined. There is still an emphasis on the clear-cut separation between the 'distribution factors' that determine income shares and those factors that determine the level of profits.

For the general case of an open economy, with no restrictions on the government budget balance or on workers' saving, Kalecki writes the national income identity in a form equivalent to

$$(P-T_p) + (W-T_w) + T_p + T_w + T_i = I + IS + G + C_c + C_w \quad (1)$$

where P, W, I, C_c and C_w represent gross profits, the total wage bill, investment expenditures, and consumption expenditures of capitalists and workers, respectively: T_p, T_w and T_i, the direct taxes on profits, on wages, and indirect taxes, respectively; IS, the international surplus; and G, the value of government expenditure on goods and services. He then adds government transfer payments (T_r) to both sides of this equation and subtracts total taxation, to obtain

$$(P-T_p) + (W-T_w+T_r) = I + IS + GD + C_e + C_w \quad (2)$$

where GD is the government budget deficit. The profits equation for this general case is then obtained by subtracting the wages item from both sides of the equation:

$$(P-T_p) = I + IS + GD + C_e - WS \quad (3)$$

where WS is the value for workers' saving.

For equation (3) to provide a causal explanation for after-tax profits, it is necessary that the other items in that equation be independent of current profits so that they determine the latter, and are not themselves determined by it. If the period of time is short, then this independence can be affirmed as it was for Kalecki's simplified model. There is, however, a possible complication with respect to the government deficit if the government revenues from profits taxes that figure in the calculation of this deficit are based on estimates of current profits. But the main direction of causation is from the items on the right-hand side of equation (3) to gross profits after tax.

Kalecki observed that the international surplus and the government deficit have the same effect on profits as investment and capitalists' consumption, and they make it possible for profits to exceed the level determined by these expenditures. He concludes:

The above shows clearly the significance of 'external' markets (including those created by budget deficits) for a capitalist economy. Without such markets profits are conditioned by the ability of capitalists to consume or to undertake capital investment. It is the export surplus and the budget deficit which enable the capitalists to make profits over and above their own purchases of goods and services.

The connection between 'external' profits and imperialism is obvious. The fight for the division of existing foreign markets and the expansion of colonial empires, which provide new opportunities for export of capital associated with export of goods, can be viewed as a drive for export surplus, the classical source of 'external' profits. Armaments and wars, usually financed by budget deficits, are also a source of this kind of profits. (ibid., p. 52)

Kalecki's statements are correct, if they are taken as interpretations of the *ex post* characteristics of equation (3), but it is necessary to be careful not to draw from them conclusions about the net effects on profits of changes in any one of the items on the right-hand side of that equation. The causal factors in this profits equation are interdependent even within a short interval of time, and a change in one could result in, at least, a partially offsetting change in the others. For example, part of capitalists' expenditures are directed to imports, so that an increase in these expenditures would adversely affect the export surplus. Imports would also be increased as a result of higher workers' consumption that accompanies the increased employment due to an increase in capitalists' expenditures. The change in these expenditures, by affecting the level of economic activity, would also alter the budget deficit. There could also be, under certain conditions, a direct relation between the government deficit and the export surplus, since both form part of the necessary equality between saving and investment. Before examining this possible connection we shall look at Kalecki's rearrangement of equation (3) to focus on the equality between saving and investment.

3.   THE SAVING–INVESTMENT EQUALITY

With the national income identity as the source of his profits equation, it is a simple matter for Kalecki to rearrange the items in that equation in order to show another consequence of this identity, the equality between saving and investment. He subtracts capitalists' consumption expenditures, and adds workers' saving, to both sides of equation (3) to obtain:

$$(P - T_p - C_c) + WS = I + IS + GD \qquad (4)$$

This equation shows that the sum of private domestic saving must be equal to private investment adjusted by the values for the export surplus and the government deficit.

This necessary equality between saving and investment is used by Kalecki as the basis for the conclusion that the rate of interest cannot be considered

> to be the factor equilibrating the demand for and supply of new capital. In the present conception investment, once carried out, automatically provides the savings necessary to finance it. Indeed, in our simplified model, profits in a given period are the direct outcome of capitalists' consumption and investment in that period. If investment increases by a certain amount, savings out of profits are *pro tanto* higher.
>
> To put it in a more concrete fashion: if some capitalists increase their investment by using for this purpose their liquid reserves, the profits of other capitalists will rise *pro tanto* and thus the liquid reserves invested will pass into the possession of the latter. If additional investment is financed by bank credit, the spending of the amounts in question will cause equal amounts of saved profits to accumulate as bank deposits. The investing capitalists will thus find it possible to float bonds to the same extent and thus to repay the bank credits.
>
> One important consequence of the above is that the rate of interest cannot be determined by the demand for and supply of new capital because investment 'finances itself'. (ibid., p. 50)

There are various traps for the unwary in these statements on the consequences of the necessary equality between saving and investment. It is true that an increase in investment at any time means, as a matter of definition, that saving must also have increased at that time by the same amount. But for 'investing capitalists . . . [to] find it possible to float bonds to the same extent and thus to repay bank credits', this saving must be short-period equilibrium saving. This means that sufficient time must have elapsed since investment increased to allow the level and distribution of income to adapt to this new value, so that the *desired* level of saving is equal to the new level of investment. But quite apart from this neglect of the passage of time needed for desired saving to adjust to the new level of investment expenditures, Kalecki's position ignores the possible role of the rate of interest in determining the amount of private investment.

Before firms make decisions to subject themselves to the risks and uncertainties of new investment projects, the values for the rates of interest are considered. Both short- and long-term interest rates are relevant in this connection. Short-term rates are considered because firms often cover the cost of investment projects during their construction phases by short-term 'bridging' loans. Long-term rates are important because firms normally fund these short-term obligations through the sale of bonds whose life to maturity tends to match the expected length of life of the investment projects being financed. In this way, firms 'lock in' their interest costs and avoid the problems that could be caused by unexpected increases in the rates of interest in subsequent years. A firm will only proceed with its investment project if current interest rates are not judged to be too onerous, given its long-term expectations of the profitability of this project.

The time sequence must be kept in mind in order to put Kalecki's statements into proper perspective. Short-term finance must first be provided by the banking system, and firms must feel confident about their ability to fund these credits at satisfactory terms, before the rate of investment can be increased.[3] This increase in investment can be said to 'finance itself', but only some time *after* it has taken place. It is the equilibrium increase in desired saving, which results from this increase in investment, that Kalecki expects to be used, directly or indirectly, to purchase the bonds of the investing firms. Kalecki assumed, in making these statements, that workers do not save and 'that both foreign trade and the government budget are balanced' (ibid., p. 49). But the terms at which bank and bond finance are available could affect investment decisions. Finance at acceptable terms is required before investment can be increased. A careful reading of Kalecki's comments thus makes clear that interest rates are involved before the increased investment 'automatically provides the savings necessary to finance it'.

The equations used by Kalecki provide a necessary framework for showing how various aggregates contribute to total profits, but they cannot be used to indicate the initiating factor in a change in profits, nor can they show the net effects on profits of a change in one of its causal determinants. The actual values for these determinants are the outcomes of a very large number of individual decisions and actions, and a given change in one of them will often affect the values of the others. For example, the favourable effects on profits of an increase in the budget deficit might, in certain circumstances, be largely dissipated by a consequent decrease in the export surplus. If this increase in the deficit is due to a decrease in tax rates that is accompanied by a tight monetary policy adopted as an anti-inflationary device, it may attract an inflow of funds from foreign countries drawn by the high interest rates. The final result could be an appreciation of the exchange rate and a sharp decrease in the international surplus that significantly reduces the beneficial effects on profits of the increase in the budget deficit. Something along these lines may have occurred in the United States economy during the 1980s.

4.   THE REAGAN YEARS

The use of the US national income accounts as the data source for the determinants of profits makes it necessary to change some of the items appearing in Kalecki's profits equation. These accounts do not distinguish between the consumption expenditures of capitalists and those of wage and salary-earners, and thus only total consumption expenditure can be used in this equation. This is one reason why personal saving, the difference between disposable personal income and total consumption expenditure, replaces workers' saving. Another difference from Kalecki's equation is the separation from profits of the incomes of proprietors of unincorporated business. He placed gross profits in a very broad category and it covered 'depreciation and undistributed profits, dividends and withdrawals from unincorporated business, rent and interest' (Kalecki, 1954, p. 45). These withdrawals from unincorporated business represent income from work, as well as from capital, and it is not clear that all of this income belongs in the profits category. The social relations that exist in capitalist firms are blurred in unincorporated businesses. The owners (and their families) often provide a significant proportion of the total labour used in these enterprises, and not all of their incomes belong in the profits category. But there is no problem with capital consumption allowances in this sector; they are a part of gross profits. Kalecki's inclusion of dividends (D) and net interest receipts (IN) in gross profits conforms to general usage. But the values for these items also appear as incomes of persons, and two 'profits' categories will be used below to reflect the two ways of treating these incomes. The broader category will be referred to as gross profits (P''), and will include dividends and the net interest item in the national income. The narrower category will be referred to as gross retained earnings (P'), and will only include the sum of undistributed profits and capital consumption allowances.

The saving-investment identity can be used to highlight the determinants of gross retained earnings. Private gross saving in the economy is equal to the sum of gross retained earnings and personal saving (PS). This sum must be equal, at each point in time, to the sum of private gross investment, net foreign investment, and the government deficit. This saving-investment equality can thus be written as:

$$P' + PS = I + GD + IS \qquad (5)$$

When personal saving is subtracted from both sides of equation (5), we obtain an equation for gross retained earnings.

$$P' = I + GD + IS - PS \qquad (6)$$

The necessary equality between the two sides of equation (6) can be interpreted as a causal explanation of P', for the reasons given in section 1 above. The current values for the items on the right-hand side of the equation must be independent of the current value for P'. This requirement will largely be met when the basic time-interval for equation (6) is a quarter of a year. The existence of time-lags in the investment process – the separation in time of investment decisions from the resulting investment expenditures – means that the value of I in a particular quarter is largely predetermined. Even unexpected changes in inventories that lead to differences between actual and planned investment are the result of mistaken short-term expectations of sales, and are not functions of current profits. There is a feedback from gross retained earnings to investment, but this is *future* investment. These earnings are an important source, directly or indirectly, of finance for investment, and they also influence the long-term expectations of the profitability of investment. The value for the government deficit (this term refers to the budget balance for *all* levels of government) depends on the tax-expenditure structure of government budgets, and the level of economic activity in the economy. The latter is a general determinant of current profits rather than the result of current profits, and thus the government deficit can be taken to be independent of current profits, even though a portion of government revenue is derived from profits taxes. The value for net foreign investment (the international surplus) depends on the international competitiveness of the domestic economy in the production of goods and services, and on the net balance of the two-way flow of interest and dividend payments.[4] It too would thus be largely independent of current profits. The value for personal saving depends on personal income and on the economy's propensity to save. Even those elements of personal income that can be considered part of gross profits, such as dividends and interest, are largely independent of current earnings in the corporate sector. Dividends reflect long-term policies, and even when they are tied to current earnings, they are declared and paid after the quarter's earnings are known. Interest receipts in a particular quarter depend on the terms and amounts of loans made in the earlier periods.

This brief consideration of the components of equation (6) leads to the conclusion that the current values for the items on the right-hand side of that equation are largely independent of current earnings in the corporate sector. The requirement that P' be equal to the sum of the values for these items thus means that they can be considered to be the causal determinants of the value for P'. As our discussion showed, the direction of causality for equation (6) is not absolute, since there is some possible feedback from the current value for P' to the current values for the items on the right-hand side of the equation. But the main causal direction in each quarter, taken separately, is from the right to the left.

Table 16.1 *Average values of quarterly data, seasonally adjusted at annual rates, for gross retained earnings and its determinants ($ billion), US 1970 to 1987*

Interval	P	I		GD		IS		PS	
	($)	($)	(% of P')	($)	(% of P')	($)	(% of P')	($)	(% of P')
1970:1 to 1980:1	203.3	276.2	(135.9)	14.1	(6.9)	4.2	(2.1)	90.0	(44.3)
1980:2 to 1987:3	469.8	572.2	(121.8)	101.7	(21.6)	−63.6	(−13.5)	140.1	(29.8)
Percentage change	131.1	107.2		621.3		—		55.7	

Note:
The sum of the determinants of profits do not add up to P' because of the statistical discrepancy and the non-zero values in some years for wage accruals less disbursements and net capital grants received by the United States.

Sources:
1970–82, *National Income and Product Accounts of the United States, 1929–82. Statistical Tables*; 1983, *Survey of Current Business*, July 1986; 1984–87, *Survey of Current Business*, July 1987.

Some perspective is provided for the examination of the determinants of profits in the Reagan years by a comparison of their relative values in an earlier interval. The two time intervals examined are 1970:1 to 1980:1, and 1980:2 to 1987:3.[5] Each of these intervals begins with the start of the contraction phase of a business cycle in order to minimize the effects of cyclical variations on this comparison. The first interval ends with the completion of an expansionary phase, while the second makes use of the most recent data available at the time of writing, and is still in an expansionary phase. The Reagan years dominate the second interval, even though it begins three quarters before his inauguration, and it is used to represent them.

The figures in Table 16.1 show substantial differences in the relative values (in current dollars) of the determinants of gross retained earnings between the two intervals being considered. The value for this profits category increased by 131 per cent with the monetary value for gross investment roughly doubling, but the government deficit increased on average over six times. There was also a drastic change in the international surplus, as it moved from a small positive value to a much larger negative value. The increase in the average value for personal saving was even smaller than the increase in investment, and since this item has a negative effect on profits, its relative decline tended to prop up gross retained earnings.

It is important to repeat again that changes in these causal determinants of profits are not independent, and that the change in the value for one of them does not translate directly into an equal change in profits. For example, an increase in investment expenditures would tend to increase economic activity, and thus to decrease the government deficit obtained with a given tax-expenditure budget structure. It would also tend to decrease the international surplus directly, with part of the increased investment expenditures being devoted to imported capital goods, and indirectly, as higher domestic economic activity and incomes pull in imported consumer goods. The net effect on profits of any initial increase in investment could thus be considerably smaller than this increase. Similarly, the net effect on profits of an increase in the government deficit due, say, to a change in the tax-expenditure structures of government budgets, could be substantially less than the increase in the deficit. There may be many reasons for the appearance of offsetting changes. One possible scenario has this increase accompanied by higher interest rates as a result of concern over the inflationary effects of this change, or as a consequence of monetary constraints taken by the monetary authorities because of this concern. This combination could affect the exchange rate. The increase in domestic interest rates relative to foreign rates could attract foreign funds in search of higher returns, and this inflow could lead to an appreciation of a country's currency. This appreciation would adversely affect the country's international competitive position, and its international surplus could decrease sharply. This policy could also have significant effects in subsequent periods. The higher interest rates might discourage some investment decisions, and thus future investment expenditures. This slowdown in the renewal of industrial facilities, added to the permanent damage caused by an over-valued currency over a period of years, means that the country's international competitive position could not be restored in the future simply by reversing the change in currency rates.

The effect on profits (and on the economic 'health' of the economy) of an initial change in one of its determinants, depends on the particular circumstances in which that change takes place. Scenarios for the effects of an increase in the government deficit other than the one sketched out above, are possible. For example, if it occurs at a time of considerable unemployment, in an environment where prices have been stable and inflationary concerns are absent, the compensating increase in saving might largely be found in higher gross retained earnings and personal saving. They would be higher as a result of the expansionary effects of the

Table 16.2   Average values of quarterly data, seasonally adjusted at annual rates, for components of gross profits and compensation of employees ($ billion)

Interval	P''	U	D	IN	NP	W+
1970:1 to 1980:1	$322.5	$41.3	$33.0	$86.2	$160.5	$986.3
1980:2 to 1987:3	$831.1	$66.3	$74.7	$286.6	$427.6	$2137.94
Percentage change	155.7	60.5	126.4	232.5	166.4	116.8

Source:
See Table 16.1.

increase in the government deficit under these circumstances. There would also be some reduction in net foreign investment as imports increase, but there is no reason to expect that they would be augmented by an appreciation of the country's exchange rate. The profits equation, of course, holds in all cases, because it is derived from the saving-investment identity. It is not possible to predict from knowledge of this equation the location of the required changes that offset an initiating change in one of the determinants. For this it is necessary to know the details of various policies, and the attitudes and expectations of individual agents. But it is clear from the requirements of the saving-investment identity, and the low propensity to save in the United States in the 1980s, that a drastic increase in the US government deficit would have to be balanced to a large extent by a decline in its net foreign investment. For a closed economy, such a combination of higher government deficits and a low propensity to save – even with investment stable – would result in sharply higher profits. The latter could then lead to increases in future investment. But in an open economy, these changes could produce a substantial deterioration in a country's international competitive position that limits their beneficial effects on investment and employment.

An equation for total gross profits can be derived from equation (6), by adding dividends, and the net interest item in the national accounts, to both sides of that equation

$$P'' = P' + D + IN = I + GD + IS - (PS - D - IN) \qquad (7)$$

The Reagan years have seen a significant change in the composition of gross profits, as shown in Table 16.2. There has been substantial growth in interest payments, reflecting the sharp increase in interest rates, and perhaps the use of higher debt ratios in the financing of investment. These interest payments increased by almost twice as much as the increase in dividends, with undistributed profits (U) only increasing by half as much as dividends. Interest payments accounted for a little over one-half of net profits (NP = U + D + IN) in the first interval, but this grew to two-thirds in the second one. This proportionate increase was at the expense of both dividend and undistributed profits, but the relative decline of the latter, from approximately 25 per cent of net profits to about 15 per cent, was especially marked. This sharp increase in interest payments – which is in large part the consequence of monetary and fiscal policy – has also affected the distribution of national income. The compensation of employees (W+) increased by 116.8 per cent, so that the ratio of net interest payments to the value for this item increased by .087 to .134. Another indication of this same change is the 25 per cent increase in the ratio of net profits to the compensation of employees from .16 to .20.

CONCLUSION

This examination of Kalecki's theory of the determination of total profits in the economy points out its important assumptions. His transformation of an identity into a causal explanation depends on the existence of time-lags between the earning of profits, and investment and consumption expenditures. The basic time-period for which data is collected should not be longer than these time lags, if these expenditures are to be considered as causal determinants of the period's profits. It is only in Kalecki's simplified model of a closed economy, with no workers' saving, and negligible government expenditures, that the level of profits depends only on capitalists' expenditures. In more general models, changes in mark-ups can affect the level of profits as well as the distribution of income.

The use of an amended version of Kalecki's profits equation to examine US profits in the 1970s and 1980s has highlighted the substantial changes in the relative values of the determinants of profits. The beneficial effects of the increase in the government deficit were offset to a considerable extent by the decrease in the international surplus. This latter could be seen as a consequence of this increase in the government deficit. The monetary policy that was adopted to limit inflationary concerns is also reflected in the marked relative increase in the net interest component of national income.

NOTES

*   A shortened version of the paper presented for the University of Tenessee Conference on Problems in Income Distribution: Functional, International, Personal. This Conference was held from 26 June to 3 July 1988 in Gatlinburg, Tennessee.

1. The material on the determinants of profits in this article was reproduced, with very minor changes, in Kalecki (1943, pp. 47–50).
2. Keynes (1983, pp. 837–41) tried, after accepting this article for publication in the *Economic Journal*, to get Kalecki to make his model more general by introducing certain features of the British economy at that time, such as workers' saving and an unbalanced budget. But Kalecki responded by emphasising the limitations of his theory. 'My theory is definitely not applicable to a war economy, not only because of my assumption that workers do not save, but also because I postulate a balanced budget' (ibid., p. 841). This response is surprising because Kalecki discussed the effects on profits of a government deficit in a 1934 article (reprinted in Kalecki, 1971, pp. 15–25). There is also his note in the 1937 taxation paper that '[I]t is quite simple to pass from this [the balanced budget] to the more general case of an unbalanced budget' (Kalecki 1971, p. 35n).
3. This was emphasized by Keynes in his December 1937 article that dealt with 'finance': 'The entrepreneur when he decides to invest has to be satisfied on two points: firstly, that he can obtain sufficient short-term finance during the period of producing the investment; and secondly, that he can eventually fund his short-term obligations by a long-term issue on satisfactory terms' (Keynes, 1973, p. 217).
4. The net foreign investment in the US national accounts is equal to the net exports of goods and services (that includes net factor income) less capital grants, transfer payments, and net interest paid by government to foreigners.
5. Two earlier studies (Asimakopulos, 1983 and 1987), contain quarterly data for the items in the equation from 1950:1 to 1985:3.

REFERENCES

Asimakopulos, A. 'A Kaleckian Theory of Income Distribution', *Canadian Journal of Economics*, *8*, August 1975, pp. 313–33.

Asimakopulos, A. 'A Kaleckian Profits Equation and the United States Economy, 1950–82'. *Metroeconomica, 35*, September–December 1983, pp. 221–33.

Asimakopulos, A. 'Kalecki on the Determinants of Profits', in G. Fink, G. Poll and M. Riese (eds), *Economic Theory, Political Power and Social Justice: Festschrift Kazimierz Laski*, Wien: Springer-Verlag, 1987, pp. 19–42.

Kalecki, Michal, 'A Theory of Profits', *Economic Journal*, *52*, June–September 1942, pp. 258–67.

Kalecki, Michal, *Studies in Economic Dynamics*, London: Allen and Unwin, 1943.

Kalecki, Michal, *Theory of Economic Dynamics*, London: Allen and Unwin, 1954.

Kalecki, Michal, *Selected Essays on the Dynamics of the Capitalist Economy: 1933–1970*, Cambridge: Cambridge University Press., 1971.

Keynes, John Maynard, *The General Theory and After: Part II Defence and Development*, Donald Moggridge (ed.), Vol.XIV of the *Collected Writings*, London: Macmillan for the Royal Economic Society, 1973.

Keynes, John Maynard, *Economic Articles and Correspondence: Investment and Editorial*, Donald Moggridge (ed.), Vol. XII of the *Collected Writings*, London: Macmillan for the Royal Economic Society, 1983.

Robinson, Joan, *Collected Economic Papers*, Vol. V, Oxford: Basil Blackwell, 1979.

17. Distribution Theory with Imperfect Competition

Y. S. Brenner

INTRODUCTION

Until a few decades ago capitalism rested upon a self-supporting mechanism, a mechanism which was sustained by 'the love of gain' and the 'fear of starvation', i.e. by a two-pronged mechanism of competition – competition between entrepreneurs for their respective shares of the market, and competition between employers and workers for their share in the fruits of production. Fearful of being driven out of business by more efficient competitors, entrepreneurs were inexorably driven to search for and introduce technological and organizational improvements; and facing an increasingly organized and powerful labour force they were pressed to introduce improvements which could help them raise output per worker sufficiently to compensate for rising wages and to maintain a level of profit necessary to finance innovations. This dual mechanism was not only the dynamic but also the progressive element in traditional capitalism – the element which increased mankind's ascendancy over nature and gave it the power to produce the material affluence which it could, and in considerable measure does, enjoy.

In new-style capitalism the operation of this mechanism has become erratic. As a result, the promise of progress inherent in traditional capitalism is in jeopardy in spite of the system's technological capability to provide higher living standards and greater social security than ever before. The threat comes from several sources: the growing power of oligopolies to reduce price competition; the decline of confidence and the spreading of corruption; the concurrence of conflicting ethical and social paradigms; the subversion of democracy and the depoliticisation of the public.

Old-style capitalism's rational self-interest assured a degree of efficiency, confidence and honesty. In new-style capitalism this link is no longer as strong as it used to be. The increasing separation of control from ownership of capital provides much greater opportunities for fraud and corruption, and these influence the cultural climate, diminish efficiency and introduce socially hazardous and economically debilitating patterns of behaviour.

Economic progress is functionally related to the accumulation of real capital and technological innovation. Given a level of technology, savings determine the upper limit of potential economic growth. The actual rate of growth and its social character are determined by income distribution. In a free enterprise economy the volume of investment depends on savings and profit-expectations, and its division between process and product innovation on the distribution of the national income between savings and consumption. A unique feature of the era of classical capitalism was that it combined a climate of confidence in property rights with the mechanism of competition in a way that made the transformation of savings into productive investment almost unavoidable. Capitalists felt that their wealth was reasonably well protected both by and against the state. At the same time, they also felt that their wealth was constantly threatened by business competitors. To protect his market share each capitalist was forced to innovate, accumulate and invest. But this implied that he was also forced to keep wages as low as was practically possible. Every successful effort of labour to obtain a greater share of the fruits of production reinforced the capitalist's need to innovate, particularly in labour-saving machinery, in order to compensate for his loss of profit. Paradoxically, however, it was precisely labour's successful struggle to obtain a greater share which kept the system going once exports no longer sufficed to clear the market of the growing volume of output. For it was labour's rising effective demand which kept the expansion of investment and production profitable.

Macroeconomic theory acknowledged the existence of this intricate relationship between investment, national income, consumers' expenditure on goods and services, employment and savings. It indicated the critical values which each of these variables must approach to sustain the system's relative stability and growth. This recognition led to what has been called the 'Keynesian compromise' which employed the state as a corrective agent to maintain the necessary balance between investment and consumption when it tended to move out of line. In spite of the system's inherent tendency to fluctuate, this kept most capitalist economies on a fairly stable upward path until the 1970s.

PRICE EFFECTS AND INCOME EFFECTS

As long as competition transmits the benefits of innovation to consumers in the form of price reductions, new investment brings with it greater efficiency and so engenders more investment and employment. A rise in productivity is, however, not always the result of an increase in consumer demand. Labour cost-reducing innovations are attractive to investors even when markets are stagnating. They increase profit margins by cost reductions. It follows that a rise in productivity without lively price competition may cause chronic unemployment. This is so because if prices do not fall, and therefore consumers' real incomes do not rise in line with productivity, they can neither buy more of the innovating firms' produce nor more of any other firms' goods. There is a contradiction here between the short-term advantages to a firm resulting from lower labour costs and the long-term disadvantages experienced by the economy as a whole from the deficiency in consumers' effective demand. It is the contradiction inherent in the pull of the 'price effect' and the push of the 'income effect'. The currently ascendant economics establishment simply ignores this contradiction by invoking Say's Law in one form or another. But the fact remains that a firm cannot avoid trying to reduce costs in the face of diminishing demand and profits, and it cannot invest in expansion without the prospect of demand and profit. So while *effective demand* is stagnating or declining, firms are compelled to reduce costs by *process innovation* or by wage reductions. But process innovation transforms market competition into a scramble for funds and, in the process, raises interest rates and sometimes also inflation; and wage reductions reduce consumer demand and consequently also employment. The firms which are unable to raise funds for innovation are forced into liquidation and the oligopolistic tendencies increase. Under these conditions there is no self-correcting mechanism like the one which turns the tide of cyclical unemployment under perfect competition and the state becomes the sole corrective 'independent variable'.

New investment is always either induced by an experienced or expected rise in demand or by the wish to reduce production costs by innovation. In both events it will have a positive effect on aggregate income and employment as long as competition is lively. But when competition fails, when prices are prevented from falling in line with cost reductions, the second type of incentives will predominate. For with the progress of technology less and less labour is required to produce a given volume of output, and so investment will raise the rate at which output is increasing in excess of the rate at which the demand for labour is growing. Consequently, with few exceptions, only cost-reducing investments can be expected to be profitable – unless the wages of those who remain employed and transfer incomes rise sufficiently to offset the loss in purchasing power of those who become redundant as a result of technological innovation. If competition fails to bring down prices sufficiently to adjust the effective demand to the growing volume of supply, producers have little alternative but to reduce production targets in line with demand, or where this is possible to try to tap the market of another income group. Their profits will depend on the difference between the ruling market price and the measure by which they can cut production costs by innovation (i.e. by how much they can reduce their labour force). As a result, investment in cost-reducing equipment will continue and employment in the production of cost-reducing equipment will remain stable or even rise slightly, while unemployment in all other sectors of the economy will progressively increase and become chronic. As only the financially most powerful businesses can invest in this manner monopolistic tendencies will accelerate in the affected sectors of the economy and influence the system as a whole.

STATE REGULATION

Until the late 1960s or early 1970s a balance between the increasing productivity and consumer demand was maintained partly by price competition, partly by the state transferring a share of profits to the collective services, and party by labour's success in raising wages more or less in line with productivity. But when these 'mechanisms' began to falter, when the share of the national product which went to capital became disproportionately larger than the share which went to labour (a fact which was successfully disguised by statistical manipulations like the AIQ in The Netherlands), and consequently supply exceeded demand, production targets were scaled down, investment was mainly directed towards process and not product innovation and unemployment soared. Before long the fall in demand for labour became self-sustained and in several countries the cost of social security rose sharply. The urge to reduce this made the disequilibrating distribution of the national product worse. In addition, it also offended the notions of equity which had developed since the war and together with the increasing unemployment abated the consensus upon which the free enterprise system rested.

In spite of this, few governments attempted (unlike Sweden) to restore the income distribution necessary for economic growth with full employment. Their economic advisers professed that a fall in interest rates, which is achieved by more saving and even less consumption, would usher in recovery – as indeed it often did in the course of conventional business cycles. They ignored the fact that low interest rates did not restore employment and prosperity in the 1930s, and overlooked the difference between cyclical and structural economic crises.

In the past, a rise in productivity in one sector of the economy, say in agriculture, led to a fall in the prices of that sector's output and consequently led to a rise in consumers' real incomes and hence to a greater demand for output of other sectors, for example for industrial products. With the growth of oligopolies increasing productivity is no longer followed by a commensurate fall in prices. If prices are administered downward, as happened with home computers, it is to include another income group in the market and not as a result of competition. On the whole, the wish to maintain profit margins restrains expansion. Prices do not fall sufficiently to have the necessary effect on the total volume of consumers' demand, and investment concentrates on labour-saving equipment. As a result, interest rates remain high in spite of large–scale unemployment and depression. The one type of cut-throat competition which remained is in the retail trade, but the retail trade does not determine the floor of prices.

In the past, competition between firms for their relative market share and competition between capital and labour for their relative shares in the fruits of production had provided a reasonably well-functioning mechanism for the mutual adjustment of income, employment, investment and technological innovation along a long-term path of economic growth. Short-term oscillations were tempered after the war by fiscal and monetary measures and the sharpest edges of the capitalist system were mitigated by progressive taxation and social security payments. The recent failure of the former mechanisms to sustain the economic system on an upward course is the result of the rising power of oligopoly and the declining power of organised labour. The failure of the latter type of mechanism is connected with the decline in political engagement of the trade unions and the public at large. The possibility of absorbing the redundant industrial labour force in the service sector was adequately demonstrated in the late 1950s and in the 1960s. In the same manner as industry had previously absorbed the redundant agricultural labour force, the service sector can very well absorb the new unemployed. The problem is that industrial goods are mainly private and services are increasingly collective. The failure of government to maintain full employment by expanding the collective services can however not be attributed to ignorance alone.

PRIVATE GOODS AND COLLECTIVE SERVICES

There are a number of substantial reasons for this: the development of *industrial feudalism*, the demise of *meaningful democracy*, the lingering belief that services are 'unproductive', and the ideological conviction of the successful, whose voice is of course loudest, that all attainment, including social security and position, ought to be the product of individual effort. In fact, the proliferation of services is inherent in the progress of technology, and a nation's economic product is the sum of all incomes earned in a determined period from work, regardless of their source of origin. Economic growth reflects increases in productivity and in the volume of employment. When the volume of employment is diminishing there can, therefore, be technological advancement without economic growth. However, if economic growth is a prerequisite for full employment it makes no difference if it is induced by industry or education – by the greater output of pinballs or by the improvement or human capital. This is particularly true where no real shortage of tangible goods can be expected and where people have to climb to the top of grain, meat and butter mountains to avoid being drowned by the floods of milk and wine.

The logic behind the refusal to expand services and thereby to restore full employment is ideological, not economic. Unemployment discourages wage claims and reintroduces the fear that, in the past, had been the main source of good work discipline. Cuts in social security payments add to this effect. From an economist's point of view only this can be argued: If extra work is created by monetary expansion it may accelerate inflation; if it is created by greater public borrowing it will reduce the fund of savings and 'crowd out' private investment. If it is done by borrowing from abroad it may upset the balance of payments. But in fact none of these need happen if the expansion of employment is financed judiciously. None of it happened in Sweden. Public expenditure does not only cost money but also earns it. It saves on unemployment benefits and causes tax revenues to increase. It can undermine the price-fixing powers of oligopolies and increase real incomes and investment in product innovation. The reason why governments fail to implement such a policy is mainly ideological, not economic. To understand this successful opposition it is essential to appreciate that the traditional struggle between employers and employees has been replaced by new contradictory interests, namely between people who depend or may come to depend upon the resources of the welfare state and people who do not. These contradictions have to date not found adequate political expression.

IDEOLOGIES AND PARADIGMS

Modern economic theory assumes the existence of an inherent mechanism in the free enterprise system which draws it toward equilibrium. It assumes that any disturbance in one or more of the system's interrelated variables will give rise to compensatory equilibrating changes in some or all its other variables. There is a good deal of disagreement among economists about the causes of disequilibrating disturbances, and even more disagreement about the desirability of stimulating or restraining them. These differences of opinion produce a variety of theories concerning the role of the state and trade unions. They range from almost total rejection of state interference (i.e. *laissez faire*) to guarded approval, which is divided between preference for intervention from the supply or from the demand side of the system. What is usually ignored in these controversies are the fundamental changes which have taken place in society and which may have altered the essential premises upon which all these theories were and continue to be based.

To understand this failing or imperfection it is necessary to be conscious of the role of theoretical paradigms in the evolution of a science and of a society. The substitution of the theoretical dominance of mercantilism by classical economics cannot be regarded merely as the result of a continual process of elimination of errors; neither can Keynesian economics and the neoclassical synthesis be regarded as such; nor the struggle between supply-side and demand-side interventionists. It is also not a matter of correct or faulty analyses. Theoretical paradigms always reflect historical realities – the dynamic character of societies – and are constantly changing. An analysis may therefore be correct at one time and totally beside the point at another.

Theoretical paradigms are sustained by people who have good reason for supporting them. The paradigm which maintains that economics is a value-free science is therefore not only upholding a proposition which is wrong, but it reflects the presence of an economic oligarchy which expects to benefit from this belief and often does. Within this paradigm the social significance of Keynes is lost and Keynesian macroeconomics is 'internalised' – emasculated, by the system and reduced to insignificance.

One change which economists who are attuned to the ruling paradigm fail to acknowledge is the growing power of multinational corporations. Whatever other effects they may have on the economy, they certainly break the direct interdependence between domestic savings and investment, an interdependence which is one of the fundamental requirements for sustaining the ruling economic theory. Even the orthodox followers of equilibrium theories cannot deny the power of multinationals to invest when and where it suits them. What they fail to admit is that this makes utter nonsense of the assumed mechanism which is supposed to steer the economic system towards a full-employment equilibrium. This is so unless it is accepted that wages in the industrial countries should be allowed to fall to the level of wages in, say, Taiwan. In addition to this the power of multinationals undermines the regulating role of prices. They have the power to determine the floor below which prices are not allowed to fall. They avoid price competition by share-swapping and other types of collusion with potential competitors; and their top functionaries cultivate personal links with each other and with top government officials that are detrimental to the proper functioning of the market system. But this presents them with a dilemma, because the survival of each individually depends upon a course of action which is injurious to the system as a whole and therefore in the long run also to themselves. Each is forced to keep prices and profits high and to reduce its labour force, while all together would be better served if prices were allowed to fall or more profits were skimmed off by the state so that full employment be sustained. But as they cannot do this there is no alternative to state intervention.

TECHNOLOGY AND UNEMPLOYMENT

This dilemma is often mistakenly conceived in terms of a threat originating from technological progress. Nothing could be further from the truth. Historically the progress of technology reflects mankind's ingenuity in overcoming the material constraints on its way to freedom from want and arduous labour. The development of the natural sciences turned spontaneous ingenuity into systematic effort: technical problems related to the creation of material affluence received systematic analysis and solutions. In contrast to this, social problems, like the persistence of poverty and unemployment, have not received a similarly dispassionate systematic treatment. The possibility that poverty and unemployment may be the product of outdated social institutions and conceptions that do not fit the new material conditions is rarely examined by economists. The most pressing problem is therefore neglected, namely the contradiction between society's objective freedom to determine how the extra labour time gained by the progress of technology can best be used to everyone's advantage, and the apparent compulsion of individuals to accept a particular choice usually determined by no more that cultural obduracy. If economics continues to ignore this contradiction and fails to adapt its theoretical framework accordingly, the fears inspired by the new technologies may very well be justified. Society may slip back into pre-industrial conditions or move into an era of abject industrial feudalism. In either event the positive aspirations of the capitalist era (such as the concern for individual freedom and human rights) will go by the board. There is no macroeconomic mechanism left, if ever there was one, to effect the income distribution which would be necessary to sustain economic growth and full employment. Without political intervention the new Captains of Industry are doomed to sail their prescribed course. They will cause the gulf between rich and poor and between employed and unemployed to widen and will lead society towards a degree of polarisation which is no longer compatible with the consensus required for the survival of democracy and 'capitalism with a human face'. A redistribution of the national income is therefore not a matter of compassion and humanity alone, but one of general self-interest; it is a legitimate and necessary concern of governments, trade unions and economists.

STRUCTURAL PROBLEMS

Most members of the economics establishment simply ignore the point that present unemployment is related to structural changes in both the economy and society and that it is a problem of income distribution. The refusal to acknowledge this leads them to the false conclusion that a return to the pre-war market structure and the demolition of the welfare state are the solution. When structural changes are admitted at all, the admission is confined to the transfer of work to low-wage countries in the Third World, and the displacement of human labour by robots and the new communications technology. Social changes are simply declared 'exogenous' or economically irrelevant. Regarding the transfer of work, the solution is presented in terms of the theory of the international division of labour, and the displacement of labour by robots, etc. in terms of a normal case of frictional unemployment. Neither of these 'solutions' has substance in reality. Structural unemployment cannot be removed by comparative costs, nor can Keynesian anti-cyclical measures eliminate it. It is not a purely economic problem but the product of social changes and changes in the mentality which accompanied the transformation of old-style competitive capitalism into the new oligopolistic system. The amelioration, and eventual removal, of structural unemployment involves much more than either the extension of regulative economic state intervention or the proliferation of job retraining schemes or work sharing. *It involves the pursuit of deliberate policies to employ more people permanently in the public sector.* This, however, will unavoidably give rise to cultural developments which are inconsistent with the survival of the capitalist era's individualistic utilitarian mentality. It will deprive the economic system of its traditional instruments for enforcing work discipline – the fear of unemployment – before new instruments, such as social pressure and responsibility, may have time fully to mature. This initial difficulty cannot be avoided, but much can be done to keep it within reasonable bounds. The gap left open by the decline of the Church in the sphere of morality and social values needs to be filled. Presently the schools are unlikely to fulfil this task. The values they disseminate are those of the establishment which emphasises material values and competition, and on the whole prefers training to education.

There is nothing new in state intervention to promote greater economic equity and ameliorate the consequences of cyclical recessions. What is required now is something more – a deliberate policy aimed at achieving a transformation of society by making full productive employment its first priority. The difference between this and the conventional approach is the reversal of order. Conventional theory stresses private investment as a key to full employment; here it is proposed that employment is not only necessary in the public sector but that it is the key to socially responsible investment in the private sector. The struggle for economic revival is, therefore, a political struggle with important cultural ramifications. There is ample room for employment in the public sector in the reconstruction of the rundown infrastructure, in education, health care, caring for the old and the infirm, in housing, in public safety, in the protection of the environment, etc., and the technological capacity also exists to produce the goods required to sustain our living standards and to improve them with less and less effort. All that is missing is the political will to correct the distribution of the national product – the will to restructure the share distribution of the national income between capital, labour and the state. Democracy can rectify this. For this reason economists must no longer spurn political involvement. They must no longer accept the myth that man is the helpless victim of mysterious economic laws that can only be understood by experts. They must acknowledge that society determines its own priorities and that these are always a matter of ideology and value judgment. They must recognise that distribution is at the very roots of the current economic difficulties.

18. Distribution of Income and Unemployment in the Netherlands 1965-85

A. H. G. M. Spithoven

This chapter is an elaboration of the summary of my thesis, 'Unemployment between Market and Planning; a Social-economic Study on the Development of Unemployment in the Netherlands since 1965' (Spithoven, 1988). The central theme of my thesis is structural unemployment. Following the structure of my thesis, here I emphasise the distribution of income as a possible cause of structural unemployment. I define this type of unemployment in the context of social and cultural developments. My definition deviates from the one commonly used in mainstream economic literature and in government documents. I needed this redefinition of the concept because the earlier one does not suit the new forms of unemployment which form part of the current economic crisis.

In my analysis of unemployment I examined the Ricardian and modern (post-)Keynesian views and confronted them with neo-classical approaches. For the supply of labour I analysed such social changes as the altered role of women in the labour market, the extension of higher education, and the new forms of withdrawal from the labour force under the Dutch Disablement Act and Early Retirement measures.

For the demand for labour I studied the effects of the conventional business cycles and also the consequences of technological developments, such as the spreading of modern communication systems and computer-integrated manufacturing. I analysed and compared the timing of the emphasis on process innovation and of product innovation, and elaborated the problem of income distribution in this context. I also studied the distribution issue in relation to the functioning of the self-regulating mechanism of prices.

1

First, I consider two approaches to the explanation of unemployment. I briefly review the approach which relates unemployment to a lack of horizontal and vertical labour mobility which recognizes only temporary and voluntary unemployment. The adherents of this view recommend wage restraint, cuts in social benefits and less government expenditure as the best means to reduce unemployment. I confront this approach with the social surplus model in which unemployment is said to be caused by institutional changes and by power factors leading to changes in income distribution. This approach, hypothetically elaborated by Brenner (1984), suggests that the distribution of income is influenced by oligopolies which tend to emphasize process innovation in recessions and product innovation in periods of expansion. Under perfect competition the self-correcting mechanisms of the price system tend to adjust supply to demand, but under imperfect competition the labour made redundant by process innovation will not find compensatory new employment opportunities. I also suggest that high and rising wages alone cannot explain the removal of certain industries from the industrialized countries to the Third World.

2

I next consider new instruments. I did not intend to develop new instruments for calculating precisely the shares of different components in total unemployment. This is impossible because *inter alia* income and price effects tend to occur simultaneously. I indicate several types of unemployment: cyclical, seasonal, frictional and structural. With the exception of the last, these are defined in more or less conventional manner. My definition of structural unemployment is limited to unemployment caused by a change in income distribution, or by changes in society, for example, by the growing labour participation of women, i.e. an absolute shortage of employment opportunities, a shortage which cannot be eliminated by the stimulation of effective demand alone. Unemployment caused by problems of labour mobility, i.e. by impediments on the movement of labour from one sector to another I regard as frictional unemployment. It is the problem of structural unemployment which forces its way to the core of my analysis.

In order to analyse structural unemployment I introduce the degree of oligopolies with a C4-coefficient. I measure product or process innovation with the help of an analysis of the share of outlay on equipment in investments in the various branches. I indicate the saving on labour costs due to new equipment with the concept of labour productivity. To analyse the international reallocation of labour I clustered the trade partners of the Netherlands on the basis of income per capita calculations as percentages of the level of per capita income in the Netherlands. The sources of market power (oligopolies), product or process innovation and international reallocation of labour are more elusive than the chosen measure suggests. Therefore the results of my analysis are limited.

3

There has been a number of fundamental changes in the Dutch economy and society since the war. One of these changes was the redistribution of employment and of production between various economic sectors. The service sector, which in the Netherlands includes government administration, public health and education, has been increasingly important for employment and production since 1965. The growth of the service sector was substantial, and not only because of a statistical redefinitions of industry. Due to government budget restraints, the growth of employment and production in the service sector, however, slackened in the late 1970s and early 1980s. For this reason I believe that only the employment figures up to 1965 reflect the conventional business cycle and the counter-cyclical measures of the government. After 1965 the effects of counter-cyclical policies are no longer traceable in the employment statistics.

4

The decline of employment opportunities since 1965 did not directly generate unemployment in the Netherlands. The official unemployment figures do not reflect the decline of employment opportunities in agriculture and industry, because the decline of employment coincided with an enormous increase in the number of people entitled to benefits under the Disablement Act. Social scientists and civil servants claim a great deal of unemployment is disguised by this Act. According to the Disablement Acts a person is defined as totally or partly disabled if, as a result of disease or other handicaps, he or she is no longer able to earn an income commensurate with his or her capabilities, education and work experience. An analysis by branches and regions of the development of employment and unemployment, and of the number of people entitled to payments under the Disablement Acts, does indeed lend credence to the proposition that some unemployment is disguised by the Act. In those branches of industry and in the regions where industrial employment declined most, the percentage of the disabled was the highest. In comparison with the sectoral pattern of employment, the share of services in unemployment is relatively high.

5

Having described the development of the demand for and supply of labour, I move to the developments in the sphere of income distribution.

The AIQ (labour's share in the net income of firms) and the primary distribution of income are frequently quoted in support of the claim that a shift in the functional distribution of income in favour of profits will stimulate savings and hence investment. But no satisfactory information is given on which part of the national income is spent by labour and which by property owners. There is no comparison of total income earned by workers as a class with that received by property owners. I therefore concentrate my analysis on the functional distribution of incomes. I assume that the division of the national income in wages and profits replicates the division of the national product in consumption and investment.

Investment in the Netherlands, especially government investment, has fallen since the early 1970s. This does not mean that there was a lack of savings. Huge amounts of money were invested abroad, mostly by large corporations. Almost 75 per cent of total Dutch investments abroad came from the ten biggest multinationals. This indicates that the rise of the multinationals has been accompanied by a change in the relationship between savings and investments. Multinationals invest where and when they want. Therefore the claim that when wages and transfer-payments are reduced more money remains for employers to invest, which will cause domestic unemployment to decline, is no longer valid. Ignoring the shift in investments and therefore in income from property of small and large corporations, I found that (as a percentage of the national product) the share of domestic investments in the Netherlands and investments abroad has been fairly stable. However, the distribution of personal incomes changed markedly. In the 1970s income differentials continued to fall, but in the mid-1980s income differentials widened. This was due largely to the greater number of people who became dependent on the *General Assistance Act for Unemployed Workers*. This development went together with a diminution of the growth in consumption and domestic investments. Overall consumption declined in absolute terms in the early 1980s. This indicates that there was no Pigou effect. Expanding exports, from which the large companies profited, did not result in a sufficient increase in employment to compensate for the decline caused by the fall in domestic demand for goods and services.

6

Since the first oil crisis investments in the Netherlands have been mainly energy cost-reducing and in substitution for labour. With the decline in the rate of investment the character of investments has also changed. During the recession of 1974–83, the share of investment in equipment (machines) was higher in all branches of industry than it had been in the period of economic growth (1964–73). But at the same time the rate of labour productivity in industry declined from 7 per cent to 3.5 per cent. Calculated by dividing the change in volume of production by the change in volume of labour with figures corrected for the changed definition of the labour volume, productivity was 0.5 per cent higher in 1974–83. It appears that employers' emphasis on labour substitution was not restricted to the recession. The explanation for the growing rate of investment in equipment seems mainly to have been in savings on energy costs. This may also explain the increased incremental capital output ratio in this period in comparison with earlier decades. Investments on saving energy costs were realized for the greater part by the large corporations.

The share of cost-reducing investments and the rise in labour productivity were on average higher in large corporations that in small firms. The proposition that in periods of recession large corporations especially engage in process innovation gains some empirical support.

The large corporations that realized savings on (labour) costs did not pass their surplus on to consumers by cutting their prices. Studies comparing different industrial branches do not show any differences in price flexibility in line with the degree of oligopoly, but the rate of profits was lower in small firms than in large corporations.

Under pressure of being designated as the cause of inflation, the unions were unable to negotiate wage increases to match the rising prices and the still rising productivity. As a consequence demand slackened and small firms dependent on the domestic market were driven out of business.

The emphasis on process innovation did not engender more employment in machine-industry. In comparison with other branches of industry, the decline of employment there was relatively small. This suggests that Ricardo's compensation theory does not accord with the empirical evidence.

The often stated marginal demand for labour is not supported by empirical evidence in the Netherlands in 1974–83. Minch (1987) came to the same conclusion for the United States in 1950–85. In spite of these facts, conservatives like Murray (1985) dismiss this evidence because (due to government welfare payments) the social structure would have changed in such a way that variations in wages and the supply of labour in the post-

1973 are irrelevant for analysing the marginal demand for labour.

To some extent wages seem to have influenced the international redistribution of labour. If the legislation concerning the production and sale of goods in low income countries is taken into account, wages differentials between countries seem to be less significant than one would expect following relocation of production abroad. A great share of the relocation of production went not to low but to high wage countries. Environmental problems and specialisation on components of production seem to have played an important role.

7

In the mid-1960s there was a labour shortage. The government therefore tried to tap a hitherto under-utilised source of labour supply by rehabilitating and reintegrating into the workforce people who were entitled to payments under the Disablement Acts. Migrant workers were also contracted. The idea was to bring in foreign workers on a temporary basis and repatriate them after the restructuring of the Dutch economy was completed. But the rehabilitation of the disabled failed, and the migrant workers were needed longer than expected. Both developments influenced the age composition of the labour force. It were mainly the elderly people who became entitled to payments under the Disablement Acts, while the migrant workers were contracted only from the productive age group. In addition, the supply of labour was influenced by raising the school leaving age and by the rising participation of women in the workforce. As a consequence the labour force was predominantly in the age group of 25–50/55 years.

Labour productivity also rose as a result of greater flexibility in work contracts. The number of part-time, volunteer, secretarial, on-call, home- and free-lance workers increased. This process increased notably after 1979. Before that date flexibility was limited to secretarial and part-time workers. With the change in the character of this process the motives for working also changed.

The increase in employment was flattened by flexibility. It diminished underemployment, and paid labour was crowded out by volunteers. This dampened incentives for innovation and investment and the the greater flexibility of employment attracted a new labour supply. As a consequence of these contradictory developments the labour market shifted further and further away from equilibrium.

8

In the 1970s and 1980s structural unemployment became the dominant type of unemployment. Cyclical unemployment also increased but structural unemployment reached an unprecedented height. Frictional unemployment diminished. In the 1980s the number of vacancies fell dramatically.

The structural developments in the economy did not directly result in unemployment. The international reallocation of labour between 1965 and 1980, and rising labour productivity, did not lead to a proportional increase in unemployment. Due to changes in the Disablement Acts and to early retirement measures, and due to the repatriation of some migrant workers, the restructuring of the economy went fairly smoothly. Only after some years of restructuring did the economy suffer from a sharp rise in (registered) unemployment. In the late 1970s and early 1980s the 'new' labour supply of women and school leavers confronted the reality of no jobs.

Government policy to reduce structural unemployment was grafted on to (re)schooling. This instrument, which meets only frictional unemployment (i.e. no absolute shortages in the demand for labour) was to no avail.

Several measures to create youth employment also failed. All the same, the growth in youth unemployment flattened out, because measures blocking the inflow of youth into the social security system discouraged its labour participation and stimulated further education.

Women's unemployment rate is higher than men's. In the early 1970s the difference was only partly cancelled by differences in the disablement rates. In the early 1980s early retirement measures, and the abolition of the duty of elderly unemployed to register, statistically favoured a lower unemployment rate for men in comparison with women. But even this did not fully cancel out the difference in unemployment rates. Women's higher unemployment rate may however be explained by their rising rate of participation in the labour force. In spite of the fact that between 1973 and 1985 the number of women who succeeded in obtaining paid work increased six times more than men, women's unemployment rate increased by a greater amount.

Unemployment rates among ethnic minorities are also high in comparison with the home population. This is explained by the government's own employment practices, and by social-cultural impediments which cannot be classified as a 'disease' under the Disablement Act. In many cases foreigners fall back on one of the Unemployment Acts which, with some restrictions, provide relatively higher incomes for a much shorter time than the those obtained by the Wage Earners Disablement Insurance Act. The same is true for women. Another cause for the difference in unemployment benefits obtained by foreigners is their age. Because the members of the ethnic minority groups are relatively young they cannot claim under the Early Retirement Act.

CONCLUSION

My analysis indicates that growth in structural unemployment is partly due to a shift in income distribution and partly to the growing participation of women in the labour force. The rise of multinational enterprises needs to review the relationship between domestic savings and domestic investments, and the policy of wage restraint, reduced social benefits and less government expenditure. This policy is advocated by politicians because the last two decades would have witnessed a dramatic shift in income in favour of labour. However, neither the often quoted statistics for labour income (*Arbeidsinkomensquote*) nor the primary income distribution of enterprises, justifies this claim. Nevertheless, investment in the Netherlands has diminished over the last fifteen years, particularly for employment-creating investments. Investments have been mainly energy cost-reducing and in substitution for labour. This does not mean that there was a lack of savings. Huge amounts of money were invested abroad, mostly by the large corporations. Thus, a policy to increase the share of property income by wage restraint and by reductions in social benefits seems to be no guarantee for more domestic investments.

REFERENCES

Brenner, Y. S., *Capitalism, Competition and Economic Crisis; Structural Changes in Advanced Industrialised Countries*, Brighton Wheatsheaf Books, 1984.
Michl, Thomas R., 'Is there Evidence for a Marginalist Demand for Labour?', *Cambridge Journal of Economics*, Vol. 11, 1987, pp. 361–73.
Murray, Charles, 'Have the Poor been "Losing Ground"?', *Political Science Quarterly*, Vol. 100, 1985, pp. 427–45.
Spithoven, A. H. G. M. *Werkloosheid tussen Markt en Regulering; een Sociaaleconomische Studie van de Ontwikkeling van de Werkloosheid in Nederland sedert 1965* (Unemployment between Market and Planning; a Social-economic Study on the Development of Unemployment in the Netherlands since 1965), thesis, Utrecht (ISOR), 1988.

INDEX